Building Mapping Applications with QGIS

Create your own sophisticated applications to analyze and display geospatial information using QGIS and Python

Erik Westra

[PACKT] open source *
PUBLISHING   community experience distilled

BIRMINGHAM - MUMBAI

Building Mapping Applications with QGIS

First published: December 2014

Production reference: 1231214

Published by Packt Publishing Ltd.
Livery Place
35 Livery Street
Birmingham B3 2PB, UK.

ISBN 978-1-78398-466-4

www.packtpub.com

Credits

Author
Erik Westra

Reviewers
David McDermott
Pablo Pardo
Heegu Park
Christopher Wesson

Commissioning Editor
Pramila Balan

Acquisition Editor
Sonali Vernekar

Content Development Editor
Rikshith Shetty

Technical Editor
Shruti Rawool

Copy Editors
Alfida Paiva
Vikrant Phadkay

Project Coordinator
Kinjal Bari

Proofreaders
Cathy Cumberlidge
Ameesha Green
Sonia Sanghera

Indexer
Monica Ajmera Mehta

Production Coordinator
Conidon Miranda

Cover Work
Conidon Miranda

About the Author

Erik Westra has been a professional software developer for over 25 years, and has worked almost exclusively with Python for the past decade. Erik's early interest in graphical user interface design led to the development of one of the most advanced urgent courier dispatch systems used by messenger and courier companies worldwide. In recent years, he has been involved in the design and implementation of systems that match seekers and providers of goods and services across a range of geographical areas. This work has included the creation of real-time geocoders and map-based views of constantly changing data. He is based in New Zealand, and works for companies worldwide.

He is the author of *Python Geospatial Development, Packt Publishing*.

I would like to thank Ruth, the love of my life, for all her support and encouragement. I would also like to thank my two children, Anneke and Oscar, for reminding me what is important in life.

About the Reviewers

David McDermott (MPhys Geog PGCE (Cantab)) is a proud Yorkshireman who has a keen interest in science fiction and Rugby League, as well as in GIS.

He studied at the University of Hull, where he acquired a 2:1 master's degree in Physical Geography. During his 4 years at university, he developed an interest in GIS, subsequently gaining his highest marks in GIS-related modules. He went on to use GIS to analyze remote sensing data as part of his master's level dissertation.

Following on his master's degree, he qualified as a secondary school geography teacher at the University of Cambridge. He spent 6 months teaching before embarking on a career in GIS.

His first GIS position was for a UK-based unaddressed mail company. He spent 18 months working with address data, promoting the use of GIS, redesigning delivery maps, and creating Python scripts to automate common repetitive tasks.

He currently works in the GIS team for a local authority in the UK. Along with working in GIS, he is the Local Land and Property Gazetteer Custodian and Street Naming and Numbering Officer. In this role, he has expanded his knowledge of database management, programming, and web GIS. He has also presented at the QGIS South East user group, and was part of the panel at GeoUtilities London 2014.

I would like to thank James Rutter for allowing me the time to peer review this book.

Pablo Pardo is a geographist from Spain. He has studied MSc in GIS, and specialized in natural risk assessment, focusing his MSc thesis on open data quality. He also received a certificate of higher education in software development.

After several years of working as a GIS technician, he is now starting his freelance career, mixing GIS consulting with data analysis and programming.

This is the first book he has helped review. He likes open data, free software, and geo stuff. You can find more about him at www.pablopardo.es.

Heegu Park began his career at an IT company as a software engineer, and developed some web programs for a famous Korean fashion company. After a short period of time as a software engineer, he moved to the gaming industry, which was booming at that time in South Korea, and he experienced technical producing and coordinating of several online games at leading online game companies.

A five-year work experience drove him to get a higher degree in business and management, so he went to the Korean Advanced Institute of Science and Technology for his MBA (Master's degree in Business Administration), and to the University of Southern California for his MSBA (Master of Science in Business Administration). During his time at two graduate schools, KAIST and USC, he mainly focused on IT and the creative industry. His studies have given him great opportunities to enhance his cooperation and management skills of various teams and people, and his knowledge, along with this work experience, has driven him to pursue successful IT business and efficient marketing strategies.

Now, he works at Gaia3D, a geospatial company based in South Korea, and is in charge of marketing and business development. Gaia3D is actively using many open source GIS to develop systems or services for clients. Also, Gaia3D participates in open source GIS activities such as FOSS4G, open source GIS training, and so on. He has conducted several lectures on open source GIS for many people from all over the world, and also participated in translating open source GIS software such as QGIS. His goal at Gaia3D is to make Gaia3D become a global open source GIS company.

Christopher Wesson is a cartographic design consultant at Ordnance Survey. Qualified with a master's degree, he studied a wide range of disciplines at the University of Southampton, including oceanography, engineering, management, and finance. He has authored and presented papers domestically and internationally, and makes time to share a blog on cartographic design (http://christopherwesson.azurewebsites.net/).

A member of the British Cartographic Society and a contributor to International Cartographic Association activities and several multi-organization projects, he has a keen interest in partnering modern technology with traditional cartographic excellence. Most of his recent work has been in automated cartography and the visualization of geographic data across different platforms.

www.PacktPub.com

Support files, eBooks, discount offers, and more

For support files and downloads related to your book, please visit www.PacktPub.com.

Did you know that Packt offers eBook versions of every book published, with PDF and ePub files available? You can upgrade to the eBook version at www.PacktPub.com and as a print book customer, you are entitled to a discount on the eBook copy. Get in touch with us at service@packtpub.com for more details.

At www.PacktPub.com, you can also read a collection of free technical articles, sign up for a range of free newsletters and receive exclusive discounts and offers on Packt books and eBooks.

PACKTLib

https://www2.packtpub.com/books/subscription/packtlib

Do you need instant solutions to your IT questions? PacktLib is Packt's online digital book library. Here, you can search, access, and read Packt's entire library of books.

Why subscribe?

- Fully searchable across every book published by Packt
- Copy and paste, print, and bookmark content
- On demand and accessible via a web browser

Free access for Packt account holders

If you have an account with Packt at www.PacktPub.com, you can use this to access PacktLib today and view 9 entirely free books. Simply use your login credentials for immediate access.

Table of Contents

Preface

As software applications become more and more a part of people's lives, the concepts of location and space become more important. Developers are regularly finding themselves having to work with location-based data. Maps, geospatial data, and spatial calculations are increasingly becoming just another part of the everyday programming repertoire.

A decade ago, geospatial concepts and development was limited to experts in the Geographic Information Sciences. These people spent years working with maps and the complex mathematics that underlie them. Often coming from a university background, these specialists would spend years becoming familiar with a particular Geographic Information System (GIS), and would make a career of using that system to draw maps and process geospatial data.

While the ever-popular Google Maps meant that anyone can view and manipulate a map, the more advanced custom display and processing of geospatial data was still limited to those who used a professional GIS system. All this changed with the advent of freely available (and often open source) tools for manipulating and displaying geospatial data. Now, anybody can learn the necessary concepts and start building their own mapping applications from scratch. Rather than being limited to the minimal capabilities and restrictive licensing terms of Google Maps, developers can now build their own mapping systems to meet their own requirements, and there are no limits to what can be done.

While the necessary tools and libraries are freely available, the developer still needs to put them together into a workable system. Often, this is a rather complex process and requires a lot of understanding of geospatial concepts, as well as how to compile the necessary wrappers and configure the tools to work on a particular computer.

Fortunately, now there is an even easier way to include geospatial programming tools and techniques within your Python applications. Thanks to the development of the freely available QGIS system, it is now easy to install a complete geospatial development environment, which you can use directly from within your Python code. Whether you choose to build your application as a plugin for the QGIS system, or write a standalone mapping application using QGIS as an external library, you have complete flexibility in how you use geospatial capabilities within your code.

What this book covers

Chapter 1, Getting Started with QGIS, shows you how to install and run the QGIS application, and introduces the three main ways in which Python can be used with QGIS.

Chapter 2, The QGIS Python Console, explores the QGIS Python Console window, and explains how it acts as a useful tool while building your own custom mapping applications. It also gives you a taste of what can be done with Python and QGIS, and improves your confidence and familiarity with the QGIS environment.

Chapter 3, Learning the QGIS Python API, introduces the Python libraries available for the QGIS Python developer, and shows how these libraries can be used to work with geospatial data and create useful and interesting maps based on your geospatial data.

Chapter 4, Creating QGIS Plugins, introduces the concept of a QGIS plugin, and explains how to write a plugin using Python. We take an in-depth look at how plugins work, and how to create a useful geospatial application as a QGIS plugin. We also look at the possibilities and limitations of QGIS plugins.

Chapter 5, Using QGIS in an External Application, completes the process of building standalone Python applications that make use of the QGIS Python libraries. You will learn how to create a wrapper script to handle platform-specific dependencies, design and build a simple but complete standalone mapping application, and learn about the structure of an application built on top of QGIS. Along the way, you will become a far more competent QGIS programmer as you build your own turnkey mapping application from scratch.

Chapter 6, Mastering the QGIS Python API, delves once more into the PyQGIS library, looking at some more advanced aspects of this library, as well as various techniques for working with QGIS using Python.

Chapter 7, Selecting and Editing Features in a PyQGIS Application, looks at how Python programs built using PyQGIS can allow the user to select, add, edit, and delete geospatial features within a map interface.

Chapter 8, Building a Complete Mapping Application Using Python and QGIS, covers the process of designing and building a complete turnkey mapping application called "ForestTrails". You will design the application, implement the overall user interface, and construct a suitable high-resolution basemap for use by the application.

Chapter 9, Completing the ForestTrails Application, covers the completion of the implementation of the "ForestTrails" mapping application by implementing the various map-editing tools, as well as writing a feature to find the shortest available path between two points on the map.

What you need for this book

To follow through the examples in this book, you will need to install the following software on your computer:

- QGIS Version 2.2 or later
- Python Version 2.6 or later (but not Python 3.x)
- GDAL/OGR Version 1.10 or later
- PyQt4 Version 4.10 or later
- Depending on your operating system, you might also need to install the Qt toolkit so that PyQt will work

All of this software can be freely downloaded, and works on Mac OS X, MS Windows, and Linux computers.

Who this book is for

This book is aimed at experienced Python developers who have some familiarity with maps and geospatial concepts. While the necessary concepts are explained as we go along, it would help to have at least some understanding of projections, geospatial data formats, and the like.

Conventions

In this book, you will find a number of text styles that distinguish between different kinds of information. Here are some examples of these styles and an explanation of their meaning.

Code words in text, database table names, folder names, filenames, file extensions, pathnames, dummy URLs, user input, and Twitter handles are shown as follows: "This uses the QGIS_PREFIX environment variable we set earlier to tell QGIS where to find its resources."

A block of code is set as follows:

```
app = QApplication(sys.argv)

viewer = MapViewer("/path/to/shapefile.shp")
viewer.show()

app.exec_()
```

When we wish to draw your attention to a particular part of a code block, the relevant lines or items are set in bold:

```
def unload(self):
    self.iface.removePluginMenu("Test Plugin", self.action)
    self.iface.removeToolBarIcon(self.action)
```

Any command-line input or output is written as follows:

```
export PYTHONPATH="$PYTHONPATH:/Applications/QGIS.app/Contents/Resources/python"
```

New terms and **important words** are shown in bold. Words that you see on the screen, for example, in menus or dialog boxes, appear in the text like this: "If you haven't already installed QGIS, click on the **Download Now** button on the main QGIS web page to download the QGIS software."

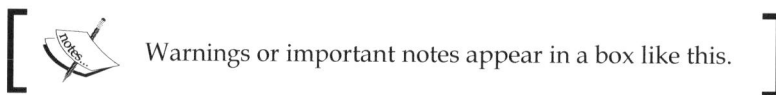

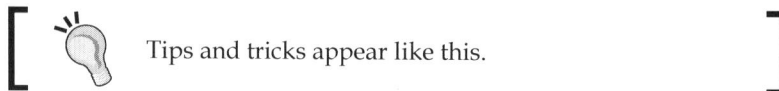

> Warnings or important notes appear in a box like this.

> Tips and tricks appear like this.

Reader feedback

Feedback from our readers is always welcome. Let us know what you think about this book—what you liked or disliked. Reader feedback is important for us as it helps us develop titles that you will really get the most out of.

To send us general feedback, simply e-mail `feedback@packtpub.com`, and mention the book's title in the subject of your message.

If there is a topic that you have expertise in and you are interested in either writing or contributing to a book, see our author guide at `www.packtpub.com/authors`.

Customer support

Now that you are the proud owner of a Packt book, we have a number of things to help you to get the most from your purchase.

Downloading the example code

You can download the example code files from your account at `http://www.packtpub.com` for all the Packt Publishing books you have purchased. If you purchased this book elsewhere, you can visit `http://www.packtpub.com/support` and register to have the files e-mailed directly to you.

Downloading the color images of this book

We also provide you with a PDF file that has color images of the screenshots/ diagrams used in this book. The color images will help you better understand the changes in the output. You can download this file from `http://www.packtpub.com/sites/default/files/downloads/4664OS_ColorImages.pdf`.

Errata

Although we have taken every care to ensure the accuracy of our content, mistakes do happen. If you find a mistake in one of our books—maybe a mistake in the text or the code—we would be grateful if you could report this to us. By doing so, you can save other readers from frustration and help us improve subsequent versions of this book. If you find any errata, please report them by visiting `http://www.packtpub.com/submit-errata`, selecting your book, clicking on the **Errata Submission Form** link, and entering the details of your errata. Once your errata are verified, your submission will be accepted and the errata will be uploaded to our website or added to any list of existing errata under the Errata section of that title.

To view the previously submitted errata, go to `https://www.packtpub.com/books/content/support` and enter the name of the book in the search field. The required information will appear under the **Errata** section.

Piracy

Piracy of copyrighted material on the Internet is an ongoing problem across all media. At Packt, we take the protection of our copyright and licenses very seriously. If you come across any illegal copies of our works in any form on the Internet, please provide us with the location address or website name immediately so that we can pursue a remedy.

Please contact us at copyright@packtpub.com with a link to the suspected pirated material.

We appreciate your help in protecting our authors and our ability to bring you valuable content.

Questions

If you have a problem with any aspect of this book, you can contact us at questions@packtpub.com, and we will do our best to address the problem.

1
Getting Started with QGIS

This chapter provides an overview of the QGIS system and how you can work with it using the Python programming language. In particular, this chapter will cover the following:

- Downloading, installing, and running QGIS
- Becoming familiar with the QGIS application
- Using Python within QGIS
- Using the Python Console as a window into the QGIS environment
- Working of a QGIS Python plugin
- Interacting with the QGIS Python API from an external Python program

About QGIS

QGIS is a popular, free, and open source **Geographic Information System (GIS)**, which runs on all major operating systems. People often use QGIS to view, edit, and analyze geospatial data. For our purposes, however, QGIS is more than just a GIS system; it is also a geospatial programming environment, which we can use to build our own geospatial applications using Python.

QGIS has a comprehensive website (`http://qgis.org`), which makes it easy to download, install, and use.

Before reading further, you should spend 15 minutes looking through the website and getting familiar with the application and the documentation available online. In particular, you should check out the **Documentation** page, where three important manuals are available: *QGIS User guide/Manual*, *QGIS Training manual*, and *PyQGIS cookbook*.

QGIS User guide/Manual provides in-depth user documentation, which you might find useful. *QGIS Training manual* is a detailed introduction to GIS systems and concepts based on QGIS; you might find it useful to work through this course if you aren't already familiar with geospatial data and techniques. Finally, *PyQGIS cookbook* will be an essential reference to use as you develop your own mapping applications built on top of QGIS.

Installing and running QGIS

If you haven't already installed QGIS, click on the **Download Now** button on the main QGIS web page to download the QGIS software. What you do next depends on which operating system you are running on your computer:

- For MS Windows, you can download a double-clickable installer that installs QGIS and all the required libraries in one go. Make sure you use the OSGeo4W installer, which includes the Python interpreter, QGIS itself, and all the required libraries.

- For Mac OS X, you'll need to visit the Kyngchaos website (`http://www.kyngchaos.com/software/qgis`) to download and install the GDAL and matplotlib libraries before installing a version of QGIS specially built for your operating system. All the required packages are available from the Kyngchaos site.

- For Unix-like systems, you'll use a package manager to download, compile, and install QGIS and the required libraries from an appropriate package repository. More information about installing on a Unix-like system can be found at `http://qgis.org/en/site/forusers/alldownloads.html#linux`.

Once you have installed the QGIS system, you can run it just like any other application on your computer, for example, by double-clicking on the QGIS icon in your `Applications` folder.

If everything goes well, the QGIS application will start up and you will be greeted with the following window:

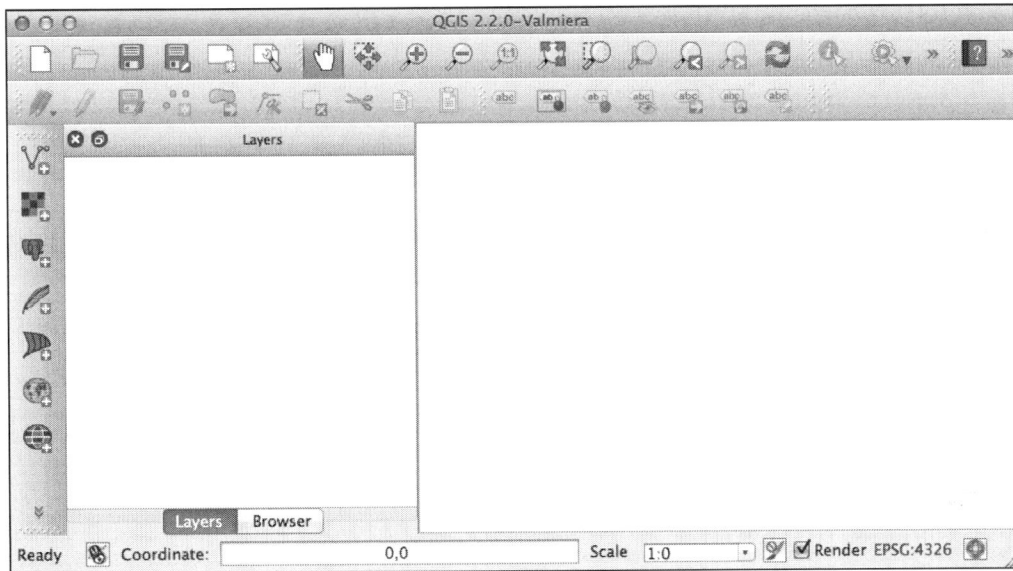

> The exact appearance of the window might vary depending on your operating system. Don't worry, as long as a window appears, which looks something like the one shown in the previous screenshot, you are running QGIS.

You don't need to worry too much about the QGIS user interface right now; the QGIS User Guide describes the interface and various options in great detail. Rather than duplicating this information, let's take a look under the hood to see how QGIS works.

Understanding QGIS concepts

To understand QGIS, you will have to become familiar with the following basic terms and concepts:

- QGIS works with geospatial information loaded from a variety of **data sources**. These data sources can include vector and raster data files on a disk, a variety of spatial databases, and even web services such as **Web Map Service (WMS)** servers that provide geospatial data from the Internet.

- Wherever the data comes from, it is retrieved by QGIS and displayed as a **map layer**. Map layers can be shown or hidden, and also customized in various ways to affect the way the data is displayed on the map.

- The map layers are then combined and displayed on a **map**.

- Finally, the various map layers, the map, and the other settings, all make up a project. QGIS always has one and only one project that it is working with. The project consists of all the map layers, the map display options, and the various settings that are currently loaded into QGIS.

These concepts are related in the following manner:

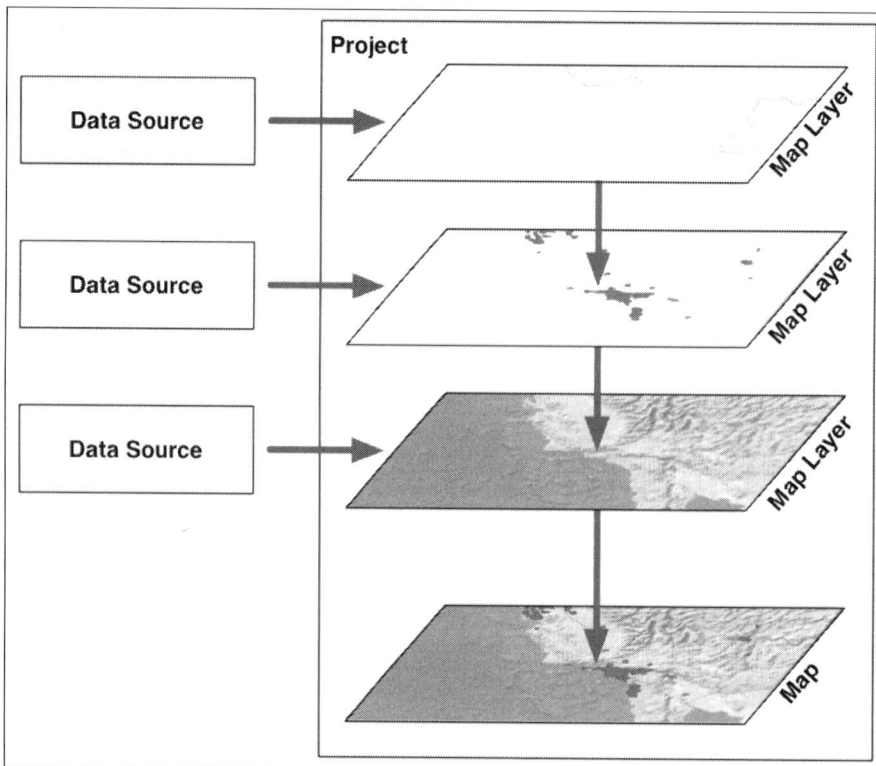

Note that the data sources are outside QGIS. While the map layer refers to a data source, the data itself is stored somewhere else, for example, in a file on a disk or within a database.

Whenever you are working with QGIS, you are always working within the current project. You can save projects and reload them later, or start a new project to reset QGIS back to its original state.

Linking QGIS and Python

While QGIS itself is written in C++, it includes extensive support for Python programming. A Python interpreter is built in, and can be used interactively via the Python Console, or to run plugins written in Python. There is also a comprehensive API for querying and controlling the QGIS application using Python code.

There are three ways in which you can use Python to work with the QGIS system:

- **Python Console**: You can open this console, which runs the interactive Python interpreter built into QGIS, allowing you to type in commands and see the results immediately.

- **Python plugin**: These are Python packages designed to be run within the QGIS environment.

- **External applications**: You can use the QGIS Python API in your own applications. This lets you use QGIS as a geospatial processing engine, or even build your own interactive applications based on QGIS.

No matter how you use Python and QGIS, you will make extensive use of the QGIS Python libraries, which are often referred to as **PyQGIS**. They provide a complete programmatic interface to the QGIS system, including calls to load data sources into layers, manipulate the map, export map visualizations, and build custom applications using the QGIS user interface. While an in-depth examination of the PyQGIS library will have to wait until *Chapter 3, Learning the QGIS Python API*, we will start dabbling with it right away in the next section on the Python Console.

For the remainder of this chapter, we will examine each of the three ways in which you can work with QGIS and Python.

Exploring the Python Console

The QGIS Python Console window can be accessed by using the **Python Console** item in the **Plugins** menu. When you select this command, the Python Console will appear in the lower-right corner of the QGIS window. Here's what the Python Console looks like when you first open it:

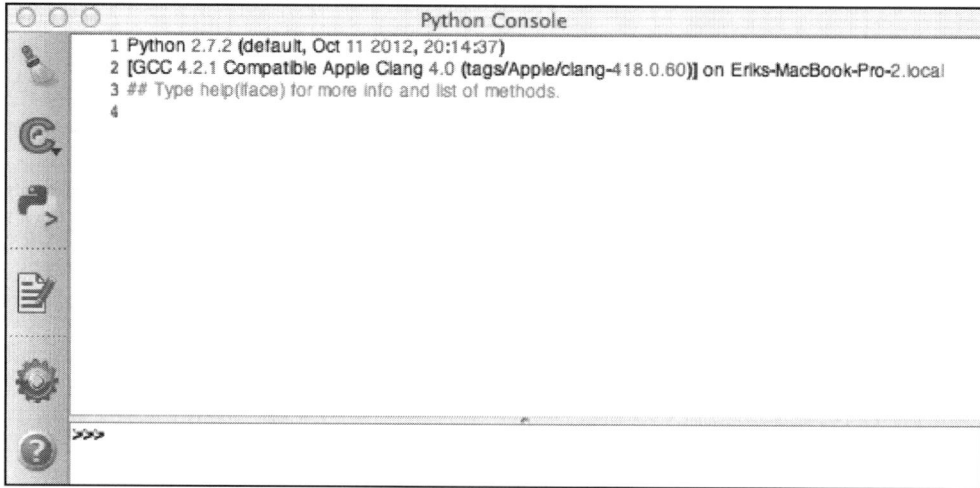

While the Python Console is an excellent tool for interacting with an existing QGIS project, we are going to use it to create a new project from scratch. Before we can do this, though, we'll need to download some geospatial data sources for our QGIS project.

We are going to need a suitable **base map** for our project, as well as some river and city information to display on top of this base map. Let's use the Natural Earth website to obtain the information we need. Go to `http://naturalearthdata.com` and click on the **Downloads** tab.

Firstly, we'll want to download a nice-looking base map for our project. To do this, select the **Raster** link under the **Medium scale data, 1:50m** section, choose the **Natural Earth 1** dataset, and click on the **Download small size** link under the *Natural Earth 1 with Shaded Relief and Water* heading.

Next, we need an overlay, which will show lakes and rivers on top of our base map. To get this information, go back to the **Downloads** tab and select the **Physical** link under the **Medium scale data, 1:50m** section. The dataset you want is called *Rivers, Lake Centerlines*, so click on the **Download rivers and lake centerlines** link to obtain this file.

Finally, we'll want to highlight the cities on top of our base map. Go back to the **Downloads** page and select the **Cultural** link under the **Medium scale data, 1:50m** heading. At the bottom is a section labelled **Urban Areas**. Click on the **Download urban areas** link to download this file.

Once you've done all this, you should have the following three files:

- A raster base map in a file named `NE1_50M_SR_W.zip`
- Lake and river vector data in a file named `ne_50m_rivers_lake_centerlines.zip`
- Urban area vector data in a file named `ne_50m_urban_areas.zip`

Since these are ZIP archives, you will need to unzip these files and store them somewhere at a convenient location on your hard disk.

> You'll need to type in the full path to these datasets, so you might want to put them somewhere convenient, for example, in your home or user directory. In this way, the path you type won't be too long.

Now that we have our data, let's use the QGIS Python Console to import this data into a project. If you've already loaded some data into QGIS (for example, by following the tutorial in the QGIS User Guide), choose the **New** option from the **Project** menu to start again with a blank project. Then, type the following into the QGIS Python Console:

```
layer1 = iface.addRasterLayer("/path/to/NE1_50M_SR_W/
NE1_50M_SR_W.tif", "basemap")
```

Make sure you replace `/path/to/` with the full path to the `NE1_50M_SR_W` directory you downloaded. Assuming you typed the path correctly, the Natural Earth 1 base map should appear in the QGIS window:

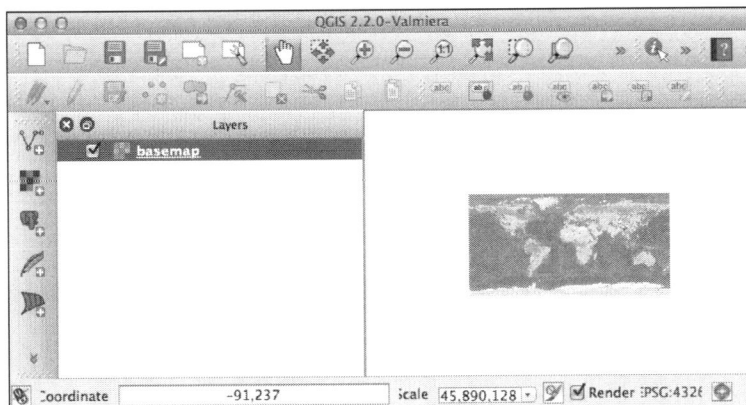

As you can see, our base map is a bit small right now. You can use the various panning and zooming commands in the toolbar at the top of the window to make it bigger, but let's use Python to do the same thing:

```
iface.zoomFull()
```

This will expand the base map to fill the entire window.

Now that we have a base map, let's add our two vector layers to the project. To do this, type the following:

```
layer2 = iface.addVectorLayer("/path/to/ne_50m_urban_areas/
  ne_50m_urban_areas.shp", "urban", "ogr")
```

Once again, make sure you replace /path/to/ with the full path to the `ne_50m_urban_areas` directory you downloaded earlier. The urban areas shapefile will be loaded into the QGIS project and will appear as a series of colored areas on top of the base map. Let's zoom in to an area of California so that we can see what this looks like more clearly. To do this, type the following commands into the Python Console window:

```
iface.mapCanvas().setExtent(QgsRectangle(-125, 31, -113, 38))
iface.mapCanvas().refresh()
```

This will zoom in on the map in so that an area of California, including Los Angeles and the southern part of San Francisco, is now shown on the map:

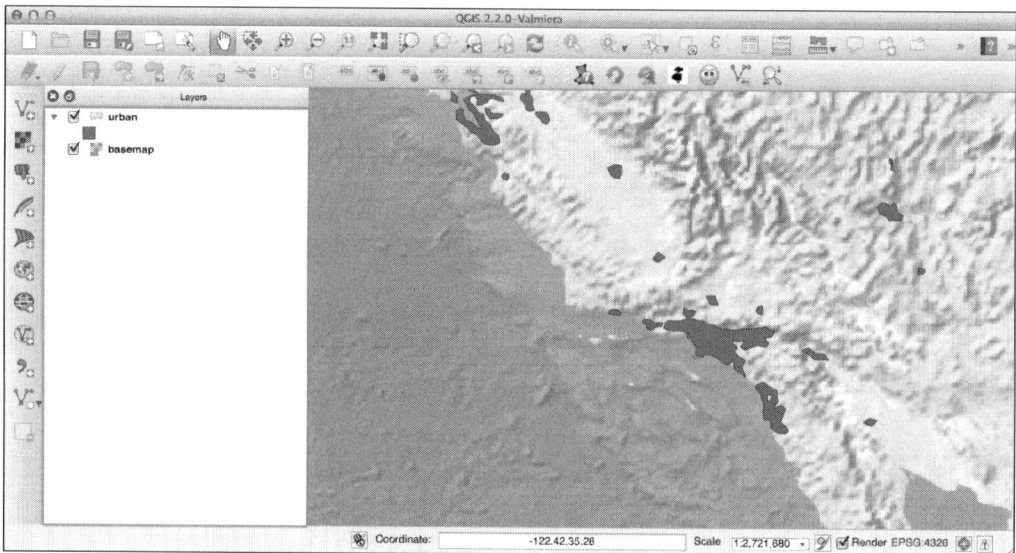

Finally, let's add our river and lake data to our project. To do this, enter the following into the Python Console:

```
layer3 = iface.addVectorLayer("/path/to/ne_50m_rivers_lake_
centerlines/ne_50m_rivers_lake_centerlines.shp", "water", "ogr")
```

If you look at the map, you'll see that the rivers and lakes are now visible. However, they are drawn in a default green color. Let's change this so that the water is now blue:

```
from PyQt4.QtGui import QColor
layer3.rendererV2().symbols()[0].setColor(QColor("#4040FF"))
iface.mapCanvas().refresh()
```

This code might be a bit confusing, but don't worry—we'll learn about renderers and symbols in *Chapter 3, Learning the QGIS Python API*.

Now that we are finished, you can save your project using the **Save As...** item in the **Project** menu. As you can see, it's quite possible to set up and customize your QGIS project using Python.

Examining a Python plugin

While the Python Console is a fantastic tool for interactive coding, it isn't all that useful if you want to use Python to extend the functionality of QGIS. This is where QGIS plugins come in; you can create (or download) a plugin that adds new features or changes the way QGIS works.

Because QGIS is written using the Qt framework, QGIS plugins make use of the Python bindings in Qt, which are called **PyQt**. We will download and install PyQt and the related tools when we start to build our own plugins in *Chapter 4, Creating QGIS Plugins*.

To get an idea of how a Python plugin works, let's take a look at the **Zoom to Point** plugin. As the name suggests, this plugin lets you zoom to display a given coordinate on the map. It's also written in Python, and is a convenient example for learning about plugins in general.

Before we can use it, we have to install this plugin. Choose the **Manage and Install Plugins...** item from the **Plugins** menu, and click on the **Not Installed** tab. You should see **Zoom to Point** listed near the bottom of the list of available plugins; click on this plugin, and then click on the **Install Plugin** button to download and install it.

Let's run this plugin to see how it works; with the project you created earlier still loaded, click on the **Zoom to Point** plugin's icon in the toolbar, which looks like this:

Try entering the longitude/latitude of your current location (if you don't know it, you might find `http://itouchmap.com/latlong.html` helpful). You should see the base map, urban areas, and waterways for your current location.

> Don't forget that x equals longitude and y equals latitude. It's easy to get them the wrong way around.

Now that we know what the plugin does, let's see how it works. The downloaded plugins are stored in a hidden directory named `.qgis2` in your user or home directory. Go to this hidden directory using your favorite file manager (for Mac OS X, you can use the **Go to Folder...** item in the Finder's **Go** menu), and find the `python/plugins` subdirectory. This is where the Python plugins are stored.

> Depending on your operating system and the version of QGIS you are using, the name of this hidden directory might be different. If you can't find it, look for a directory named `.qgis` or `.qgis2` or something similar.

You should see a directory named `zoomtopoint` (the full path to this directory will be `~/.qgis2/python/plugins/zoomtopoint`). Inside this directory, you will find the various files that make up the Zoom to Point plugin:

Name	Date Modified	Size	Kind
__init__.py	Today 6:54 AM	1 KB	Python Source File
COPYING	Today 6:54 AM	19 KB	Document
icon.png	Today 6:54 AM	1 KB	Portable Network Graphics image
Makefile	Today 6:54 AM	2 KB	Document
metadata.txt	Today 6:54 AM	516 bytes	Plain Text File
resources.py	Today 6:54 AM	6 KB	Python Source File
resources.qrc	Today 6:54 AM	107 bytes	Document
ui_zoomtopoint.py	Today 6:54 AM	5 KB	Python Source File
ui_zoomtopoint.ui	Today 6:54 AM	5 KB	Document
zoomtopoint.py	Today 6:54 AM	4 KB	Python Source File
zoomtopointdialog.py	Today 6:54 AM	1 KB	Python Source File
zoomtopointdialog.ui	Today 6:54 AM	5 KB	Document

Let's see what these various files do:

Filename	Used for
`__init__.py`	This is a standard Python package initialization file. This file also initializes the plugin and makes it available to the QGIS system.
`COPYING`	This is a copy of the GNU **General Public License (GPL)**. Since the Zoom to Point plugin is generally available, this defines the license under which it can be used.
`icon.png`	As the name suggests, this is the plugin's toolbar icon.
`Makefile`	This is a standard *nix Makefile used to automate the process of compiling and deploying the plugin.
`metadata.txt`	This file contains the plugin's metadata, including the full name of the plugin, a description, the current version number, and so on.
`resources.qrc`	This is a Qt resource file that defines the various resources such as images and sound files used by the plugin.
`resources.py`	This indicates the contents of the `resources.qrc` file, compiled into a Python module.
`ui_zoomtopoint.ui`	This is a Qt user interface template that defines the main UI for the plugin.
`ui_zoomtopoint.py`	This indicates the contents of the `ui_zoomtopoint.ui` file compiled into a Python module.
`zoomtopoint.py`	This file contains the main Python code for the plugin.
`zoomtopointdialog.ui`	This is a copy of the `ui_zoomtopoint.ui` file. It looks like this file was included by accident, as the plugin can run without it.
`zoomtopointdialog.py`	This Python module defines a `QtGui.QDialog` subclass that loads the dialog box's contents from `ui_zoomtopoint.py`.

Open the `zoomtopoint.py` module in your favorite text editor. As you can see, this contains the main Python code for the plugin, in the form of a `ZoomToPoint` class. This class has the following basic structure:

```python
class ZoomToPoint:
    def __init__(self, iface):
        self.iface = iface
```

```
def initGui(self):
    ...

def unload(self):
    ...

def run(self):
    ...
```

If you open the __init__.py module, you'll see how this class is used to define the plugin's behavior:

```
def classFactory(iface):
    from zoomtopoint import ZoomToPoint
    return ZoomToPoint(iface)
```

When the plugin is loaded, a parameter named `iface` is passed to the `ClassFactory` function. This parameter is an instance of `QgsInterface`, and provides access to the various parts of the running QGIS application. As you can see, the class factory creates a `ZoomToPoint` object, and passes the `iface` parameter to the initializer so that `ZoomToPoint` can make use of it.

Notice how `ZoomToPoint.__init__()`, in the `Zoomtopoint.py` module, stores a reference to the `iface` parameter in an instance variable, so that the other methods can refer to the QGIS interface using `self.iface`. For example:

```
def __init__(self, iface):
    self.iface = iface

def initGui(self):
    ...
    self.iface.addPluginToMenu("&Zoom to point...", self.action)
```

This allows the plugin to interact with and manipulate the QGIS user interface.

The four methods defined by the `ZoomToPoint` class are all quite straightforward:

- `__init__()`: This method initializes a new `ZoomToPoint` object.
- `initGui()`: This method initializes the plugin's user interface, preparing it to be used.
- `unload()`: This method removes the plugin from the QGIS user interface.
- `run()`: This method is called when the plugin is activated, that is, when the user clicks on the plugin's icon in the toolbar, or selects the plugin from the Plugins menu.

Don't worry too much about all the details here; we'll look at the process of initializing and unloading a plugin in a later chapter. For now, take a closer look at the `run()` method. This method essentially looks like the following:

```
def run(self):
    dlg = ZoomToPointDialog()
    ...
    dlg.show()
    result = dlg.exec_()
    if result == 1:
        x = dlg.ui.xCoord.text()
        y = dlg.ui.yCoord.text()
        scale = dlg.ui.spinBoxScale.value()
        rect = QgsRectangle(float(x) - scale,
                            float(y) - scale,
                            float(x) + scale,
                            float(y) + scale)
        mc=self.iface.mapCanvas()
        mc.setExtent(rect)
        mc.refresh()
    ...
```

We've excluded the code that remembers the values the user entered previously, and copies those values back into the dialog when the plugin is run. Looking at the previous code, the logic seems to be fairly straightforward and is explained as follows:

- Create a `ZoomToPointDialog` object.
- Display the dialog box to the user.
- If the user clicks on the **OK** button, extract the entered values, use them to create a new bounding rectangle, and set the extent of the map to this rectangle.

While this plugin is quite straightforward and the actual code doesn't do all that much, it is a useful example of what a Python plugin should look like, as well as the various files that are needed by a Python plugin. In particular, you should note that:

- A plugin is simply a directory that contains a Python package initialization file (`__init__.py`), some Python modules, and other files created using Qt Designer.
- The `__init__.py` module must define a top-level function named `ClassFactory` that accepts an `iface` parameter and returns an object that represents the plugin.

- The plugin object must define an `initGui()` method, which is called to initialize the plugin's user interface, and an `unload()` method, which is called to remove the plugin from the QGIS application.

- The plugin can interact with and manipulate the QGIS application via the `iface` object passed to the class factory.

- The `resources.qrc` file lists various resources such as images, which are used by the plugin.

- The `resources.qrc` file is compiled into a `resources.py` file using the PyQt command-line tools.

- Dialog boxes and other windows are created using a Qt Designer template, which are typically stored in a file with a name of the form `ui_Foo.ui`.

- The UI template files are then compiled into Python code using the PyQt command-line tools. If the template is named `ui_foo.ui`, then the associated Python module will be named `ui_foo.py`.

- Once the user interface for a dialog box has been defined, you create a subclass of `QtGui.QDialog`, and load that user interface module into it. This defines the contents of the dialog box based on your template.

- Your plugin can then display the dialog box as required, extracting the entered values and using the results to interact with QGIS via the `iface` variable.

Plugins are a useful way of extending and customizing QGIS. We will return to the topic of QGIS plugins in *Chapter 4, Creating QGIS Plugins*, where we will create our own plugin from scratch.

Writing an external application

The final way to work with Python and QGIS is to write a completely standalone Python program that imports the QGIS libraries and works with them directly. In many ways, this is an ideal way of writing your own custom mapping applications, because your program doesn't have to run within the existing QGIS user interface. There are, however, a few things you need to be aware of when you attempt to use Python and QGIS in this way:

1. Your Python program needs to be able to find the QGIS Python libraries before it can be run. Since these are bundled into the QGIS application itself, you will need to add the directory where the PyQGIS libraries are installed in your Python path.

2. You also need to tell the PyQGIS libraries where the QGIS application's resources are stored.

3. As the application is running outside the QGIS application, you won't have access to the `iface` variable. You also can't use those parts of the PyQGIS library that assume you are running inside QGIS.

None of this is too onerous, though it can trip you up the first time you attempt to access PyQGIS from your external Python code. Let's take a look at how we can avoid these traps when writing your own Python programs.

Firstly, to allow your program to access the PyQGIS libraries, you need to modify your Python path (and possibly some other environment variables) before you can import any of the QGIS packages. For MS Windows, you can do this by running the following in the command line:

```
SET OSGEO4W_ROOT=C:\OSGeo4W
SET QGIS_PREFIX=%OSGEO4W_ROOT%\apps\qgis
SET PATH=%PATH%;%QGIS_PREFIX%\bin
SET PYTHONPATH=%QGIS_PREFIX%\python;%PYTHONPATH%
```

If you are running Mac OS X, the following commands will set up the Python path for you:

```
export PYTHONPATH="$PYTHONPATH:/Applications/QGIS.app/Contents/Resources/python"
export DYLD_FRAMEWORK_PATH="/Applications/QGIS.app/Contents/Frameworks"
export QGIS_PREFIX="/Applications/QGIS.app/Contents/Resources"
```

For computers that run a version of Linux, you can use the following:

```
export PYTHONPATH="/path/to/qgis/build/output/python/"
export LD_LIBRARY_PATH="/path/to/qgis/build/output/lib/"
export QGIS_PREFIX="/path/to/qgis/build/output/"
```

> Obviously, you will need to replace /path/to/qgis with the actual path of your QGIS installation.

If you have QGIS installed in a nonstandard location, you might need to modify these commands before they will work. To check if they have worked, start up the Python interpreter and enter the following command:

```
>>> import qgis
```

If everything goes well, you'll simply see the Python prompt:

```
>>>
```

On the other hand, you might see the following error:

```
ImportError: No module named qgis
```

In this case, the PYTHONPATH variable has not been set up correctly, and you will have to check the commands you entered earlier to set this environment variable, and possibly modify it to allow for a nonstandard location of the QGIS libraries.

> Note that in some cases, this isn't enough because the Python libraries are only wrappers around the underlying C++ libraries; you might also need to tell your computer where to find these C++ libraries. To see if this is a problem, you can try to do the following:
>
> ```
> import qgis.core
> ```
>
> You might get an error that looks like this:
>
> ```
> ImportError: libqgis_core.so.1.5.0: cannot open shared
> object file: No such file or directory
> ```
>
> You will to have to tell your computer where to find the underlying shared libraries. We will return to this later when we look at writing our own external applications; if you want to see the details, skip ahead to *Chapter 5, Using QGIS in an External Application.*

With the path set, you can now import the various parts of the PyQGIS library that you want to use, for example:

```
from qgis.core import *
```

Now that we have access to the PyQGIS libraries, our next task is to initialize these libraries. As mentioned earlier, we have to tell PyQGIS where to find the various QGIS resources. We do this using the QgsApplication.setPrefixPath() function, like this:

```
import os
QgsApplication.setPrefixPath(os.environ['QGIS_PREFIX'], True)
```

This uses the QGIS_PREFIX environment variable we set earlier to tell QGIS where to find its resources. With this done, you can then initialize the PyQGIS library by making the following call:

```
QgsApplication.initQgis()
```

We can now use PyQGIS to do whatever we want in our application. When our program exits, we also need to inform the PyQGIS library that we are exiting:

```
QgsApplication.exitQgis()
```

Putting all this together, our minimal Python application looks like this:

```
import os
from qgis.core import *

QgsApplication.setPrefixPath(os.environ['QGIS_PREFIX'], True)
QgsApplication.initQgis()

# ...

QgsApplication.exitQgis()
```

Of course, this application doesn't do anything useful yet—it simply starts up and shuts down the PyQGIS libraries. So let's replace the "..." line with some useful code that displays a basic map widget. To do this, we need to define a QMainWindow subclass, which displays the map widget, and then create and use a QApplication object to display this window and handle the various user-interface events while the application is running.

> Both QMainWindow and QApplication are PyQt classes. We will be working extensively with the various PyQt classes as we develop our own external applications using QGIS and Python.

Let's start by replacing the "..." line with the following code, which displays a map viewer and then runs the application's main event loop:

```
app = QApplication(sys.argv)

viewer = MapViewer("/path/to/shapefile.shp")
viewer.show()

app.exec_()
```

As you can see, a MapViewer instance (which we will define shortly) is created and displayed, and the QApplication object is run by calling the exec_() method. For simplicity, we pass the name of a shapefile to display within the map viewer.

Running this code will cause the map viewer to be displayed, and the application will run until the user closes the window or chooses the **Quit** command from the menu.

Now, let's define the `MapViewer` class. Here is what the class definition looks like:

```python
class MapViewer(QMainWindow):
    def __init__(self, shapefile):
        QMainWindow.__init__(self)
        self.setWindowTitle("Map Viewer")

        canvas = QgsMapCanvas()
        canvas.useImageToRender(False)
        canvas.setCanvasColor(Qt.white)
        canvas.show()

        layer = QgsVectorLayer(shapefile, "layer1", "ogr")
        if not layer.isValid():
            raise IOError("Invalid shapefile")

        QgsMapLayerRegistry.instance().addMapLayer(layer)
        canvas.setExtent(layer.extent())
        canvas.setLayerSet([QgsMapCanvasLayer(layer)])

        layout = QVBoxLayout()
        layout.addWidget(canvas)

        contents = QWidget()
        contents.setLayout(layout)
        self.setCentralWidget(contents)
```

Don't worry too much about the details of this class; we basically just create a window and place a `QgsMapCanvas` object within it. We then create a map layer (an instance of `QgsVectorLayer`) and add it to the map canvas. Finally, we add the canvas to the window's contents.

Notice that `QgsMapCanvas` and `QgsVectorLayer` are both part of PyQGIS, while `QMainWindow`, `QVBoxLayout`, and `QWidget` are all PyQt classes. This application uses the PyQGIS classes within a PyQt application, mixing the classes from both sources. This is possible because QGIS is built using Qt, and the various PyQGIS classes are based on PyQt.

To turn the preceding code into a working application, all we need to do is add some more `import` statements to the top of the module:

```
import sys
from PyQt4.QtGui import *
from PyQt4.QtCore import Qt
```

> **Downloading the example code**
>
> You can download the example code files from your account at `http://www.packtpub.com` for all the Packt Publishing books you have purchased. If you purchased this book elsewhere, you can visit `http://www.packtpub.com/support` and register to have the files e-mailed directly to you.

If you run this application, the map viewer will be displayed, showing the contents of the shapefile referred to by the code. For example:

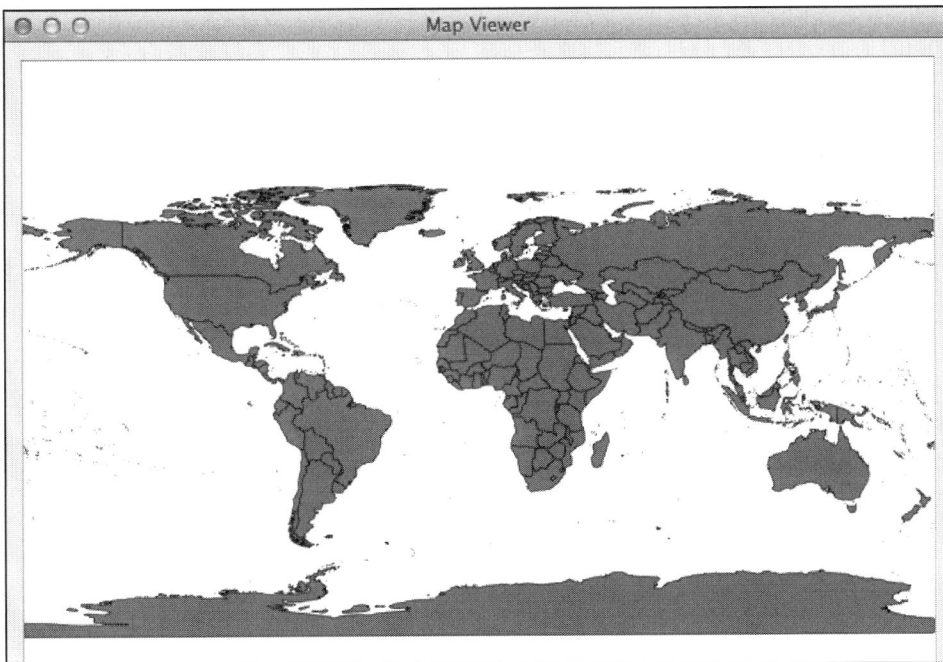

This application is still a bit ugly — you can see white space at the top and bottom this map because it doesn't take into account the aspect ratio of the map data. There's also no feature of zooming in or scrolling around the map. However, these can be added quite easily, and as you can see, it's not very difficult to create your own standalone mapping applications built on top of QGIS.

Summary

In this chapter, we became familiar with QGIS and the various ways in which it can be used as a Python geospatial development system. We installed and explored the QGIS application itself, and then looked at how Python can be used with QGIS. We saw how QGIS uses data sources, map layers, maps, and projects to organize and work with geospatial data. Next, we examined the three ways in which you can use Python and QGIS: by typing commands into the Python Console, by writing a Python plugin or by writing an external application that makes use of the QGIS Python API.

We then looked at the extensive set of Python libraries that come with QGIS, called PyQGIS, which you can use for geospatial development. We saw how to use the QGIS Python Console to directly manipulate the QGIS project, add layers, zoom in and out, change options, and so on.

Next up, we downloaded and examined a QGIS Python plugin. In doing this, we learned that QGIS plugins are simply Python packages installed in a hidden directory named .qgis2 (or .qgis) within your home or user directory. A plugin makes use of the Qt library to define and build resources such as user interface templates.

Finally, we saw how we can write external Python applications that load the PyQGIS libraries from within the QGIS system, and then use those libraries within a larger PyQt application.

In the next chapter, we will explore the QGIS Python Console in more detail, and use it to become more familiar with the PyQGIS library, and also see how we can use it within our own Python geospatial development projects.

2
The QGIS Python Console

In this chapter, we will look at the ways in which you can use the QGIS Python Console as a geospatial development tool. We will also use the console as a looking-glass to examine the world of QGIS programming. In particular, we will learn the following:

- Explore the ways in which the console can be used to develop and execute Python code

- Learn how to write Python scripts using the console's built-in source code editor

- Discover various tips and techniques to work with the QGIS Console

- Figure out how to manipulate the current project within QGIS using Python commands

- Access geospatial data and perform geospatial calculations using the console

- Use various QGIS user-interface elements within our Python programs

Using the console

While you briefly used the QGIS Console in the previous chapter, it is worth examining the QGIS Console window in more detail, so that you are aware of the various features that are available.

If you don't already have it open, choose the **Python Console** item from the **Plugins** menu to open the console. The following screenshot shows the various parts of the console window:

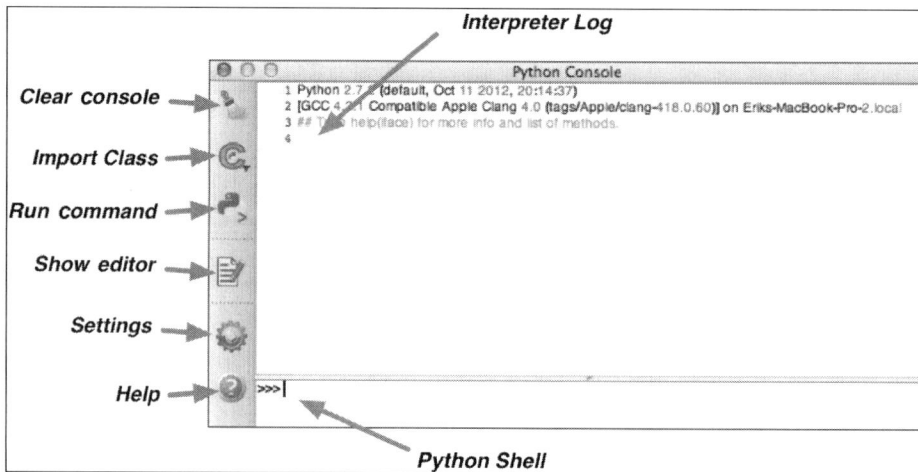

Let's take a closer look at these various parts:

- The **Clear console** button wipes out the contents of the interpreter log

- The **Import Class** pop up contains shortcuts to import some commonly-used PyQGIS classes

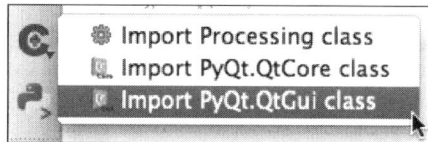

These are equivalent to typing `import Processing`, `from PyQt4.QtCore import *`, and `from PyQt4.QtGui import *`.

- The **Run command** button simply executes the command you have typed in the Python shell field

> Of course, you can also run the entered command by pressing the *Return* key, so this command is only useful if you really want to run a command using the mouse.

- The **Show editor** button shows or hides the built-in source code editor. We'll look at this shortly

- The **Settings** button displays the console's Settings window, allowing you to customize the way the console looks and behaves

- The **Help** button brings up the built-in help viewer page, which contains useful information about how to use the console

- The **Python Shell** field is where you type your Python commands and other input

- The **Interpreter Log** shows a complete history of the commands you have typed and the Python interpreter's output

As we've already seen, you can type Python commands in the shell and press the *Return* key to execute them. The commands you type, along with the Python interpreter's output, appear in the Interpreter Log.

The Python Shell has been designed to make it easier to work with Python interactively. The following features are currently supported:

- Pressing the up and down arrow keys will move through the command history, making it easy to re-enter the Python commands you typed earlier.

- You can display a list of previously-entered commands by pressing *Ctrl + Shift + Space* (*command + Shift + Space* on Mac).

- If you select some text in the Interpreter Log, you can use the **Enter Selected** command to move that text to the shell and execute it. This command is available in the console's pop-up menu, or it can be accessed by pressing *Ctrl + E* (*command + E* if you are running Mac OS X).

- The Python Shell supports **auto-completion**. As you type, a pop-up menu appears, showing you the matching class, function, and method names within the PyQGIS and PyQt APIs. You can then press the up and down arrow keys to select the exact name you want, and press the *Tab* key to select it.

- When you type an opening parenthesis, the console automatically enters the closing parenthesis for you. You can turn this off by using the **Settings** window if you wish.

- When you type `from XXX`, the console enters the word `import` for you automatically. Once again, you can turn this off in the **Settings** window if you don't like this behavior.

- When you type the opening parenthesis for a function or method, the C++ signature for that function or method will be displayed. Despite being in C++ format, this tells you which parameters are expected and the type of value being returned.

- You can type _api into the shell; your web browser will open the PyQGIS API reference documentation. Similarly, if you type _pyqgis, your web browser will display the PyQGIS Developer Cookbook.

While typing commands into the Python Shell is a useful way of exploring the QGIS Python libraries, and is good for one-off commands, it quickly gets tedious if you have to type multiple lines of Python text or repeat the same set of commands over and over. After all, this is why we store Python code in .py files and execute them, rather than just typing everything into the Python command-line interface.

The QGIS Console comes with its own editor, allowing you to write Python scripts and execute them directly within the console. Let's take a quick look at how this works.

With the QGIS Console open, click on the **Show Editor** icon ( ). The console window will be split in half, with the Python source code editor now taking up the right-hand side of the window:

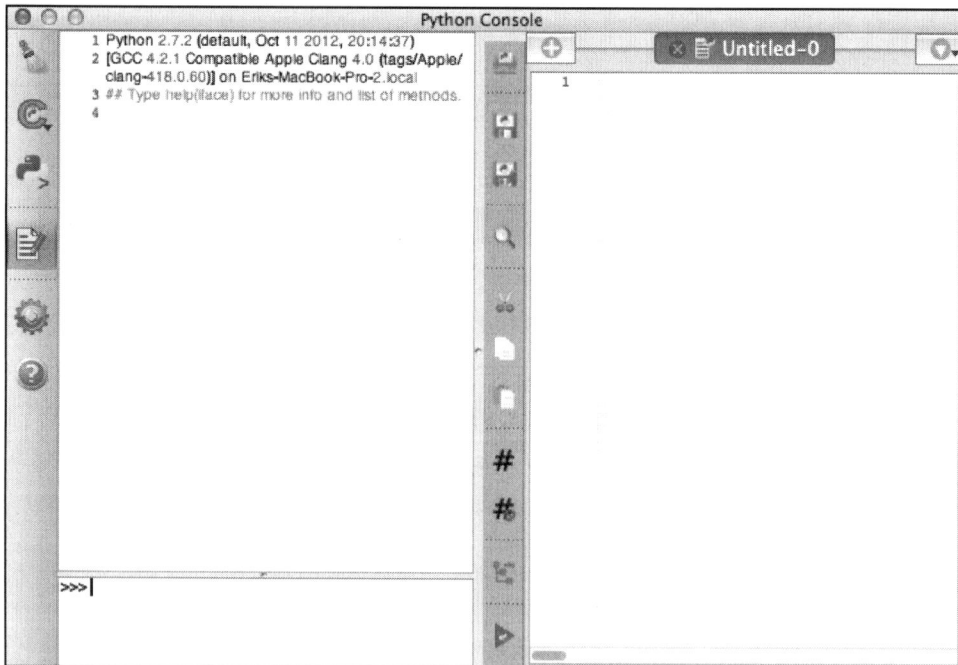

The various toolbar icons provide standard editing behavior such as loading and saving files, copying and pasting text, checking syntax, and executing your script:

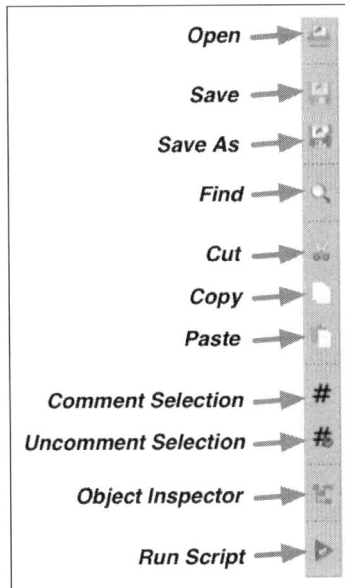

You'll probably want to memorize the top three icons as there are currently no keyboard shortcuts to open and save Python scripts.

Let's use the console editor to create a simple Python program and run it. With a QGIS project loaded, type the following into the editor:

```
for layer in iface.legendInterface().layers():
    print layer.name()
```

As you can probably guess, this program prints out the names of the various layers within the current project. To run this program, save it by clicking on the **Save As...** toolbar icon; then, either click on the **Run script** toolbar icon ( ), or type the keyboard shortcut, *Ctrl + Shift + E* (that's *command + Shift + E* on Mac). You should see something like the following appear in the Interpreter Log:

```
>>> execfile(u'/.../tmp1NR24f.py'.encode('utf-8'))
water
urban
basemap
```

Note that QGIS uses the `execfile()` function (which is part of the Python standard library) to execute your script.

> If your program didn't display the names of any layers, make sure you have a project loaded with at least one layer. In this example, we've used the example project we created in the previous chapter, which had three layers in it.

Of course, there is a lot more that we can do with the QGIS Console and its built-in Python editor, and we'll be using it to do useful work shortly. Before we do, though, there are two final things you should know about the QGIS Console.

Firstly, the console itself is written in Python using PyQt and the `PyQScintilla2` editor. You can learn a lot about how QGIS has been implemented by looking through the source code to the console, which is available at `https://github.com/qgis/QGIS/tree/master/python/console`.

The second thing you should know is that the console is implemented as a Qt "Dockable" window; that is, it can be dragged into a pane within the main QGIS window. If you click and hold the console's title bar, you can drag it inside the main window, as shown in the following illustration:

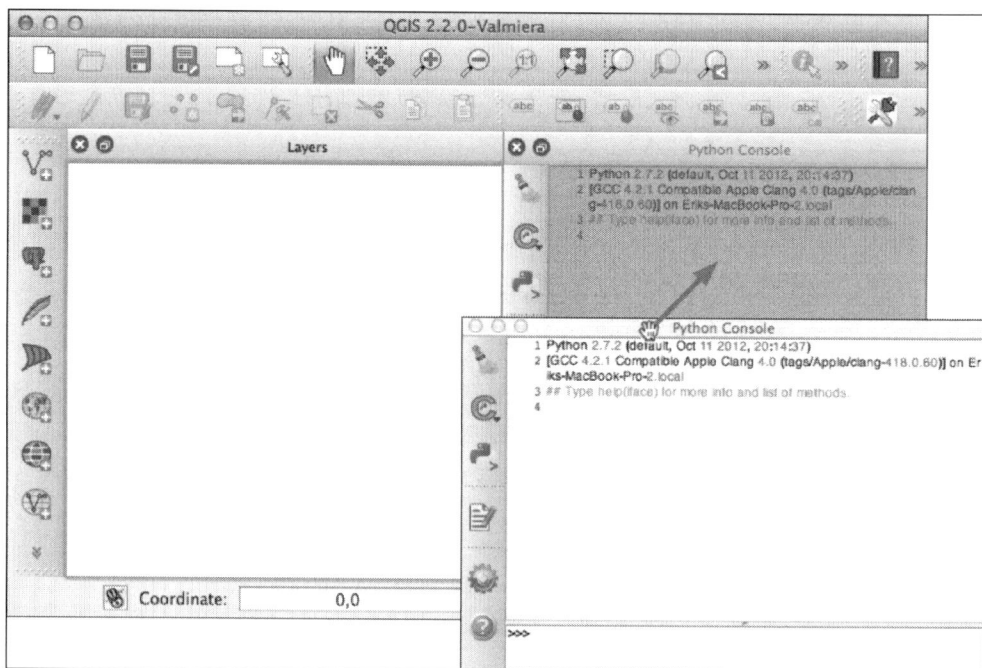

The console can be moved into any of the existing panes within the QGIS window, and it will stay there until you move it out.

To turn the console into a window again, click on the title bar and drag it out of the QGIS window. Alternatively, you can double-click on the console's title bar to switch between having it as a standalone window or a docked pane.

This docking behavior can be annoying if you're working on a small screen, where you can accidentally dock the console window while moving it out of the way so you can see what is beneath it. Fortunately, since the QGIS Console is implemented in PyQt, you can disable this quite easily by running the following Python code:

```
from console import console
from PyQt4.QtCore import Qt
console._console.setAllowedAreas(Qt.DockWidgetAreas(Qt.
NoDockWidgetArea))
```

If you want, you can create a startup script that automatically shows the console and makes it nondockable whenever QGIS starts up. The startup script is stored in a hidden directory in your user or home folder. Using your file manager, look for a hidden directory named `.qgis2` (or `.qgis`, depending on which version of QGIS you are running) in your user or home directory (for Mac OS X, you can use the **Go to Folder...** item in the Finder's **Go** menu). Inside this directory, there will be a subdirectory named `python`. Inside the `python` directory, create a file named `startup.py` and place the following into this file:

```
from console import console
from PyQt4.QtCore import Qt
console.show_console()
console._console.setAllowedAreas(Qt.DockWidgetAreas(Qt.
NoDockWidgetArea))
```

As you can see, the only thing we changed was to add a call to `console.show_console()` to open the console window when QGIS starts.

> If the console is currently docked, this script won't undock it, although it will prevent you from accidentally docking the console again.

Working with geospatial data in the console

So far, we have used the QGIS Console as a glorified Python interpreter, running standard Python programs and manipulating the QGIS user interface. But QGIS is a Geographical Information System (GIS), and one of the main uses of a GIS is to manipulate and query geospatial data. So, let's write some Python code to work with geospatial data directly within the QGIS Console.

In the previous chapter, we loaded three shapefiles into a QGIS project using Python. Here is a typical instruction we used to load a shapefile into a QGIS map layer:

```
layer = iface.addVectorLayer("/path/to/shapefile.shp", "layer_name",
"ogr")
```

While this is useful if you want to create a QGIS project programmatically, you may just want to load a shapefile so you can analyze its contents, without putting the data into a map layer. To do this, we have to get an appropriate **data provider** and ask it to open the shapefile, like this:

```
registry = QgsProviderRegistry.instance()
provider = registry.provider("ogr","/path/to/shapefile.shp")
if not provider.isValid():
    print "Invalid shapefile."
    return
```

The isValid() method will return False if the shapefile cannot be loaded; this allows us to fail gracefully if there is an error.

Once we have the data provider, we can ask it for the list of fields used to hold the attribute values for each of the shapefile's features:

```
for field in provider.fields():
    print field.name(), field.typeName()
```

We can also scan through the features within the shapefile using a QgsFeatureRequest object. For example:

```
for feature in provider.getFeatures(QgsFeatureRequest()):
    print feature.attribute("name")
```

Of course, this is just a taste of what can be done using the QGIS libraries to query and manipulate geospatial data. However, let's use what we've learned to build a simple program that calculates and displays information about the contents of a shapefile. Shapefiles hold geospatial features such as polygons, lines and points, and each feature can have any number of attributes associated with it. We'll write a program that opens and scans through a shapefile, identifying the features and calculating the length of each line feature and the area of each polygon feature. We'll also calculate the total length and area across all the features.

One of the challenges we'll have to deal with is the fact that the shapefile can be in any map projection. This means that our calculation of the area and length has to take the map projection into account; if, for example, we simply calculated the linear length of a feature in a shapefile that uses the EPSG 4326 projection (that is, lat/long coordinates), then the calculated length will be in degrees of latitude and longitude — which is a completely meaningless figure. We'll want to calculate the feature lengths in kilometers, and the areas in square kilometers. This is possible but requires us to do a bit more work.

Let's get started with our program. Start by creating a new Python script and enter the following:

```
from PyQt4.QtGui import *
```

To make the program easier to use, we're going to define a function and place all our program logic inside this function, like this:

```
def analyze_shapefile():
    ...

analyze_shapefile()
```

Now, let's start writing the contents of the `analyze_shapefile()` function. So far, we've been hardwiring the name of the shapefile, but this time, let's use QGIS's graphical interface to prompt the user to select a shapefile:

```
def analyze_shapefile():
    filename = QFileDialog.getOpenFileName(iface.mainWindow(),
                                           "Select Shapefile",
                                           "~", '*.shp')

    if not filename:
        print "Cancelled."
        return
```

We can then open the selected shapefile:

```
registry = QgsProviderRegistry.instance()
provider = registry.provider("ogr",filename)
if not provider.isValid():
    print "Invalid shapefile."
    return
```

In order to identify a feature, we need to display a meaningful label for the feature. To do this, we'll look for an attribute with a likely-looking name. If there is no suitable attribute, we'll have to use the feature's ID instead.

Let's start by building a list of the various attributes stored in this shapefile:

```
attr_names = []
for field in provider.fields():
    attr_names.append(field.name())
```

We're now ready to start scanning through the shapefile's features. Before we do this, though, let's initialize a couple of variables to hold the totals we need to calculate:

```
tot_length = 0
tot_area = 0
```

We also need to set up a `QgsDistanceArea` object to do the distance and area calculations for us.

```
crs = provider.crs()
calculator = QgsDistanceArea()
calculator.setSourceCrs(crs)
calculator.setEllipsoid(crs.ellipsoidAcronym())
calculator.setEllipsoidalMode(crs.geographicFlag())
```

We'll use this object to calculate the true length and area of the shapefile's features in meters and square meters respectively.

We're now ready to scan through the contents of the shapefile, processing each feature in turn:

```
for feature in provider.getFeatures(QgsFeatureRequest()):
    ...
```

For each feature, we want to calculate a label that identifies that feature. We'll do this by looking for an attribute called `"name"`, `"NAME"`, or `"Name"`, and using that attribute's value as the feature label. If there is no attribute with one of these field names, we'll fall back to using the feature's ID instead. Here is the relevant code:

```
if "name" in attr_names:
    feature_label = feature.attribute("name")
elif "Name" in attr_names:
    feature_label = feature.attribute("Name")
elif "NAME" in attr_names:
    feature_label = feature.attribute("NAME")
else:
    feature_label = str(feature.id())
```

Next, we need to obtain the geometry object associated with the feature. The geometry object represents a polygon, line, or point. Getting a reference to the feature's underlying geometry object is simple:

```
geometry = feature.geometry()
```

We can now use the `QgsDistanceArea` calculator we initialized earlier to calculate the length of a line feature and the area of a polygon feature. To do this, we'll first have to identify the type of feature we are dealing with:

```
if geometry.type() == QGis.Line:
    ...
elif geometry.type() == QGis.Polygon:
    ...
else:
    ...
```

For line geometries, we'll calculate the length of the line and update the total length:

```
if geometry.type() == QGis.Line:
    length = int(calculator.measure (geometry) / 1000)
    tot_length = tot_length + length
    feature_info = "line of length %d kilometers" % length
```

For polygon geometries, we'll calculate the area of the polygon and update the total area:

```
elif geometry.type() == QGis.Polygon:
    area = int(calculator.measure (geometry) / 1000000)
    tot_area = tot_area + area
    feature_info = "polygon of area %d square kilometers" %
area
```

Finally, for the other types of geometries, we'll simply display the geometry's type:

```
else:
    geom_type = qgis.vectorGeometryType(geometry.type())
    feature_info = "geometry of type %s" % geom_type
```

Now that we've done these calculations, we can display the feature's label together with the information we calculated about this feature:

```
print "%s: %s" % (feature_label, feature_info)
```

Finally, when we've finished iterating over the features, we can display the total line length and polygon area for all the features in the shapefile:

```
print "Total length of all line features: %d" % tot_length
print "Total area of all polygon features: %d" % tot_area
```

This completes our program for analyzing the contents of a shapefile. The full source for this program is available in the code samples provided with this book. To test our program, type or copy and paste it into the console's script editor, save the file, and click on the **Run Script** button (or press *Ctrl + Shift + E*). Here's an example of what the program's output looks like:

```
Antigua and Barbuda: polygon of area 549 square kilometers

Algeria: polygon of area 2334789 square kilometers

Azerbaijan: polygon of area 86109 square kilometers

Albania: polygon of area 28728 square kilometers

Armenia: polygon of area 29732 square kilometers

...

Jersey: polygon of area 124 square kilometers

South Georgia South Sandwich Islands: polygon of area 3876 square
kilometers

Taiwan: polygon of area 36697 square kilometers

Total length of all line features: 0

Total area of all polygon features: 147363163
```

> This output was produced using the World Borders dataset, available at http://thematicmapping.org/downloads/world_borders.php. This is a useful set of geospatial data, which provides simple world maps and associated metadata. If you haven't already done so, you should grab yourself a copy of this dataset, as we'll be using this shapefile throughout this book.

As you can see, it is quite possible to create Python programs that read and analyze geospatial data, and you can run these programs directly from within the QGIS Console. It is also possible to create and manipulate geospatial data sources using the PyQGIS libraries.

Scripting the QGIS user interface

While the example program we created earlier has very limited user interaction, it is quite possible to build your program to directly use the QGIS user interface elements such as the status bar, the message bar, progress indicators, and the QGIS logging window. You can also create custom forms and windows so that the output of your program looks just like any other feature of QGIS itself. Let's take a closer look at how some of these QGIS user-interface elements can be used from within your Python programs.

The status bar

The QGIS window has a status bar. You can use it to display the current status of your Python program, for example:

```
iface.mainWindow().statusBar().showMessage("Please wait...")
```

The status message will appear at the bottom of the window, like this:

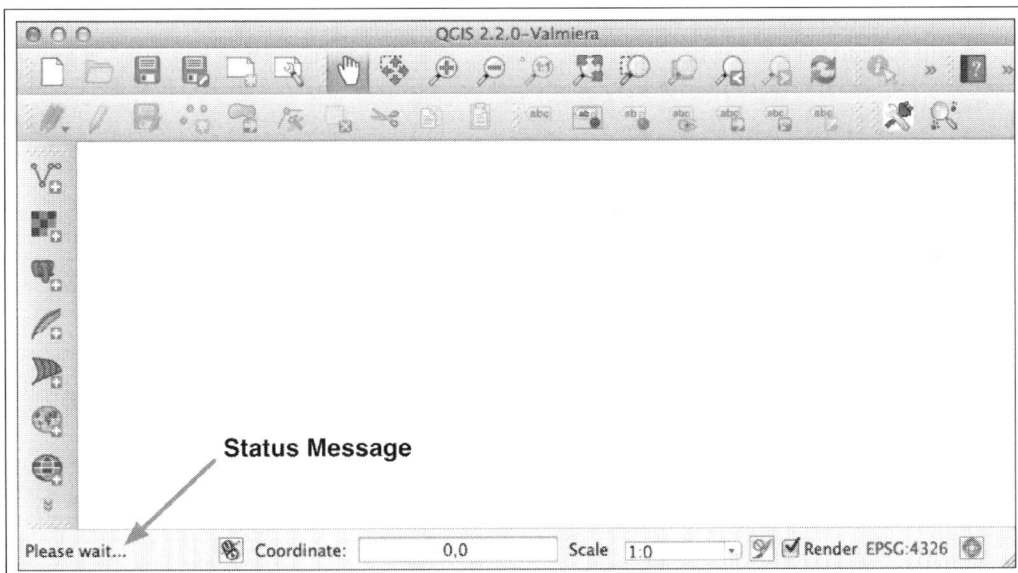

As you can see, there isn't much room on the status bar, so you'll need to keep your status message short. To hide the message again, do the following:

```
iface.mainWindow().statusBar().clearMessage()
```

The message bar

A message bar appears within a window to display messages to the user, for example:

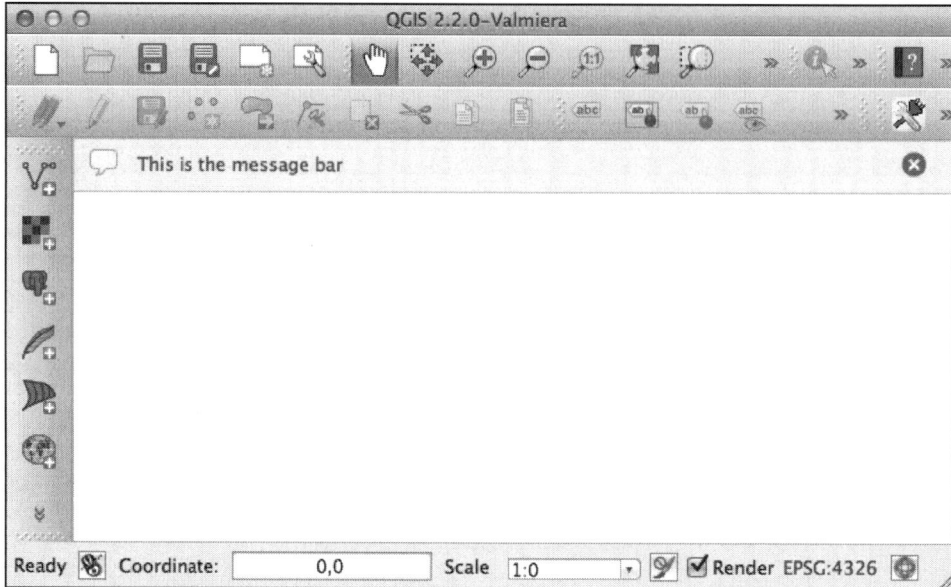

Message bars have several useful features:

- Messages can be stacked so that if multiple messages appear at once, the user won't miss the earlier messages
- Messages have a level, which indicates the importance of the message, and affects how the message is displayed
- Messages have an optional title as well as the text to be displayed
- Messages can stay on the screen until the user closes them, or they can time out, disappearing automatically after a given number of seconds
- You can add various Qt widgets to the message bar to customize its behavior and appearance

Any window in QGIS can have its own message bar. The `iface` variable has a `messageBar()` method, which returns the message bar for the main QGIS window, but you can also add a message bar to your own custom windows if you wish.

To add a message to a message bar, you call the message bar's `pushMessage()` method. To create a message without a title, you use the following method signature:

```
messageBar.pushMessage(text, level=QsgMessageBar.INFO, duration=None)
```

For example:

```
from qgis.gui import *
iface.messageBar().pushMessage("Hello World",
        level=QgsMessageBar.INFO)
```

To include a title, use the following method signature:

```
messageBar.pushMessage(title, text, level=QgsMessageBar.INFO,
duration=None)
```

In both cases, the `level` parameter can be set to `QgsMessageBar.INFO`, `QgsMessageBar.WARNING`, or `QgsMessageBar.CRITICAL`, and if the `duration` parameter is specified, it will be the number of seconds before the message is hidden.

To remove all the messages currently being shown, you can call the `messageBar.clearWidgets()` method.

Progress indicators

You can also make use of the message bar to display a Qt progress indicator. To do this, use the `messageBar.createMessage()` method to create a widget to display your message, then modify the widget to include additional Qt controls, and finally call the `messageBar.pushWidget()` method to display the message and the controls you added. For example:

```
progressMessage = iface.messageBar().createMessage("Please wait")
progressBar = QProgressBar()
progressBar.setMaximum(100)
progressBar.setAlignment(Qt.AlignLeft | Qt.AlignVCenter)
progressMessage.layout().addWidget(progressBar)
iface.messageBar().pushWidget(progressMessage)
...
progressBar.setValue(n)
...
iface.messageBar().clearWidgets()
```

> There is a bug in the Mac version of QGIS 2.2, which prevents the user interface from updating while your Python code is running. A workaround for this is to use threads, as described in the following article: http://snorf.net/blog/2013/12/07/multithreading-in-qgis-python-plugins

QGIS logging

You can use the built-in logging facilities of QGIS to display the output in a separate window. For example:

```
for i in range(100):
    QgsMessageLog.logMessage("Message %d" % i)
```

The log messages will be shown in the log view, which you can show by navigating to **View | Panels | Log Messages**.

If you wish, you can change the importance of your message by adding a message level to the `logMessage()` call, for example:

```
QgsMessageLog.logMessage("Something is wrong",
                    level=QgsMessageLog.CRITICAL)
```

Rather than being mixed in with other QGIS messages, you can also choose to have all your log messages appear in a pane by themselves, by adding a tag to the `logMessage()` call as follows:

```
QgsMessageLog.logMessage("Test Message", tag="my panel")
```

Your log messages will then appear in a panel by themselves, like this:

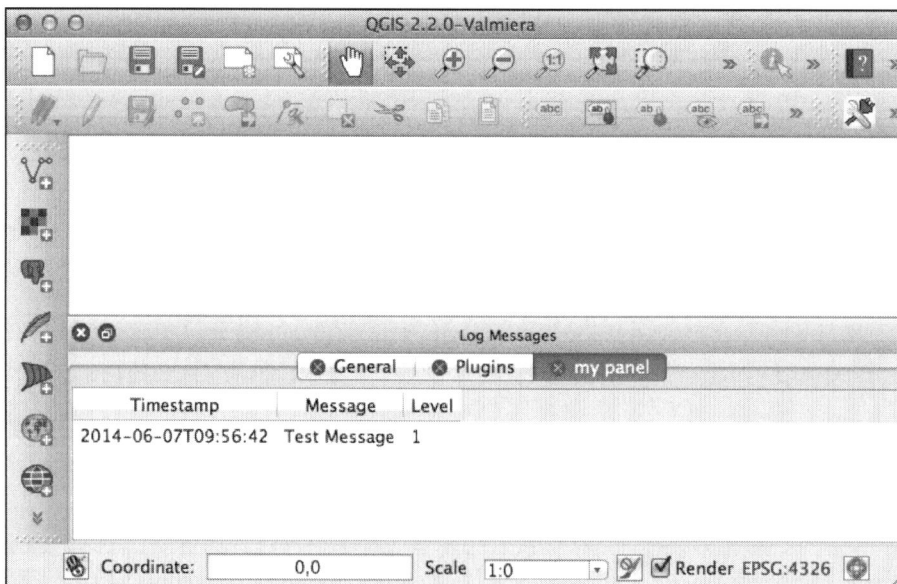

Custom dialogs and windows

As QGIS is built on top of Qt, you can use the PyQt classes to create your own windows and dialog boxes, and display them directly from within your Python code. For example, here's a script that displays a custom dialog box that prompts the user to enter a latitude and longitude value:

```
from PyQt4.QtGui import *

class MyDialog(QDialog):
    def __init__(self):
        QDialog.__init__(self)
        self.setWindowTitle("Enter Coordinate")

        layout = QFormLayout(self)

        self.lat_label = QLabel("Latitude", self)
        self.lat_field = QLineEdit(self)

        self.long_label = QLabel("Longitude", self)
        self.long_field = QLineEdit(self)

        self.ok_btn = QPushButton("OK", self)
        self.ok_btn.clicked.connect(self.accept)

        self.cancel_btn = QPushButton("Cancel", self)
        self.cancel_btn.clicked.connect(self.reject)

        btn_layout = QHBoxLayout(self)
        btn_layout.addWidget(self.ok_btn)
        btn_layout.addWidget(self.cancel_btn)

        layout.addRow(self.lat_label, self.lat_field)
        layout.addRow(self.long_label, self.long_field)
        layout.addRow(btn_layout)

        self.setLayout(layout)

dialog = MyDialog()
if dialog.exec_() == QDialog.Accepted:
    lat = dialog.lat_field.text()
    long = dialog.long_field.text()
    print lat,long
```

Running this script will cause the following dialog box to be displayed:

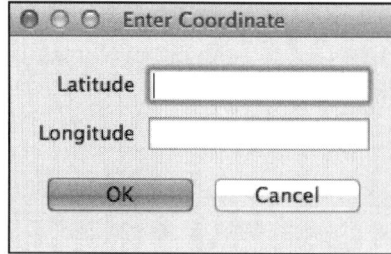

If the user clicks on the **OK** button, the entered latitude and longitude values will be printed to the console. Of course, this is just a simple example—there's no error checking or conversion of the entered values from text back to numbers. However, this is just a simple example. There's a lot more that can be done using the PyQt libraries, and people have written entire books on the subject. However, the main thing to realize now is that, because QGIS is built on top of Qt, you can use all of the features of PyQt to build sophisticated user interfaces. You're certainly not limited to using the Python console to interact with the user.

Summary

In this chapter, we explored the QGIS Python Console, and how to use it for a variety of programming tasks. We also used the console to delve more deeply into the QGIS Python programming environment.

As we worked through this chapter, we learned what the various toolbar buttons and controls do within the QGIS Console, and how to enter commands using the Python Shell. We looked at how we can use the Python Interpreter Log to view the previous output and re-enter commands you executed earlier. We saw the ways in which you can use autocompletion to enter your Python code more quickly, and also learned about the parameters that the various PyQGIS functions and methods accept.

We then looked at how to enter and execute Python scripts using the built-in source code editor. We discovered that the Python Console is itself written in Python, allowing you to explore the source code and manipulate the console itself using the Python code.

We learned how to create a startup script that is run automatically whenever QGIS starts up, and how you can use this to set up the console to open automatically and prevent it from acting as a dockable window.

Next, we examined the process of loading geospatial data directly using your Python scripts, without first having to load it into a QGIS map layer. We saw how to identify the attributes defined by a shapefile, how to scan through the features within a shapefile, and the ways in which the PyQGIS libraries allow you to perform common geospatial calculations.

We then looked at the various ways in which you can make use of QGIS user interface elements within your Python scripts, including the status bar, message bars, progress indicators, and the QGIS message log.

Finally, we saw how you can use standard PyQt classes to create your own windows and dialog boxes to provide a sophisticated user interface for your Python scripts.

In the following chapter, we will work more directly with the QGIS Python libraries, learning how these libraries are structured and how you can use them to perform various sorts of geospatial data manipulation and display the results on a map.

3
Learning the QGIS Python API

In this chapter, we will take a closer look at the Python libraries available for the QGIS Python developer, and also look at the various ways in which we can use these libraries to perform useful tasks within QGIS.

In particular, you will learn:

- How the QGIS Python libraries are based on the underlying C++ APIs
- How to use the C++ API documentation as a reference to work with the Python APIs
- How the PyQGIS libraries are organized
- The most important concepts and classes within the PyQGIS libraries and how to use them
- Some practical examples of performing useful tasks using PyQGIS

About the QGIS Python APIs

The QGIS system itself is written in C++, and has its own set of APIs that are also written in C++. The Python APIs are implemented as wrappers around these C++ APIs. For example, there is a Python class named `QgisInterface` that acts as a wrapper around a C++ class of the same name. All the methods, class variables, and the like that are implemented by the C++ version of `QgisInterface` are made available through the Python wrapper.

What this means is that when you access the Python QGIS APIs, you aren't accessing the API directly. Instead, the wrapper connects your code to the underlying C++ objects and methods, as follows:

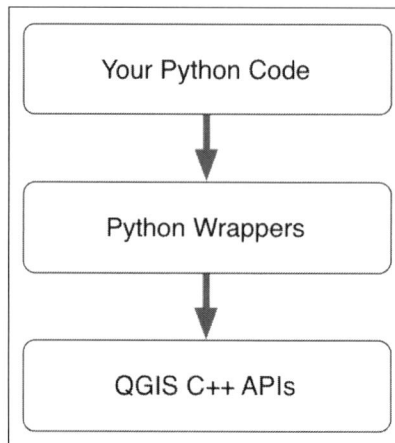

Fortunately, in most cases, the QGIS Python wrappers simply hide away the complexity of the underlying C++ code, so the PyQGIS libraries work as you would expect them to. There are some gotchas, however, and we will cover these as they come up.

Deciphering the C++ documentation

As QGIS is implemented in C++, the documentation for QGIS APIs is all based on C++. This can make it difficult for Python developers to understand and work with the QGIS APIs. For example, the API documentation for the `QgsInterface.zoomToActiveLayer()` method:

> **virtual void QgsInterface::zoomToActiveLayer ( )**   `pure virtual` `slot`
>
> Zoom to extent of the active layer.

If you're not familiar with C++, this can be quite confusing. Fortunately, as a Python programmer, you can skip over much of the complexity as it doesn't apply to you. In particular:

- The `virtual` keyword is an implementation detail you don't need to worry about
- `void` indicates that the method doesn't return a value
- The double colons in `QgisInterface::zoomToActiveLayer` are simply a C++ convention for separating the class name from the method name

Just like in Python, the parentheses show that the method doesn't take any parameters. So if you have an instance of `QgisInterface` (for example, as the standard `iface` variable available in the Python Console), you can call this method simply by typing the following:

```
iface.zoomToActiveLayer()
```

Now, let's take a look at a slightly more complex example: the C++ documentation for the `QgisInterface.addVectorLayer()` method looks like the following:

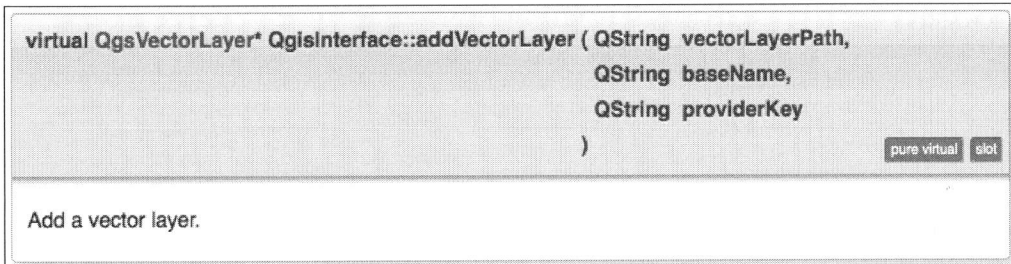

```
virtual QgsVectorLayer* QgisInterface::addVectorLayer ( QString  vectorLayerPath,
                                                        QString  baseName,
                                                        QString  providerKey
                                                      )                          pure virtual  slot

Add a vector layer.
```

Notice how the `virtual` keyword is followed by `QgsVectorLayer*` instead of `void`. This is the return value for this method; it returns a `QgsVector` object.

> Technically speaking, `*` means that the method returns a **pointer** to an object of type `QgsVectorLayer`. Fortunately, Python wrappers automatically handle pointers, so you don't need to worry about this.

Notice the brief description at the bottom of the documentation for this method; while many of the C++ methods have very little, if any, additional information, other methods have more extensive information. Obviously, you should read these descriptions carefully as they tell you more about what the method does.

Even without any description, the C++ documentation is still useful as it tells you what the method is called, what parameters it accepts, and what type of data is being returned.

In the preceding method, you can see that there are three parameters listed in between the parentheses. As C++ is a *strongly typed* language, you have to define the type of each parameter when you define a function. This is helpful for Python programmers as it tells you what type of value to supply. Apart from QGIS objects, you might also encounter the following data types in the C++ documentation:

Data type	Description
int	A standard Python integer value
long	A standard Python long integer value
float	A standard Python floating point (real) number
bool	A Boolean value (true or false)
QString	A string value. Note that the QGIS Python wrappers automatically convert Python strings to C++ strings, so you don't need to deal with QString objects directly
QList	This object is used to encapsulate a list of other objects. For example, QList<QString*> represents a list of strings

Just as in Python, a method can take default values for each parameter. For example, the QgisInterface.newProject() method looks like the following:

```
virtual void QgisInterface::newProject ( bool  thePromptToSaveFlag = false )    pure virtual  slot

Start a blank project.
```

In this case, the thePromptToSaveFlag parameter has a default value, and this default value will be used if no value is supplied.

In Python, classes are initialized using the __init__ method. In C++, this is called a *constructor*. For example, the constructor for the QgsLabel class looks like the following:

QgsLabel::QgsLabel (const QgsFields & fields)

Definition at line **47** of file **qgslabel.cpp**.

References fields(), LabelFieldCount, mFields, mLabelAttributes, and mLabelFieldIdx.

Just as in Python, C++ classes *inherit* the methods defined in their superclass. Fortunately, QGIS doesn't have an extensive class hierarchy, so most of the classes don't have a superclass. However, don't forget to check for a superclass if you can't find the method you're looking for in the documentation for the class itself.

Finally, be aware that C++ supports the concept of *method overloading*. A single method can be defined more than once, where each version accepts a different set of parameters. For example, take a look at the constructor for the QgsRectangle class—you will see that there are four different versions of this method.

The first version accepts the four coordinates as floating point numbers:

QgsRectangle::QgsRectangle (double xmin = 0,
                            double ymin = 0,
                            double xmax = 0,
                            double ymax = 0
)

Constructor.

Definition at line **31** of file **qgsrectangle.cpp**.

References normalize().

Referenced by buffer(), and intersect().

The second version constructs a rectangle using two `QgsPoint` objects:

```
QgsRectangle::QgsRectangle ( const QgsPoint &  p1,
                             const QgsPoint &  p2
                           )
```

Construct a rectangle from two points. The rectangle is normalized after construction.

Definition at line 37 of file **qgsrectangle.cpp**.

The third version copies the coordinates from `QRectF` (which is a Qt data type) into a `QgsRectangle` object:

```
QgsRectangle::QgsRectangle ( const QRectF &  qRectF )
```

Construct a rectangle from a QRectF.

The rectangle is normalized after construction.

Note
     added in 2.0

Definition at line 42 of file **qgsrectangle.cpp**.

References **xmax, xmin, ymax,** and **ymin.**

The final version copies the coordinates from another `QgsRectangle` object:

```
QgsRectangle::QgsRectangle ( const QgsRectangle &  other )
```

Copy constructor.

Definition at line 50 of file **qgsrectangle.cpp**.

References **xmax, xMaximum(), xmin, xMinimum(), ymax, yMaximum(), ymin,** and **yMinimum().**

The C++ compiler chooses the correct method to use based on the parameters that have been supplied. Python has no concept of method overloading; just choose the version of the method that accepts the parameters you want to supply, and the QGIS Python wrappers will automatically choose the correct method for you.

If you keep these guidelines in mind, deciphering the C++ documentation for QGIS isn't all that hard. It just looks more complicated than it really is, thanks to all the complexity specific to C++. However, it doesn't take long for your brain to start filtering out the C++ gobbledygook, and you'll be able to use the QGIS reference documentation almost as easily as if it was written for Python rather than C++.

Organizing the QGIS Python libraries

Now that we can understand the C++-oriented documentation, let's see how the PyQGIS libraries are structured. All of the PyQGIS libraries are organized under a package named `qgis`. You wouldn't normally import `qgis` directly, however, as all the interesting libraries are subpackages within this main package; here are the five packages that make up the PyQGIS library:

`qgis.core`	This provides access to the core GIS functionality used throughout QGIS.
`qgis.gui`	This defines a range of GUI widgets that you can include in your own programs.
`qgis.analysis`	This provides spatial analysis tools to analyze vector and raster format data.
`qgis.networkanalysis`	This provides tools to build and analyze topologies.
`qgis.utils`	This implements miscellaneous functions that allow you to work with the QGIS application using Python.

The first two packages (`qgis.core` and `qgis.gui`) implement the most important parts of the PyQGIS library, and it's worth spending some time to become more familiar with the concepts and classes they define. Let's take a closer look at these two packages now.

The qgis.core package

The `qgis.core` package defines fundamental classes used throughout the QGIS system. A large part of this package is dedicated to working with vector and raster format geospatial data, and displaying these types of data within a map. Let's see how this is done.

Maps and map layers

A map consists of multiple layers drawn one on top of the other:

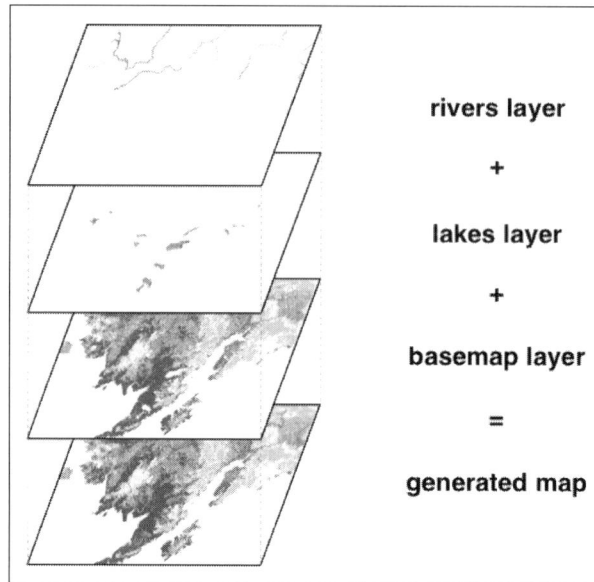

rivers layer

+

lakes layer

+

basemap layer

=

generated map

There are three types of map layers supported by QGIS:

- **Vector layer**: This layer draws geospatial features such as points, lines, and polygons
- **Raster layer**: This layer draws raster (bitmapped) data onto a map
- **Plugin layer**: This layer allows a plugin to draw directly onto a map

Each of these types of map layers has a corresponding class within the `qgis.core` library. For example, a vector map layer will be represented by an object of type `qgis.core.QgsVectorLayer`.

We will take a closer look at vector and raster map layers shortly. Before we do this, though, we need to learn how geospatial data (both vector and raster data) is positioned on a map.

Coordinate reference systems

Since the Earth is a three-dimensional object, while maps represent the Earth's surface as a two-dimensional plane, there has to be a way of translating from points on the Earth's surface into (x,y) coordinates within a map. This is done using a **Coordinate Reference System (CRS)**:

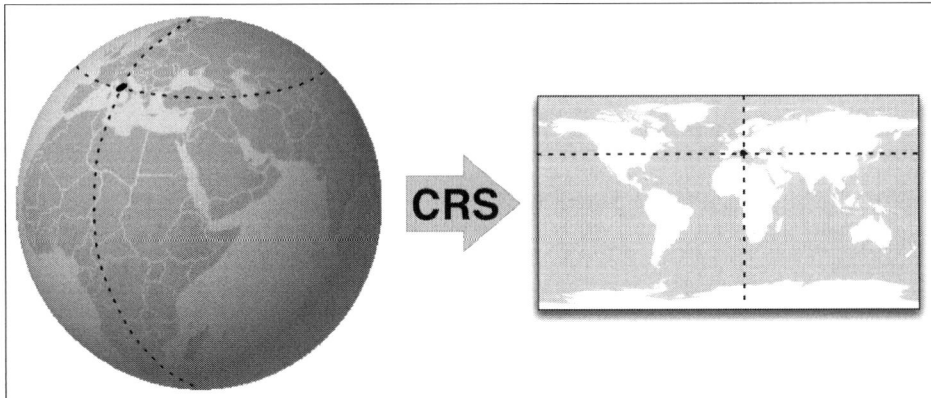

Globe image courtesy Wikimedia (http://commons.wikimedia.org/wiki/File:Rotating_globe.gif)

A CRS has two parts: an **ellipsoid**, which is a mathematical model of the Earth's surface, and a **projection**, which is a formula that converts points on the surface of the spheroid into (x,y) coordinates on a map.

Fortunately, most of the time you can simply select the appropriate CRS that matches the CRS of the data you are using. However, because many different coordinate reference systems have been devised over the years, it is vital that you use the correct CRS when plotting your geospatial data. If you don't do this, your features will be displayed in the wrong place or have the wrong shape.

The majority of geospatial data available today uses the **EPSG 4326** coordinate reference system (sometimes also referred to as WGS84). This CRS defines coordinates as latitude and longitude values. This is the default CRS used for new data imported into QGIS. However, if your data uses a different coordinate reference system, you will need to create and use a different CRS for your map layer.

The `qgis.core.QgsCoordinateReferenceSystem` class represents a CRS. Once you create your coordinate reference system, you can tell your map layer to use that CRS when accessing the underlying data. For example:

```
crs = QgsCoordinateReferenceSystem(4326,
        QgsCoordinateReferenceSystem.EpsgCrsId)
layer.setCrs(crs)
```

Note that different map layers can use different coordinate reference systems. Each layer will use its CRS when drawing the contents of the layer onto the map.

Vector layers

A vector layer draws geospatial data onto a map in the form of points, lines, polygons, and so on. Vector-format geospatial data is typically loaded from a **vector data source** such as a shapefile or database. Other vector data sources can hold vector data in memory, or load data from a web service across the Internet.

A vector-format data source has a number of features, where each feature represents a single *record* within the data source. The `qgis.core.QgsFeature` class represents a feature within a data source. Each feature has the following components:

- **ID**: This is the feature's unique identifier within the data source

- **Geometry**: This is the underlying point, line, polygon, and so on, which represents the feature on the map. For example, a **city** data source would have one feature for each city, and the geometry would typically be either a point that represents the center of the city, or a polygon (or a multipolygon) that represents the city's outline.

- **Attributes**: These are key/value pairs that provide additional information about the feature. For example, a city data source representing cities might have attributes such as `total_area`, `population`, `elevation`, and so on. Attribute values can be strings, integers, or floating point numbers.

In QGIS, a **data provider** allows the vector layer to access the features within the data source. The data provider, an instance of `qgis.core.QgsVectorDataProvider`, includes:

- A **geometry type** that is stored in the data source

- A list of **fields** that provide information about the attributes stored for each feature

- The ability to search through the features within the data source, using the `getFeatures()` method and the `QgsFeatureRequest` class

You can access the various vector (and also raster) data providers by using the `qgis.core.QgsProviderRegistry` class.

The vector layer itself is represented by a `qgis.core.QgsVectorLayer` object. Each vector layer includes:

- **Data provider**: This is the connection to the underlying file or database that holds the geospatial information to be displayed
- **Coordinate reference system**: This indicates which CRS the geospatial data uses
- **Renderer**: This chooses how the features are to be displayed

Let's take a closer look at the concept of a renderer and how features are displayed within a vector map layer.

Displaying vector data

The features within a vector map layer are displayed using a combination of **renderer** and **symbol** objects. The renderer chooses the symbol that has to be used for a given feature, and the symbol that does the actual drawing.

There are three basic types of symbols defined by QGIS:

- **Marker symbol**: This displays a point as a filled circle
- **Line symbol**: This draws a line using a given line width and color
- **Fill symbol**: This draws the interior of a polygon with a given color

These three types of symbols are implemented as subclasses of the `qgis.core.QgsSymbolV2` class:

- `qgis.core.QgsMarkerSymbolV2`
- `qgis.core.QgsLineSymbolV2`
- `qgis.core.QgsFillSymbolV2`

> You might be wondering why all these classes have "V2" in their name. This is a historical quirk of QGIS. Earlier versions of QGIS supported both an "old" and a "new" system of rendering, and the "V2" naming refers to the new rendering system. The old rendering system no longer exists, but the "V2" naming continues to maintain backward compatibility with existing code.

Internally, symbols are rather complex, using "symbol layers" to draw multiple elements on top of each other. In most cases, however, you can make use of the "simple" version of the symbol. This makes it easier to create a new symbol without having to deal with the internal complexity of symbol layers. For example:

```
symbol = QgsMarkerSymbolV2.createSimple({'width' : 1.0,
                                         'color' : "255,0,0"})
```

While symbols draw the features onto the map, a renderer is used to choose which symbol to use to draw a particular feature. In the simplest case, the same symbol is used for every feature within a layer. This is called a **single symbol renderer**, and is represented by the `qgis.core.QgsSingleSymbolRenderV2` class. Other possibilities include:

- **Categorized symbol renderer** (`qgis.core.QgsCategorizedSymbolRendererV2`): This renderer chooses a symbol based on the value of an attribute. The categorized symbol renderer has a mapping from attribute values to symbols.

- **Graduated symbol renderer** (`qgis.core.QgsGraduatedSymbolRendererV2`): This type of renderer uses ranges of attribute values, and maps each range to an appropriate symbol.

Using a single symbol renderer is very straightforward:

```
symbol = ...
renderer = QgsSingleSymbolRendererV2(symbol)
layer.setRendererV2(renderer)
```

To use a categorized symbol renderer, you first define a list of `qgis.core.QgsRendererCategoryV2` objects, and then use that to create the renderer. For example:

```
symbol_male = ...
symbol_female = ...

categories = []
categories.append(QgsRendererCategoryV2("M", symbol_male, "Male"))
categories.append(QgsRendererCategoryV2("F", symbol_female,
                  "Female"))

renderer = QgsCategorizedSymbolRendererV2("", categories)
renderer.setClassAttribute("GENDER")
layer.setRendererV2(renderer)
```

Notice that the `QgsRendererCategoryV2` constructor takes three parameters: the desired value, the symbol used, and the label used to describe that category.

Finally, to use a graduated symbol renderer, you define a list of `qgis.core.QgsRendererRangeV2` objects and then use that to create your renderer. For example:

```
symbol1 = ...
symbol2 = ...

ranges = []
ranges.append(QgsRendererRangeV2(0, 10, symbol1, "Range 1"))
ranges.append(QgsRendererRange(11, 20, symbol2, "Range 2"))

renderer = QgsGraduatedSymbolRendererV2("", ranges)
renderer.setClassAttribute("FIELD")

layer.setRendererV2(renderer)
```

Accessing vector data

In addition to displaying the contents of a vector layer within a map, you can use Python to directly access the underlying data. This can be done using the data provider's `getFeatures()` method. For example, to iterate over all the features within the layer, you can do the following:

```
provider = layer.dataProvider()
for feature in provider.getFeatures(QgsFeatureRequest()):
    ...
```

If you want to search for features based on some criteria, you can use the `QgsFeatureRequest` object's `setFilterExpression()` method, as follows:

```
provider = layer.dataProvider()
request = QgsFeatureRequest()
request.setFilterExpression('"GENDER" = "M"')
for feature in provider.getFeatures(QgsFeatureRequest()):
    ...
```

Once you have the features, it's easy to get access to the feature's geometry, ID, and attributes. For example:

```
geometry = feature.geometry()
id = feature.id()
name = feature.attribute("NAME")
```

The object returned by the `feature.geometry()` call, which will be an instance of `qgis.core.QgsGeometry`, represents the feature's geometry. This object has a large number of methods you can use to extract the underlying data and perform various geospatial calculations.

Spatial indexes

In the previous section, we searched for features based on their attribute values. There are times, though, when you might want to find features based on their position in space. For example, you might want to find all features that lie within a certain distance of a given point. To do this, you can use a **spatial index**, which indexes features according to their location and extent. Spatial indexes are represented in QGIS by the `QgsSpatialIndex` class.

For performance reasons, a spatial index is not created automatically for each vector layer. However, it's easy to create one when you need it:

```
provider = layer.dataProvider()
index = QgsSpatialIndex()
for feature in provider.getFeatures(QgsFeatureRequest()):
  index.insertFeature(feature)
```

Don't forget that you can use the `QgsFeatureRequest.setFilterExpression()` method to limit the set of features that get added to the index.

Once you have the spatial index, you can use it to perform queries based on the position of the features. In particular:

- You can find one or more features that are closest to a given point using the `nearestNeighbor()` method. For example:

```
features = index.nearestNeighbor(QgsPoint(long, lat), 5)
```

  Note that this method takes two parameters: the desired point as a `QgsPoint` object and the number of features to return.

- You can find all features that intersect with a given rectangular area by using the `intersects()` method, as follows:

```
features = index.intersects(QgsRectangle(left, bottom,
                   right, top))
```

Raster layers

Raster-format geospatial data is essentially a bitmapped image, where each pixel or "cell" in the image corresponds to a particular part of the Earth's surface. Raster data is often organized into **bands**, where each band represents a different piece of information. A common use for bands is to store the red, green, and blue component of the pixel's color in a separate band. Bands might also represent other types of information, such as moisture level, elevation, or soil type.

There are many ways in which raster information can be displayed. For example:

- If the raster data only has one band, the pixel value can be used as an index into a **palette**. The palette maps each pixel value maps to a particular color.

- If the raster data has only one band but no palette is provided, the pixel values can be used directly as a **grayscale** value; that is, larger numbers are lighter and smaller numbers are darker. Alternatively, the pixel values can be passed through a **pseudocolor algorithm** to calculate the color to be displayed.

- If the raster data has multiple bands, then typically, the bands would be combined to generate the desired color. For example, one band might represent the red component of the color, another band might represent the green component, and yet another band might represent the blue component.

- Alternatively, a multiband raster data source might be drawn using a palette, or as a grayscale or a pseudocolor image, by selecting a particular band to use for the color calculation.

Let's take a closer look at how raster data can be drawn onto the map.

How raster data is displayed

The **drawing style** associated with the raster band controls how the raster data will be displayed. The following drawing styles are currently supported:

Drawing style	Description
PalettedColor	For a single band raster data source, a palette maps each raster value to a color.
SingleBandGray	For a single band raster data source, the raster value is used directly as a grayscale value.
SingleBandPseudoColor	For a single band raster data source, the raster value is used to calculate a pseudocolor.

Drawing style	Description
PalettedSingleBandGray	For a single band raster data source that has a palette, this drawing style tells QGIS to ignore the palette and use the raster value directly as a grayscale value.
PalettedSingleBandPseudoColor	For a single band raster data source that has a palette, this drawing style tells QGIS to ignore the palette and use the raster value to calculate a pseudocolor.
MultiBandColor	For multiband raster data sources, use a separate band for each of the red, green, and blue color components. For this drawing style, the setRedBand(), setGreenBand(), and setBlueBand() methods can be used to choose which band to use for each color component.
MultiBandSingleBandGray	For multiband raster data sources, choose a single band to use as the grayscale color value. For this drawing style, use the setGrayBand() method to specify the band to use.
MultiBandSingleBandPseudoColor	For multiband raster data sources, choose a single band to use to calculate a pseudocolor. For this drawing style, use the setGrayBand() method to specify the band to use.

To set the drawing style, use the layer.setDrawingStyle() method, passing in a string that contains the name of the desired drawing style. You will also need to call the various setXXXBand() methods, as described in the preceding table, to tell the raster layer which bands contain the value(s) to use to draw each pixel.

Note that QGIS doesn't automatically update the map when you call the preceding functions to change the way the raster data is displayed. To have your changes displayed right away, you'll need to do the following:

1. Turn off raster image caching. This can be done by calling layer.setImageCache(None).

2. Tell the raster layer to redraw itself, by calling layer.triggerRepaint().

Accessing raster data

As with vector-format data, you can access the underlying raster data via the data provider's `identify()` method. The easiest way to do this is to pass in a single coordinate and retrieve the value or values at that coordinate. For example:

```
provider = layer.dataProvider()
values = provider.identify(QgsPoint(x, y),
              QgsRaster.IdentifyFormatValue)
if values.isValid():
  for band,value in values.results().items():
    ...
```

As you can see, you need to check whether the given coordinate exists within the raster data (using the `isValid()` call). The `values.results()` method returns a dictionary that maps band numbers to values.

Using this technique, you can extract all the underlying data associated with a given coordinate within the raster layer.

> You can also use the `provider.block()` method to retrieve the band data for a large number of coordinates all at once. We will look at how to do this later in this chapter.

Other useful qgis.core classes

Apart from all the classes and functionality involved in working with data sources and map layers, the `qgis.core` library also defines a number of other classes that you might find useful:

Class	Description
QgsProject	This represents the current QGIS project. Note that this is a singleton object, as only one project can be open at a time. The QgsProject class is responsible for loading and storing properties, which can be useful for plugins.
QGis	This class defines various constants, data types, and functions used throughout the QGIS system.
QgsPoint	This is a generic class that stores the coordinates for a point within a two-dimensional plane.
QgsRectangle	This is a generic class that stores the coordinates for a rectangular area within a two-dimensional plane.

Class	Description
QgsRasterInterface	This is the base class to use for processing raster data, for example, to reproject a set of raster data into a new coordinate system, to apply filters to change the brightness or color of your raster data, to resample the raster data, and to generate new raster data by rendering the existing data in various ways.
QgsDistanceArea	This class can be used to calculate distances and areas for a given geometry, automatically converting from the source coordinate reference system into meters.
QgsMapLayerRegistry	This class provides access to all the registered map layers in the current project.
QgsMessageLog	This class provides general logging features within a QGIS program. This lets you send debugging messages, warnings, and errors to the QGIS "Log Messages" panel.

The qgis.gui package

The qgis.gui package defines a number of user-interface widgets that you can include in your programs. Let's start by looking at the most important qgis.gui classes, and follow this up with a brief look at some of the other classes that you might find useful.

The QgisInterface class

QgisInterface represents the QGIS system's user interface. It allows programmatic access to the map canvas, the menu bar, and other parts of the QGIS application. When running Python code within a script or a plugin, or directly from the QGIS Python console, a reference to QgisInterface is typically available through the iface global variable.

> The QgisInterface object is only available when running the QGIS application itself. If you are running an external application and import the PyQGIS library into your application, QgisInterface won't be available.

Some of the more important things you can do with the QgisInterface object are:

- Get a reference to the list of layers within the current QGIS project via the legendInterface() method.

- Get a reference to the map canvas displayed within the main application window, using the mapCanvas() method.

- Retrieve the currently active layer within the project, using the `activeLayer()` method, and set the currently active layer by using the `setActiveLayer()` method.

- Get a reference to the application's main window by calling the `mainWindow()` method. This can be useful if you want to create additional Qt windows or dialogs that use the main window as their parent.

- Get a reference to the QGIS system's message bar by calling the `messageBar()` method. This allows you to display messages to the user directly within the QGIS main window.

The QgsMapCanvas class

The **map canvas** is responsible for drawing the various map layers into a window. The `QgsMapCanvas` class represents a map canvas. This class includes:

- A list of the currently shown **map layers**. This can be accessed using the `layers()` method.

> Note that there is a subtle difference between the list of map layers available within the map canvas and the list of map layers included in the `QgisInterface.legendInterface()` method. The map canvas's list of layers only includes the list of layers currently visible, while `QgisInterface.legendInterface()` returns all the map layers, including those that are currently hidden.

- The **map units** used by this map (meters, feet, degrees, and so on). The map's map units can be retrieved by calling the `mapUnits()` method.

- An **extent**, **which** is the area of the map currently shown within the canvas. The map's extent will change as the user zooms in and out, and pans across the map. The current map extent can be obtained by calling the `extent()` method.

- **A current map tool** that is used to control the user's interaction with the contents of the map canvas. The current map tool can be set using the `setMapTool()` method, and you can retrieve the current map tool (if any) by calling the `mapTool()` method.

- A **background color** used to draw the background behind all the map layers. You can change the map's background color by calling the `canvasColor()` method.

- A **coordinate transform** that converts from map coordinates (that is, coordinates in the data source's coordinate reference system) to pixels within the window. You can retrieve the current coordinate transform by calling the `getCoordinateTransform()` method.

The QgsMapCanvasItem class

A **map canvas item** is an item drawn on top of the map canvas. The map canvas item will appear in front of the map layers. While you can create your own subclass of QgsMapCanvasItem if you want to draw custom items on top of the map canvas, you will find it easier to use an existing subclass that does much of the work for you. There are currently three subclasses of QgsMapCanvasItem that you might find useful:

- QgsVertexMarker: This draws an icon (an "X", a "+", or a small box) centered around a given point on the map.

- QgsRubberBand: This draws an arbitrary polygon or polyline onto the map. It is intended to provide visual feedback as the user draws a polygon onto the map.

- QgsAnnotationItem: This is used to display additional information about a feature, in the form of a balloon that is connected to the feature. The QgsAnnotationItem class has various subclasses that allow you to customize the way the information is displayed.

The QgsMapTool class

A **map tool** allows the user to interact with and manipulate the map canvas, capturing mouse events and responding appropriately. A number of QgsMapTool subclasses provide standard map interaction behavior such as clicking to zoom in, dragging to pan the map, and clicking on a feature to identify it. You can also create your own custom map tools by subclassing QgsMapTool and implementing the various methods that respond to user-interface events such as pressing down the mouse button, dragging the canvas, and so on.

Once you have created a map tool, you can allow the user to activate it by associating the map tool with a toolbar button. Alternatively, you can activate it from within your Python code by calling the mapCanvas.setMapTool(...) method.

We will look at the process of creating your own custom map tool in the section *Using the PyQGIS library*.

Other useful qgis.gui classes

While the `qgis.gui` package defines a large number of classes, the ones you are most likely to find useful are given in the following table:

Class	Description
QgsLegendInterface	This provides access to the map legend, that is, the list of map layers within the current project. Note that map layers can be grouped, hidden, and shown within the map legend.
QgsMapTip	This displays a tip on a map canvas when the user holds the mouse over a feature. The map tip will show the display field for the feature; you can set this by calling `layer.setDisplayField("FIELD")`.
QgsColorDialog	This is a dialog box that allows the user to select a color.
QgsDialog	This is a generic dialog with a vertical box layout and a button box, making it easy to add content and standard buttons to your dialog.
QgsMessageBar	This is a bar that displays non-blocking messages to the user. We looked at the message bar class in the previous chapter.
QgsMessageViewer	This is a generic class that displays long messages to the user within a modal dialog.
QgsBlendModeComboBox QgsBrushStyleComboBox QgsColorRampComboBox QgsPenCapStyleComboBox QgsPenJoinStyleComboBox QgsScaleComboBox	These `QComboBox` user-interface widgets allow you to prompt the user for various drawing options. With the exception of the `QgsScaleComboBox`, which lets the user choose a map scale, all the other `QComboBox` subclasses let the user choose various Qt drawing options.

Using the PyQGIS library

In the previous section, we looked at a number of classes provided by the PyQGIS library. Let's make use of these classes to perform some real-world geospatial development tasks.

Analyzing raster data

We're going to start by writing a program to load in some raster-format data and analyze its contents. To make this more interesting, we'll use a **Digital Elevation Model (DEM)** file, which is a raster format data file that contains elevation data.

The **Global Land One-Kilometer Base Elevation Project (GLOBE)** provides free DEM data for the world, where each pixel represents one square kilometer of the Earth's surface. GLOBE data can be downloaded from `http://www.ngdc.noaa.gov/mgg/topo/gltiles.html`. Download the E tile, which includes the western half of the USA. The resulting file, which is named `e10g`, contains the height information you need. You'll also need to download the `e10g.hdr` header file so that QGIS can read the file—you can download this from `http://www.ngdc.noaa.gov/mgg/topo/elev/esri/hdr`. Once you've downloaded these two files, put them together into a convenient directory.

You can now load the DEM data into QGIS using the following code:

```
registry = QgsProviderRegistry.instance()
provider = registry.provider("gdal", "/path/to/e10g")
```

Unfortunately, there is a slight complexity here. Since QGIS doesn't know which coordinate reference system is used for the data, it displays a dialog box that asks you to choose the CRS. Since the GLOBE DEM data is in the WGS84 CRS, which QGIS uses by default, this dialog box is redundant. To disable it, we need to add the following to the top of our program:

```
from PyQt4.QtCore import QSettings
QSettings().setValue("/Projections/defaultBehaviour", "useGlobal")
```

Now that we've loaded our raster DEM data into QGIS, we can analyze it. While there are lots of things we can do with DEM data, let's calculate how often each unique elevation value occurs within the data.

> Notice that we're loading the DEM data directly using `QgsRasterDataProvider`. We don't want to display this information on a map, so we don't want (or need) to load it into `QgsRasterLayer`.

Since the DEM data is in a raster format, you need to iterate over the individual pixels or cells to get each height value. The `provider.xSize()` and `provider.ySize()` methods tell us how many cells are there in the DEM, while the `provider.extent()` method gives us the area of the Earth's surface covered by the DEM. Using this information, we can extract the individual elevation values from the contents of the DEM in the following way:

```
raster_extent = provider.extent()
raster_width = provider.xSize()
raster_height = provider.ySize()
block = provider.block(1, raster_extent, raster_width,
            raster_height)
```

The returned `block` variable is an object of type `QgsRasterBlock`, which is essentially a two-dimensional array of values. Let's iterate over the raster and extract the individual elevation values:

```
for x in range(raster_width):
  for y in range(raster_height):
    elevation = block.value(x, y)
    ....
```

Now that we've loaded the individual elevation values, it's easy to build a histogram out of those values. Here is the entire program to load the DEM data into memory, and then calculate and display the histogram:

```
from PyQt4.QtCore import QSettings
QSettings().setValue("/Projections/defaultBehaviour", "useGlobal")

registry = QgsProviderRegistry.instance()
provider = registry.provider("gdal", "/path/to/e10g")

raster_extent = provider.extent()
raster_width = provider.xSize()
raster_height = provider.ySize()
no_data_value = provider.srcNoDataValue(1)

histogram = {} # Maps elevation to number of occurrences.

block = provider.block(1, raster_extent, raster_width,
            raster_height)
```

```
if block.isValid():
  for x in range(raster_width):
    for y in range(raster_height):
      elevation = block.value(x, y)
      if elevation != no_data_value:
        try:
          histogram[elevation] += 1
        except KeyError:
          histogram[elevation] = 1

for height in sorted(histogram.keys()):
  print height, histogram[height]
```

Note that we've added a *no data value* check to the code. Raster data often includes pixels that have no value associated with them. In the case of a DEM, elevation data is only provided for areas of land; pixels over the sea have no elevation, and we have to exclude them, or our histogram will be inaccurate.

Manipulating vector data and saving it to a shapefile

Let's create a program that takes two vector data sources, subtracts one set of vectors from the other, and saves the resulting geometries into a new shapefile. Along the way, we'll learn a few important things about the PyQGIS library.

We'll be making use of the QgsGeometry.difference() function. This function performs a geometrical subtraction of one geometry from another, like this:

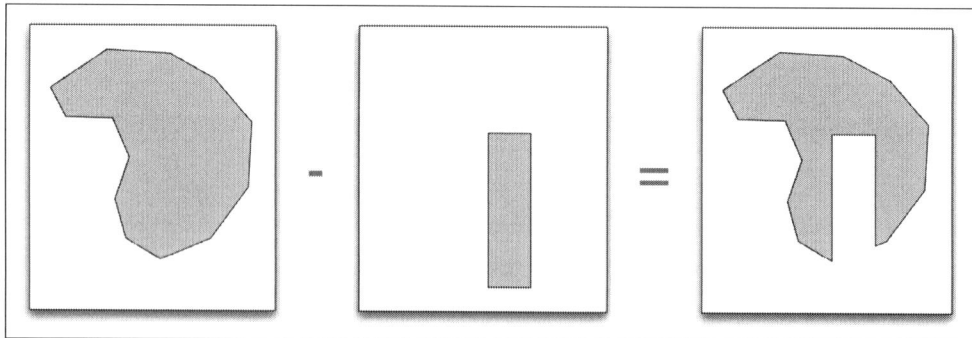

Let's start by asking the user to select the first shapefile and open up a vector data provider for that file:

```
filename_1 = QFileDialog.getOpenFileName(iface.mainWindow(),
                    "First Shapefile",
                    "~", "*.shp")
if not filename_1:
  return

registry = QgsProviderRegistry.instance()
provider_1 = registry.provider("ogr", filename_1)
```

We can then read the geometries from that file into memory:

```
geometries_1 = []
for feature in provider_1.getFeatures(QgsFeatureRequest()):
  geometries_1.append(QgsGeometry(feature.geometry()))
```

This last line of code includes an important feature. Notice that we use the following:

```
QgsGeometry(feature.geometry())
```

We use the preceding line instead of the following:

```
feature.geometry()
```

This is to get the geometry object to add to the list. In other words, we had to create a new geometry object based on the feature's existing geometry object. This is a limitation of the way the QGIS Python wrappers work: the `feature.geometry()` method returns a reference to the geometry, but the C++ code doesn't know that you are storing this reference away in your Python code. So, when the feature is no longer needed, the memory used by the feature's geometry is also released. If you then try to access that geometry later on, the entire QGIS system will crash. To get around this, we make a copy of the geometry so that we can refer to it even after the feature's memory has been released.

Now that we've loaded our first set of geometries into memory, let's do the same for the second shapefile:

```
filename_2 = QFileDialog.getOpenFileName(iface.mainWindow(),
                    "Second Shapefile",
                    "~", "*.shp")
if not filename_2:
```

```
    return

provider_2 = registry.provider("ogr", filename_2)

geometries_2 = []
for feature in provider_2.getFeatures(QgsFeatureRequest()):
  geometries_2.append(QgsGeometry(feature.geometry()))
```

With the two sets of geometries loaded into memory, we're ready to start subtracting one from the other. However, to make this process more efficient, we will combine the geometries from the second shapefile into one large geometry, which we can then subtract all at once, rather than subtracting one at a time. This will make the subtraction process much faster:

```
combined_geometry = None
for geometry in geometries_2:
  if combined_geometry == None:
    combined_geometry = geometry
  else:
    combined_geometry = combined_geometry.combine(geometry)
```

We can now calculate the new set of geometries by subtracting one from the other:

```
dst_geometries = []
for geometry in geometries_1:
  dst_geometry = geometry.difference(combined_geometry)
  if not dst_geometry.isGeosValid(): continue
  if dst_geometry.isGeosEmpty(): continue
  dst_geometries.append(dst_geometry)
```

Notice that we check to see whether the destination geometry is mathematically valid and is not empty.

> Invalid geometries are a common problem when manipulating complex shapes. There are options for fixing them, such as splitting apart multi-geometries and performing a buffer operation. However, doing this is beyond the scope of this book.

Our last task is to save the resulting geometries into a new shapefile. We'll first ask the user for the name of the destination shapefile:

```
dst_filename = QFileDialog.getSaveFileName(iface.mainWindow(),
                 "Save results to:",
                 "~", "*.shp")
if not dst_filename:
  return
```

We'll make use of a **vector file writer** to save the geometries into a shapefile. Let's start by initializing the file writer object:

```
fields = QgsFields()
writer = QgsVectorFileWriter(dst_filename, "ASCII", fields,
              dst_geometries[0].wkbType(),
              None, "ESRI Shapefile")
if writer.hasError() != QgsVectorFileWriter.NoError:
  print "Error!"
  return
```

We don't have any attributes in our shapefile, so the fields list is empty. Now that the writer has been set up, we can save the geometries into the file:

```
for geometry in dst_geometries:
  feature = QgsFeature()
  feature.setGeometry(geometry)
  writer.addFeature(feature)
```

Now that all the data has been written to the disk, let's display a message box that informs the user that we've finished:

```
QMessageBox.information(iface.mainWindow(), "",
              "Subtracted features saved to disk.")
```

As you can see, creating a new shapefile is very straightforward in PyQGIS, and it's easy to manipulate geometries using Python—just so long as you copy the QgsGeometry objects you want to keep around. If your Python code starts to crash while manipulating geometries, this is probably the first thing you should look for.

Using different symbols for different features within a map

Let's use World Borders Dataset that you downloaded in the previous chapter to draw a world map, using different symbols for different continents. This is a good example of using a categorized symbol renderer, though we'll combine it into a script that loads the shapefile into a map layer and sets up the symbols and map renderer to display the map exactly as you want. We'll then save the resulting map as an image.

Let's start by creating a map layer to display the contents of the World Borders Dataset shapefile:

```
layer = iface.addVectorLayer("/path/to/TM_WORLD_BORDERS-0.3.shp",
              "continents", "ogr")
```

Each unique region code in the World Borders Dataset shapefile corresponds to a continent. We want to define the name and color to use for each of these regions, and use this information to set up the various categories to use when displaying the map:

```
from PyQt4.QtGui import QColor
categories = []
for value,color,label in [(0,   "#660000", "Antarctica"),
                          (2,   "#006600", "Africa"),
                          (9,   "#000066", "Oceania"),
                          (19,  "#660066", "The Americas"),
                          (142, "#666600", "Asia"),
                          (150, "#006666", "Europe")]:
    symbol = QgsSymbolV2.defaultSymbol(layer.geometryType())
    symbol.setColor(QColor(color))
    categories.append(QgsRendererCategoryV2(value, symbol, label))
```

With these categories set up, we simply update the map layer to use a categorized renderer based on the value of the region attribute, and then redraw the map:

```
layer.setRendererV2(QgsCategorizedSymbolRendererV2("region",
                        categories))
layer.triggerRepaint()
```

There's only one more thing to do, since this is a script that can be run multiple times, let's have our script automatically remove the existing continents layer, if it exists, before adding a new one. To do this, we can add the following to the start of our script:

```
layer_registry = QgsMapLayerRegistry.instance()
for layer in layer_registry.mapLayersByName("continents"):
    layer_registry.removeMapLayer(layer.id())
```

Now when our script is run, it will create one (and only one) layer that shows the various continents in different colors. These will appear as different shades of gray in the printed book, but the colors will be visible on the computer screen:

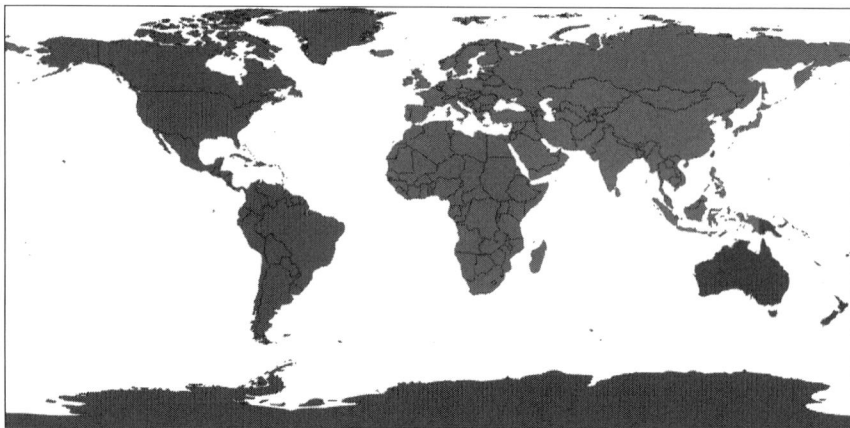

Now, let's use the same data set to color each country based on its relative population. We'll start by removing the existing "population" layer, if it exists:

```
layer_registry = QgsMapLayerRegistry.instance()
for layer in layer_registry.mapLayersByName("population"):
  layer_registry.removeMapLayer(layer.id())
```

Next, we open the World Borders Dataset into a new layer called "population":

```
layer = iface.addVectorLayer("/path/to/TM_WORLD_BORDERS-0.3.shp",
                "population", "ogr")
```

We then need to set up our various population ranges:

```
from PyQt4.QtGui import QColor
ranges = []
for min_pop,max_pop,color in [(0,          99999,     "#332828"),
                              (100000,     999999,    "#4c3535"),
                              (1000000,    4999999,   "#663d3d"),
                              (5000000,    9999999,   "#804040"),
                              (10000000,   19999999,  "#993d3d"),
                              (20000000,   49999999,  "#b33535"),
                              (50000000,   999999999, "#cc2828")]:
  symbol = QgsSymbolV2.defaultSymbol(layer.geometryType())
  symbol.setColor(QColor(color))
  ranges.append(QgsRendererRangeV2(min_pop, max_pop,
                  symbol, ""))
```

Now that we have our population ranges and their associated colors, we simply set up a graduated symbol renderer to choose a symbol based on the value of the pop2005 attribute, and tell the map to redraw itself:

```
layer.setRendererV2(QgsGraduatedSymbolRendererV2("pop2005",
                          ranges))
layer.triggerRepaint()
```

The result will be a map layer that shades each country according to its population:

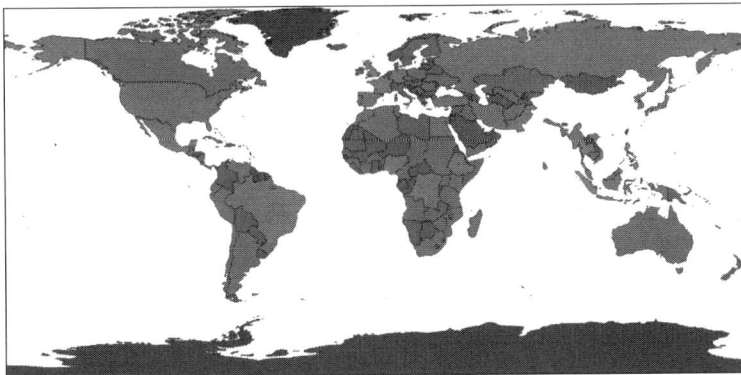

Calculating the distance between two user-defined points

In our final example of using the PyQGIS library, we'll write some code that, when run, starts listening for mouse events from the user. If the user clicks on a point, drags the mouse, and then releases the mouse button again, we will display the distance between those two points. This is a good example of how to add your own map interaction logic to QGIS, using the `QgsMapTool` class.

This is the basic structure for our `QgsMapTool` subclass:

```
class DistanceCalculator(QgsMapTool):
    def __init__(self, iface):
        QgsMapTool.__init__(self, iface.mapCanvas())
        self.iface = iface

    def canvasPressEvent(self, event):
        ...

    def canvasReleaseEvent(self, event):
        ...
```

To make this map tool active, we'll create a new instance of it and pass it to the `mapCanvas.setMapTool()` method. Once this is done, our `canvasPressEvent()` and `canvasReleaseEvent()` methods will be called whenever the user clicks or releases the mouse button over the map canvas.

Let's start with the code that responds when the user clicks on the canvas. In this method, we're going to convert from the pixel coordinates that the user clicked on to the corresponding map coordinates (that is, a latitude and longitude value). We'll then remember these coordinates so that we can refer to them later. Here is the necessary code:

```
def canvasPressEvent(self, event):
    transform = self.iface.mapCanvas().getCoordinateTransform()
    self._startPt = transform.toMapCoordinates(event.pos().x(),
                        event.pos().y())
```

When the `canvasReleaseEvent()` method is called, we'll want to do the same with the point at which the user released the mouse button:

```
def canvasReleaseEvent(self, event):
    transform = self.iface.mapCanvas().getCoordinateTransform()
    endPt = transform.toMapCoordinates(event.pos().x(),
                        event.pos().y())
```

Now that we have the two desired coordinates, we'll want to calculate the distance between them. We can do this using a `QgsDistanceArea` object:

```
crs = self.iface.mapCanvas().mapRenderer().destinationCrs()
distance_calc = QgsDistanceArea()
distance_calc.setSourceCrs(crs)
distance_calc.setEllipsoid(crs.ellipsoidAcronym())
distance_calc.setEllipsoidalMode(crs.geographicFlag())
distance = distance_calc.measureLine([self._startPt,
                endPt]) / 1000
```

Notice that we divide the resulting value by 1000. This is because the `QgsDistanceArea` object returns the distance in meters, and we want to display the distance in kilometers.

Finally, we'll display the calculated distance in the QGIS message bar:

```
messageBar = self.iface.messageBar()
messageBar.pushMessage("Distance = %d km" % distance,
            level=QgsMessageBar.INFO,
            duration=2)
```

Now that we've created our map tool, we need to activate it. We can do this by adding the following to the end of our script:

```
calculator = DistanceCalculator(iface)
iface.mapCanvas().setMapTool(calculator)
```

With the map tool activated, the user can click and drag on the map. When the mouse button is released, the distance (in kilometers) between the two points will be displayed in the message bar:

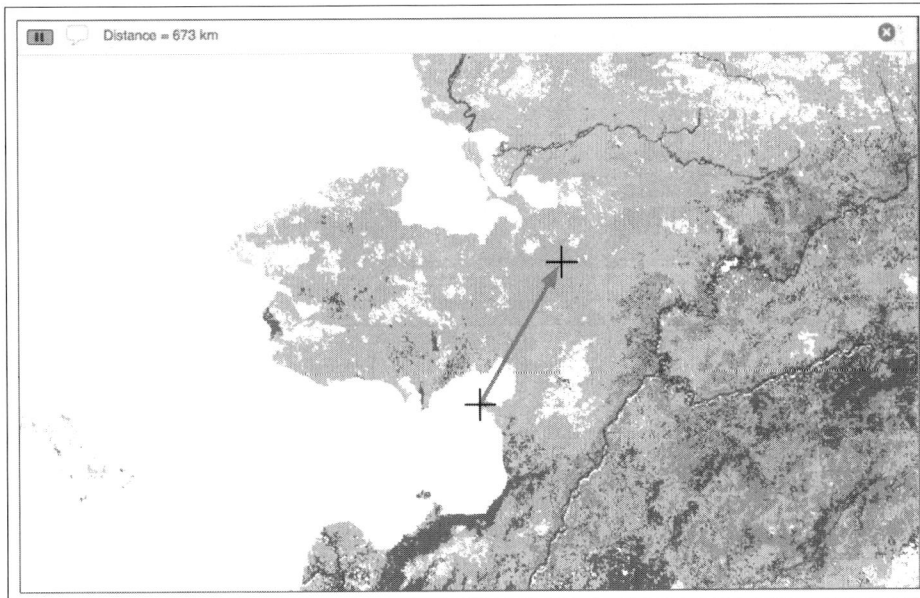

Summary

In this chapter, we took an in-depth look at the PyQGIS libraries and how you can use them in your own programs. We learned that the QGIS Python libraries are implemented as wrappers around the QGIS APIs implemented in C++. We saw how Python programmers can understand and work with the QGIS reference documentation, even though it is written for C++ developers. We also looked at the way the PyQGIS libraries are organized into different packages, and learned about the most important classes defined in the qgis.core and qgis.gui packages.

We then saw how a coordinate reference systems (CRS) is used to translate from points on the three-dimensional surface of the Earth to coordinates within a two-dimensional map plane.

We learned that vector format data is made up of features, where each feature has an ID, a geometry, and a set of attributes, and that symbols are used to draw vector geometries onto a map layer, while renderers are used to choose which symbol to use for a given feature.

We learned how a spatial index can be used to speed up access to vector features.

Next, we saw how raster format data is organized into bands that represent information such as color, elevation, and so on, and looked at the various ways in which a raster data source can be displayed within a map layer. Along the way, we learned how to access the contents of a raster data source.

Finally, we looked at various techniques for performing useful tasks using the PyQGIS library.

In the next chapter, we will learn more about QGIS Python plugins, and then go on to use the plugin architecture as a way of implementing a useful feature within a mapping application.

4
Creating QGIS Plugins

In *Chapter 1*, *Getting Started with QGIS*, we took a brief look at how QGIS Python plugins are organized. In this chapter, we will use this knowledge to create two plugins: a simple "Hello World" style plugin, so you can understand the process, and a much more sophisticated and useful plugin that displays information about a clicked-on geometry. In the process, we will learn how plugins work, how to create and distribute plugins, what plugins will allow us to do, and some of the possibilities and limitations involved in implementing your mapping applications as QGIS plugins.

Getting ready

Before we can delve into the plugin development process, there are three things you will need to do:

1. Install the **Qt developer tools** from the Qt developer website (`http://qt-project.org`).

2. Install the Python bindings for Qt, called **PyQt**, from `http://www.riverbankcomputing.co.uk/software/pyqt`. While we won't be using the Python bindings directly, there are two command-line tools included with PyQt that we will need.

> QGIS is currently based on PyQt4. Make sure you install Version 4 of the Qt Developer tools and the PyQt bindings so that you get the compatible version.
>
> PyQt is available as an installer for MS Windows and in source code form for Linux. For Mac OS X users, a binary installer is available at `http://sourceforge.net/projects/pyqtx`.

3. You should install and enable the **Plugin Reloader** plugin for QGIS. This makes it much easier to develop and test your plugins. To do this, you will need to turn on experimental plugin support by selecting the **Manage and Install Plugins...** item from the **Plugins** menu, clicking on the **Settings** tab, and then turning on the **Show also experimental plugins** checkbox. You can then see the experimental plugins, including the Plugin Reloader. Select this plugin and then click on the **Install Plugin** button to install it.

The Plugin Reloader adds buttons to the QGIS toolbar that you can click on in order to reload your plugin:

This allows you to make changes to your plugin and see the result right away. Without the Plugin Reloader, you would have to quit and restart QGIS for your changes to take effect.

Understanding the QGIS plugin architecture

As we saw in *Chapter 1*, *Getting Started with QGIS*, QGIS plugins are stored as Python packages in the `~/.qgis2/python/plugins` directory.

> Depending on your operating system and the version of QGIS you're using, the `.qgis2` directory might be named `.qgis`.

The plugin's package includes a number of Python modules and other files. At a minimum, the plugin package must include:

- `__init__.py`: This is a package initialization module that contains the **class factory** function, which creates and initializes the plugin.

- `metadata.txt`: This is a text file that contains information about the plugin, including the plugin's version number, the name of the plugin, and the plugin's author.

In addition, most plugins will include:

- A separate Python module that contains a class definition for the plugin. The plugin class implements a number of specially named methods that get called to start up and shut down the plugin.
- One or more user-interface template files with the extension .ui.
- The compiled version of each user-interface template in the form of a Python module with the same name as that of the template.
- A resources.qrc file, which is an XML format file that lists the various images and other resources used by the plugin.
- The compiled version of the resources file, in the form of a Python module named resources.py.

The various .ui template files are created using **Qt Designer**, which is a part of the standard Qt installation. The command-line tools to convert the .qrc and .ui files into Python modules are part of PyQt.

When it starts up, QGIS looks through the various Python packages it finds in the ~/.qgis2/python/plugins directory. For each package, it attempts to call the top-level function named ClassFactory() in the plugin's __init__.py file. This function should import and return an instance of the plugin's object, like this:

```
def ClassFactory(iface):
from myPlugin import MyPlugin
return MyPlugin(iface)
```

> Obviously, you should change the name of myPlugin (and MyPlugin) to something more meaningful when you write a real plugin.

While it's usual to define the plugin in a separate module, you can create it directly within the __init__.py module if you prefer. The important thing is to define a class that provides the following methods:

- __init__(iface): This initializes the plugin object. Note that this should accept the iface variable passed to the class factory and store it in an instance variable for later use.
- initGui(): This initializes the plugin's user interface. This would typically involve adding the plugin to the QGIS menus and toolbar, and setting up the signal handlers to respond to various events.

- unload(): This removes the plugin's user-interface elements. This would normally include removing the plugin from the QGIS menus and toolbar, and disconnecting the signal handlers defined in the plugin's initGui() method.

The __init__(iface) method is called by your class factory function to initialize the plugin object itself. The initGui() method is then called by QGIS when the program starts up, or when the user installs the plugin. Finally, the unload() method is called by QGIS when the user uninstalls the plugin or when QGIS shuts down.

A plugin doesn't usually run right away when QGIS starts up. Instead, it installs various menu and toolbar items, which the user can then select to perform various actions. For example, a simple plugin may have just one menu item and one toolbar item, and when the user selects one of these, the plugin performs its one and only action. More sophisticated plugins might have a range of menu and toolbar items, each one performing a different action.

Many plugins add their menu items to the **Plugins** menu using the iface. addPluginToMenu() method. This creates a submenu within the **Plugins** menu for the plugin's menu items, making it easy for the user to see which menu items have been provided by a given plugin. Alternatively, the plugin might choose to add its menu items to one of the existing submenus within the **Vector**, **Raster**, or **Database** menu, as appropriate.

In the same way, the plugin might add icons or widgets to the plugin toolbar, or to one of the other toolbars if it prefers. A plugin might also add a whole new toolbar to the QGIS window if it wants to.

Creating a simple plugin

Now that we've seen how plugins are structured and used, let's create a very simple "Hello World" style plugin to see what's involved in making one. While there are various tools such as the **Plugin Builder** plugin, which will create the various files for you, we're going to eschew them in favor of creating our plugin manually. This will make the process clearer and avoid the situation where your code just magically works without knowing why or how.

Go to the ~/.qgis2/python/plugins directory and create a subdirectory named testPlugin. In this directory, create a file named metadata.txt and enter the following values into it:

```
[general]
name=Test Plugin
email=test@example.com
```

```
author_My Name Here
qgisMinimumVersion=2.0
description=Simple test plugin.
about=A very simple test plugin.
version=version 0.1
```

This is the minimum metadata you need to enter for a plugin. Obviously, you can change these values if you want. Now, create a package initialization file, __init__. py, and enter the following into that file:

```
def classFactory(iface):
    from testPlugin import TestPlugin
    return TestPlugin(iface)
```

As you can see, we're going to define a class named TestPlugin that represents our plugin object, and implement it in a module named testPlugin.py. Let's create this module now:

```
from PyQt4.QtCore import *
from PyQt4.QtGui import *

class TestPlugin:
  def __init__(self, iface):
    self.iface = iface

  def initGui(self):
    self.action = QAction("Run", self.iface.mainWindow())
    QObject.connect(self.action, SIGNAL("triggered()"),
            self.onRun)
    self.iface.addPluginToMenu("Test Plugin", self.action)

  def unload(self):
    self.iface.removePluginMenu("Test Plugin", self.action)

  def onRun(self):
    QMessageBox.information(self.iface.mainWindow(), "debug",
                "Running")
```

As you can see, we created a Qt QAction object for our menu item, named it Run, and added it to the **Plugin** menu in a submenu named "Test Plugin". We then connected that action to our onRun() method, which simply displays a message to the user stating that the plugin is running.

This is all we need for a very minimal plugin. Let's test it out. Start QGIS and choose the **Manage and Install Plugins…** item from the **Plugins** menu. The QGIS **Plugin Manager** window will appear, and if you scroll down, you should see your plugin listed:

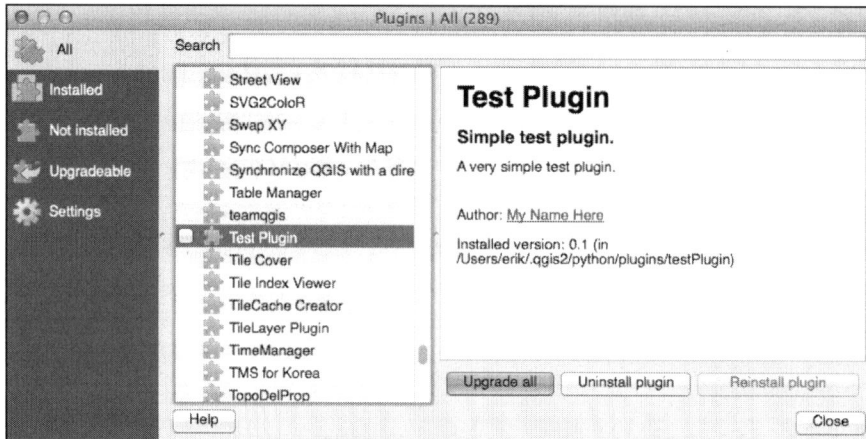

If you click on the checkbox, the plugin will be activated. If you then look in the **Plugins** menu, you should see your plugin listed, and if you select the **Run** item from your plugin's submenu, the "Running" message box should be displayed.

If your plugin isn't working, or if it isn't listed in the Plugin Manager window, you might have made a mistake in your code. If the plugin can't be loaded for some reason, a window will appear, giving you the Python traceback when you attempt to install or reload the plugin:

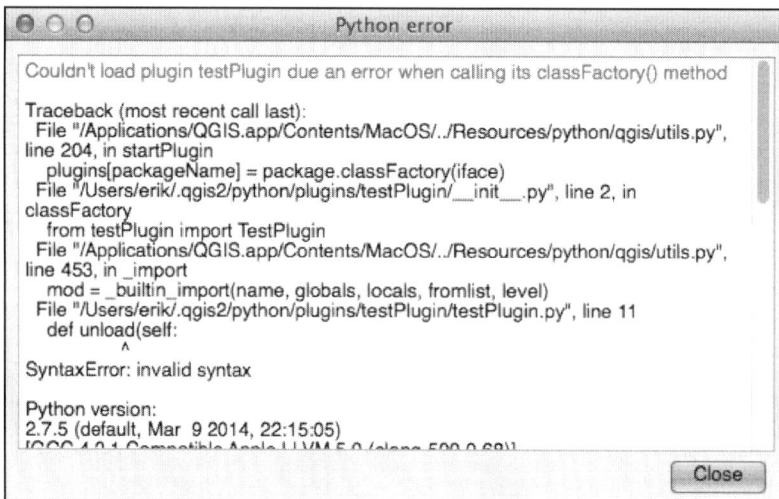

This window will also appear if your plugin's code generates an exception while it is running.

> If there's a problem with your plugin that prevents it from even being loaded (for example, a mistake in the metadata.txt file), you might need to check the **Log Messages** panel to see the error. You can show this panel by selecting it from the **Panels** submenu in the **View** menu; make sure you click on the **Plugins** tab to see the log messages associated with your plugin:

Timestamp	Message	Level
2014-08-08T06:19:36	Loaded Plugin Reloader (package: plugin_reloader)	0
2014-08-08T06:19:36	Error when reading metadata of plugin testPlugin	1
2014-08-08T06:19:36	Loaded Zoom to Point (package: zoomtopoint)	0
2014-08-08T06:19:36	Loaded DB Manager (package: db_manager)	0
2014-08-08T06:19:36	Loaded fTools (package: fTools)	0
2014-08-08T06:19:37	Loaded GdalTools (package: GdalTools)	0
2014-08-08T06:19:37	Loaded Processing (package: processing)	0

Let's add one more feature to our test plugin: a toolbar item, which, when clicked on, also calls the onRun() method. Find a suitable PNG format image that is 24 x 24 pixels (the default size for a QGIS toolbar icon), and save that image into your plugin's directory under the name icon.png. Then, change your initGui() method to look like the following:

```
def initGui(self):
    icon = QIcon(":/plugins/testPlugin/icon.png")
    self.action = QAction(icon, "Run",
                self.iface.mainWindow())
    QObject.connect(self.action, SIGNAL("triggered()"),
            self.onRun)
    self.iface.addPluginToMenu("Test Plugin", self.action)
    self.iface.addToolBarIcon(self.action)
```

The changed lines have been highlighted. As you can see, we've added an icon to our QAction object, and then also called the addToolBarIcon() method to add our action to the Plugins toolbar.

We'll also have to add one extra line to our unload() method to remove the toolbar icon when the plugin is unloaded:

```
def unload(self):
    self.iface.removePluginMenu("Test Plugin", self.action)
    self.iface.removeToolBarIcon(self.action)
```

There's one last thing we need to do before our toolbar icon will work; we need to tell QGIS that the `icon.png` file is a **resource** used by our plugin. This is done through the `resources.qrc` file. Create this file now, placing it into your plugin's directory, and edit it using your favorite text editor, so that it contains the following XML format text:

```
<RCC>
  <qresource prefix="/plugins/testPlugin">
    <file>icon.png</file>
  </qresource>
</RCC>
```

QGIS can't use this file directly; it has to be compiled into a `resources.py` module using the **pyrcc4** command-line tool. This tool is installed as part of PyQt; once you've created your `resources.qrc` file, use the following command to compile it:

```
pyrcc4 resources.qrc -o resources.py
```

> Depending on where PyQt installed it, you might need to include the path to the `pyrcc4` command. If you run this command from a directory other than the plugin directory, you will also need to include the path to the `resources.qrc` and `resource.py` files.

Finally, we need to add the following to the top of our `testPlugin.py` module:

```
import resources
```

This makes the compiled resources available for our plugin to use. When you reload your plugin, an icon should appear in the QGIS toolbar, and if you click on that icon, the "Running" message box should be displayed.

While this plugin is very basic, we've actually learned a lot: how to create and install a plugin, how a plugin can add itself to the QGIS user interface, how plugins interact with the user, how errors in a plugin are handled, and how to deal with images and other plugin resources. Let's take a closer look now at the processes typically used to develop and distribute plugins, before going on to create a plugin that actually does something useful.

The plugin development process

In the previous section, we created a plugin by hand, directly storing the necessary files in the hidden `~/.qgis2` directory. This isn't a particularly robust way of building plugins. In this section, we will look at some of the best practices for developing and distributing plugins, as well as some of the things you need to be aware of when creating your own plugins.

Using the Plugin Builder

QGIS provides a plugin called **Plugin Builder** that you can use to create your new plugin from a standard template. Plugin Builder is a sophisticated and useful tool for creating plugins, but it does make some assumptions about the way your plugin will be structured and what it will do. For this reason, we deliberately didn't use the Plugin Builder for our example plugins.

More information on the Plugin Builder can be found at `http://geoapt.net/pluginbuilder`. You can install the Plugin Builder directly from within QGIS, using the **Manage and Install Plugins...** item from the **Plugins** menu. Once installed, you simply click on the Plugin Builder's icon in the toolbar, and you will be prompted to fill in various details about your new plugin:

After filling in the information, you will be prompted to select the directory in which your plugin's source code is stored. The Plugin Builder will then create the necessary files for you.

It is up to you whether to use Plugin Builder or not, and whether or not to use all the features it provides. For example, the Plugin Builder provides a *make* target to create the HTML format help files for your plugin, using Sphynx. If you prefer to create your help files in a different way, or don't want to create help files at all, you can simply ignore this option.

One of the problems with using Plugin Builder is the complexity of the generated plugin. Right from the outset, your plugin will include:

- Help files, both in reStructuredText and in HTML format, as well as directories for holding images and HTML templates

- Support for internationalization

- A Makefile to automate the plugin building process

- A Python script for uploading the plugin to the QGIS plugin repository

- A `pylintrc` file, allowing you to check your plugin's Python source files using the Pylint code-analysis system

- Two separate README files, one in HTML and another in plain text format

- Various shell scripts

- A range of standard unit tests

- The UI template and Python code that displays a dialog box when the plugin is run

All of this leads to a rather complex directory structure, with lots of files that may or may not be relevant to you. You can certainly remove the various files and directories you don't need, but this can be risky if you don't know what the files and directories are for.

Due to all this complexity, we won't be using Plugin Builder in this book. Instead, we'll create our plugins manually, only adding the files and directories you need so that you can understand what everything does.

Automating the build process

For our example plugin, we had to create the `resources.qrc` file and then compile this file into a `resources.py` file using the `pyrcc4` command-line tool. Whenever we made a change to the `resources.qrc` file, we had to remember to recompile it. The same thing applies to any user-interface template (`.ui`) files in our plugin.

Manually running the compiler each time you make a change is poor programming practice. Instead, you should use a **Makefile** to automate the process. We won't go into the details of how to use *make* here (there are complete books on this topic), but we will use it to compile all the necessary files with a single command. We will also store the plugin's source files in a different directory, and use *make* to compile and copy all the necessary files into the `~/.qgis2` directory:

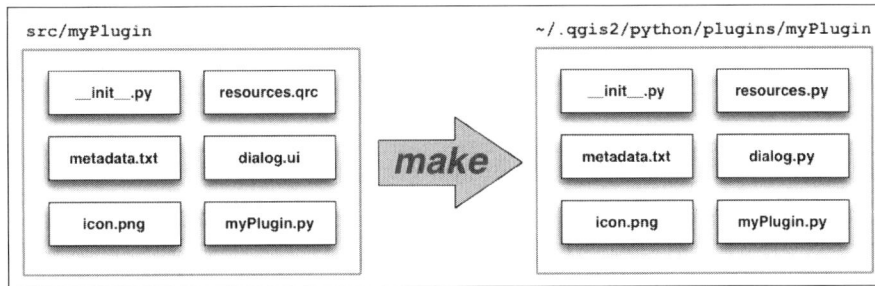

This ensures that the various files in the running plugin are all consistent—you can't forget to compile a template, or break the running plugin by running an updated Python source file before a template has been recompiled. Keeping your source files separate from your running code is also an excellent programming practice.

By using *make* in this way, you end up with a highly productive process for developing and testing your plugin:

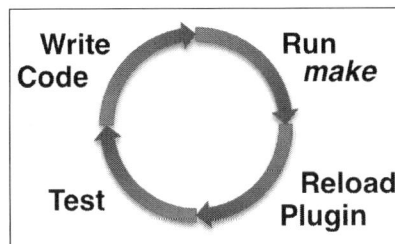

A typical Makefile for building and running QGIS plugins looks like this:

```
PLUGINNAME = testPlugin
PY_FILES = testPlugin.py __init__.py
EXTRAS = icon.png metadata.txt
UI_FILES = testPluginDialog.py
RESOURCE_FILES = resources.py

default: compile

compile: $(UI_FILES) $(RESOURCE_FILES)

%.py : %.qrc
   pyrcc4 -o $@ $<

%.py : %.ui
```

```
    pyuic4 -o $@ $<

deploy: compile
    mkdir -p $(HOME)/.qgis2/python/plugins/$(PLUGINNAME)
    cp -vf $(PY_FILES) $(HOME)/.qgis2/python/plugins/$(PLUGINNAME)
    cp -vf $(UI_FILES) $(HOME)/.qgis2/python/plugins/$(PLUGINNAME)
    cp -vf $(RESOURCE_FILES) $(HOME)/.qgis2/python/plugins/$(PLUGINNAME)
    cp -vf $(EXTRAS) $(HOME)/.qgis2/python/plugins/$(PLUGINNAME)

clean:
    rm $(UI_FILES) $(RESOURCE_FILES)
```

The top portion of the Makefile sets five variables that tell *make* about your plugin:

- `PLUGINNAME` is, of course, the name of your plugin.

- `PY_FILES` is a list of the Python source files that make up your plugin's source code.

- `EXTRAS` is a list of additional files that should be included with your plugin. You would typically include the `metadata.txt` file and any additional images or other files used by your plugin.

- `UI_FILES` is a list of the UI templates that need to be compiled for your plugin to work. Note that you have to use the `.py` suffix for each template file, as you're telling *make* which file you want to have recompiled when the corresponding `.ui` file is changed.

- `RESOURCE_FILES` is a list of the resource files used by your application. Once again, you have to use the `.py` suffix for each resource file rather than the `.qrc` version of the file.

Typically, you would only have to change the values of these five variables to set up your Makefile. However, if the `pyrcc4` or `pyuic4` command-line tools are in a nonstandard location, or if QGIS uses a directory other than `~/.qgis2/python/plugins` for its Python plugins, then you will have to modify the other parts of the Makefile so that it works with your particular development setup.

Once it has been set up, the Makefile provides three **make targets** that you can use:

- `make compile` (or just `make`) will compile your plugin's `.ui` and `.qrc` files into the corresponding `.py` modules.

- `make deploy` will compile the `.ui` and `.qrc` files, and then copy all the necessary files into the QGIS plugin directory.

- `make clean` will remove the `.py` version of your `.ui` and `.qrc` files.

You can use `make deploy` and then click on the Plugin Reloader tool in QGIS to run the latest version of your plugin so you can test it out.

Plugin help files

QGIS allows you to include an HTML-formatted help file for your plugin. This file will be displayed using the built-in QGIS help browser if your plugin calls the `qgis.utils.showPluginHelp()` function. This function has the following signature:

```
showPluginHelp(packageName=None, filename='index', section='')
```

The various parameters are as follows:

- `packageName`: This is the name of the Python package where the help file can be found. If a package is specified, QGIS will look for the help files inside the given package directory. Otherwise, it will look for the help files in the same directory as the Python module that called `showPluginHelp()`. Note that it's quite unusual for a plugin to use this parameter, and you would normally just leave it set to `None`.

- `filename`: This is the base name for the HTML help file to display. Note that an appropriate suffix (for example, `.html`) will be added to this base name.

- `section`: This is the name of an optional HTML anchor tag, which the help file will be scrolled to when it is opened.

Note that the `filename` parameter is the *base* name for the desired HTML file. QGIS allows you to have your help files translated into multiple languages, and will automatically choose the appropriate version of the file based on the current locale. If a translated version of the help file is not available in the current language, then QGIS will fall back to displaying the US English version of the help file, and if that's not available, it will use the file named `filename.html`.

This allows you to include translated versions of your help files if you want (for example, `index-es.html`, `index-de.html`, and `index-fr-ca.html`), but if you don't want to have translated help files, a single `index.html` file will suffice.

There are several ways in which you can organize your plugin's online help. The following are some examples:

1. You can put all the documentation for your plugin in a single file named `index.html`, and then simply call `showPluginHelp()` with no parameters to display that help file when the user asks for help.

2. You can use a different filename for your help file and supply that name in the `filename` parameter when calling `showPluginHelp()`, for example, `showPluginHelp(filename="plugin_help")`.

3. You're not just limited to having one help file. You can have a whole directory of help files, and have the `index.html` file act as a table of contents for the plugin's online help. To do this, call `showPluginHelp` with `filename` set to something like `os.path.join("help_files", "index")` so that the help file is found in a subdirectory rather than the main plugin directory.

4. If you have multiple help files, for example, one for each of your plugin's main features, you might choose to display the appropriate help file based on which feature the user is using at that time. For example, you might add a **Help** button to a complex dialog or window and have that button call `showPluginHelp(filename="my_dialog")`.

5. Finally, you might put all your documentation into a single file, and use HTML anchor tags (for example, `<a id="my_dialog">My Dialog</a>`) to define the various sections of your documentation. You will then use the `section` parameter to jump directly to that section of your plugin's documentation, like this: `showPluginHelp(section="my_dialog")`.

Of course, while your help file has to end up in HTML format, you might not want to write HTML directly. Instead, you can write your documentation using a markup language such as Markdown, reStructuredText, or Latex, and then use a documentation generator to convert your marked-up files into HTML. This is a perfect example of something that can be automated using a Makefile, and indeed, the Plugin Builder's default Makefile includes support for using Sphinx to convert reStructuredText markup into HTML.

Unit testing

Unit tests are a common programming technique to make sure each part of your code works as it should. The following is a very simple example of a unit test written in Python:

```
import unittest

def double(n):
    return n * 2

class TestDouble(unittest.TestCase):
    def test(self):
        self.assertEqual(double(2), 4)
```

You can run this unit test either directly from the command line, or by adding extra code to create a `TestRunner` object that you can then use to run the test.

We're not going to describe the rationale behind unit testing, or how to use the `unittest` library to test your Python code. However, it is worth spending some time learning how you can write and run unit tests for your QGIS plugins.

> If you haven't worked with the `unittest` module before, check out
> `http://docs.python-guide.org/en/latest/writing/tests`.

Unit testing is done outside of QGIS itself; that is, the unit tests run as an external Python application that loads your plugin and then tests it. Doing this isn't as bad as it sounds; in *Chapter 1, Getting Started with QGIS*, we looked at a simple external application built on top of QGIS, and we can use pretty much the same process to write our testing code. Here's the boilerplate example of an external application, copied from *Chapter 1, Getting Started with QGIS*:

```
import os

from qgis.core import *

QgsApplication.setPrefixPath(os.environ['QGIS_PREFIX'], True)
QgsApplication.initQgis()

# ...

QgsApplication.exitQgis()
```

You will also need to use an appropriate wrapper script, as described in *Chapter 1, Getting Started with QGIS*, so that the Python path and other environment variables are set correctly.

With QGIS unit tests, you have to set up the QGIS environment before the test is run, and then shut it down again once the test finishes. This is done by placing the appropriate parts of the boilerplate code into the unit test's `setup()` and `tearDown()` methods, like this:

```
import unittest

import os

from qgis.core import *

class MyTest(unittest.TestCase):
  def setup(self):
    QgsApplication.setPrefixPath(os.environ['QGIS_PREFIX'], True)
```

```
    QgsApplication.initQgis()

def tearDown(self):
    QgsApplication.exitQgis()

def test_plugin(self):
    ...
```

You can then import and test your plugin's Python code within the `test_plugin()` method.

> You can, of course, have multiple `test_XXX()` methods in your test case. The PyQGIS library will be initialized before the first test is run, and shut down after the last test finishes.

Testing plugins in this way does reveal a major limitation of this approach: there is no `QgisInterface` object available for your plugin to use. This means that the parts of the plugin you're testing can't interact with the rest of the QGIS system via the `iface` variable.

Unit tests get around this limitation by creating a fake QGIS environment (including a Python implementation of `QgisInterface`), which the plugin can use for testing. The plugin is then loaded by adding the plugin's directory to `sys.path` and then calling the plugin's `ClassFactory()` function with the fake `QgisInterface`:

```
sys.path.append("/path/to/my/plugin")
import MyPlugin
plugin = MyPlugin.classFactory(fake_iface)
```

While it seems complex and might introduce errors that only occur while the plugin is being tested, this process is actually very useful. If you want to use unit tests, you can either implement your own `QgsInterface` or make use of the unit testing framework provided by the Plugin Builder.

> If you want to roll your own unit tests, a good starting point is available at `http://snorf.net/blog/2014/01/04/writing-unit-tests-for-qgis-python-plugins`.

If you are doing unit testing, then you would normally add an extra target to your Makefile so you can run the unit tests simply by typing:

```
make test
```

Chapter 4

Distributing your plugin

To share your plugin with others, you have to upload it to a plugin repository. Let's look at the steps involved in doing this.

Firstly, you need to ensure that your plugin adheres to the following rules:

- The name of your plugin's folder must contain only upper- and lowercase letters, digits, underscores, and hyphens, and must not start with a digit.
- Your `metadata.txt` file must exist and include the following entries:

Metadata entry	Description
`name`	The name of your plugin.
`qgisMinimumVersion`	The minimum version of QGIS that your plugin will run under.
`description`	A brief textual description of your plugin and what it does.
`version`	The version number of your plugin, as a string. Note that you can't upload two copies of a plugin with the same version.
`author`	The name of the plugin's author.
`email`	The author's e-mail address.

If you don't follow these rules, your plugin will be rejected when you attempt to upload it.

The next step is to compress the plugin into a ZIP archive. Note that you should compress the folder that contains your plugin, so that the ZIP archive has only one entry (the plugin's directory) rather than a collection of individual files.

The final step is to upload the ZIP archive to a QGIS plugin repository. You have two options here:

- You can use the official plugin repository at `http://plugins.qgis.org`. This will make your plugin available to all QGIS users.
- You can set up your own plugin repository. This means that only people who know about your repository or have access to it (for example, via a VPN) can download your plugins.

Setting up your own plugin repository isn't nearly as daunting as it sounds; you simply create an XML file that lists the plugins that you want to make available, and then upload that XML file and the plugins themselves to a web server. Here is what the XML file looks like:

```
<?xml version="1.0"?>
<plugins>
 <pyqgis_plugin name="MyPlugin" version="0.1">
  <description>This is a test plugin</description>
  <homepage>http://my-site.com/qgis/myplugin</homepage>
  <qgis_minimum_version>2.2</qgis_minimum_version>
  <file_name>myplugin.zip</file_name>
  <author_name>My Name</author_name>
  <download_url>http://my-site.com/myplugin.zip</download_url>
 </pyqgis_plugin>
</plugins>
```

Create a `<pyqgis_plugin>` section for each of your repository's plugins. Once this file has been uploaded, the user simply goes to the QGIS Plugin Manager window, clicks on the **Settings** tab, and clicks on the **Add** button in the **Plugin repositories** section of the window. The user will be asked to enter the details of the new repository:

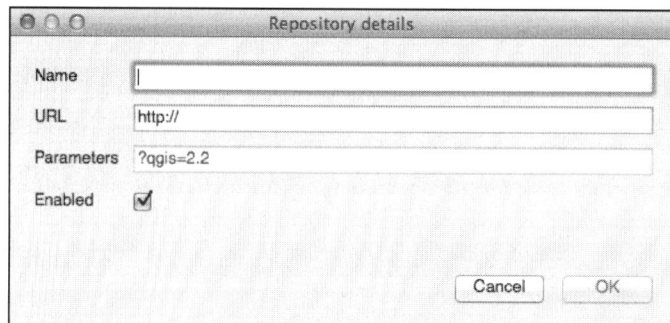

The **URL** field should be set to the complete URL for the XML file you uploaded, for example `http://my-site.com/qgis_plugins.xml`. Once the repository has been added, the plugins listed in the XML file will appear in the Plugin Manager, and the user can install them directly.

Writing a useful plugin

Let's now apply the knowledge we've gained to build a plugin that does something useful and interesting. While there are built-in tools in QGIS to query a feature and identify the feature's attributes, there is no easy way of getting information about the *geometry* associated with a feature. So let's write a plugin that lets the user click on a feature and display various statistics about that feature's geometry.

We're going to call our new plugin **Geometry Info**. When the user clicks on our plugin's toolbar icon, we will activate a map tool that listens for mouse clicks on the map canvas. When the user clicks on the map canvas, we'll find the feature that the user clicked on, and calculate and display statistics about that feature's geometry.

Let's start by setting up the basic template for our plugin. Create a directory named geometryInfo, put it somewhere convenient, and create an __init__.py file within that directory. In that file, place the following code:

```
def classFactory(iface):
    from geometryInfo import GeometryInfoPlugin
    return GeometryInfoPlugin(iface)
```

Next, we need to define the metadata for our plugin. Create the metadata.txt file and add the following to this file:

```
[general]
name=Geometry Info
email=your email address
author=your name
qgisMinimumVersion=2.0
description=Displays information about the clicked-on geometry.
about=Plugin used as an example in Chapter 4 of Building Mapping
    Applications with QGIS.
version=version 0.1
```

Next, we need an icon for our plugin. We're going to use the following icon:

A copy of this icon is available with the sample code that comes with this book, though you can create your own icon or find a different one to use somewhere; just make sure that the resulting image file is named icon.png, and that the icon is 24 x 24 pixels. Place this file into your geometryInfo directory along with the other files.

We next need to define the `resources.qrc` file that tells QGIS about our icon. Create this file and put the following text into it:

```
<RCC>
  <qresource prefix="/plugins/geometryInfo">
    <file>icon.png</file>
  </qresource>
</RCC>
```

Finally, let's create a Makefile to automate the process of compiling and deploying our plugin. Here's a suitable Makefile to get you started:

```
PLUGINNAME = geometryInfo
PY_FILES = geometryInfo.py __init__.py
EXTRAS = icon.png metadata.txt
RESOURCE_FILES = resources.py

default: compile

compile: $(RESOURCE_FILES)

%.py : %.qrc
	pyrcc4 -o $@ $<

deploy: compile
	mkdir -p $(HOME)/.qgis2/python/plugins/$(PLUGINNAME)
	cp -vf $(PY_FILES) $(HOME)/.qgis2/python/plugins/$(PLUGINNAME)
	cp -vf $(RESOURCE_FILES) $(HOME)/.qgis2/python/plugins/$(PLUGINNAME)
	cp -vf $(EXTRAS) $(HOME)/.qgis2/python/plugins/$(PLUGINNAME)

clean:
	rm $(RESOURCE_FILES)
```

You may need to modify the paths in this file to suit your development setup. Notice that because our plugin won't have any UI templates, we've removed the portions of the Makefile that compile and deploy the template files.

Now that we've created the framework for our plugin, let's start writing the code that does the actual work. The final file we need for our plugin will be named `geometryInfo.py`. Create this file and put the following code into it:

```
from PyQt4.QtCore import *
from PyQt4.QtGui import *
import resources
from qgis.core import *
from qgis.gui import *

class GeometryInfoPlugin:
```

```
def __init__(self, iface):
    self.iface = iface

def initGui(self):
    icon = QIcon(":/plugins/geometryInfo/icon.png")
    self.action = QAction(icon, "Get Geometry Info",
            self.iface.mainWindow())
    QObject.connect(self.action, SIGNAL("triggered()"),
            self.onClick)
    self.iface.addPluginToMenu("Geometry Info", self.action)
    self.iface.addToolBarIcon(self.action)

def unload(self):
    self.iface.removePluginMenu("Geometry Info", self.action)
    self.iface.removeToolBarIcon(self.action)

def onClick(self):
    QMessageBox.information(self.iface.mainWindow(), "debug",
            "Click")
```

Apart from a few extra `import` statements (which we'll need later on), this is almost identical to our earlier example plugin. The `onClick()` method, of course, is just a placeholder so we can tell if the plugin is working.

We can now run our plugin by typing `make deploy` in the command line, starting up QGIS, and enabling the plugin using the **Manage and Install Plugins...** command, just like we did earlier. If all goes well, the plugin's icon should appear in the QGIS toolbar, and when you select it, the "Click" message should be displayed.

Next, we want to make our toolbar icon *checkable*. That is, when the user clicks on our icon, we want to highlight it, activate our map tool, and keep the icon highlighted until the user either clicks on the icon again or switches to a different tool. To make the toolbar icon checkable, add the following line to your `initGui()` method, immediately after the `self.action = QAction(...)` statement:

```
self.action.setCheckable(True)
```

We then have to respond to the checking and unchecking of our toolbar icon by activating and deactivating our map tool. Here is what the code will look like:

```
def onClick(self):
    if not self.action.isChecked():
        # ...deactivate map tool...
        return
    self.action.setChecked(True)
    # ...activate map tool...
```

The first thing we do is see if the user has unchecked our icon, and if this is the case, we deactivate the map tool. Otherwise, we visually highlight the icon by calling `self.action.setChecked(True)`, and then activate our map tool. In this way, our plugin will act like a mode within QGIS; clicking on the icon will activate the map tool, and clicking on it again (or selecting a different icon) will deactivate it.

We're now ready to implement our map tool. Earlier, we looked at how you can use the `QgsMapTool` class to respond to mouse clicks within the map canvas. In this case, we'll use a subclass of `QgsMapTool`, called `QgsMapToolIdentify`. This class makes it easy to find the feature at a given point. When the user clicks on the map canvas, we'll use the `QgsMapToolIdentify.identify()` method to find the first clicked-on feature, and then calculate and display various statistics about that feature's geometry.

Add the following code to the end of your `geometryInfo.py` module:

```
class GeometryInfoMapTool(QgsMapToolIdentify):
    def __init__(self, iface):
        QgsMapToolIdentify.__init__(self, iface.mapCanvas())
        self.iface = iface

    def canvasReleaseEvent(self, event):
        QMessageBox.information(self.iface.mainWindow(), "debug",
                    "Canvas Click")
```

This defines our `QgsMapToolIdentify` subclass. It doesn't do anything useful yet, but it will respond with a simple "Canvas Click" message when the user clicks on the map canvas. Now, let's finish writing our plugin's `onClick()` method to activate and deactivate our map tool as the user clicks on our toolbar icon. This is what the `onClick()` method should look like:

```
def onClick(self):
    if not self.action.isChecked():
        self.iface.mapCanvas().unsetMapTool(self.mapTool)
        self.mapTool = None
        return
    self.action.setChecked(True)
    self.mapTool = GeometryInfoMapTool(self.iface)
    self.mapTool.setAction(self.action)
    self.iface.mapCanvas().setMapTool(self.mapTool)
```

You should now be able to run your plugin by typing `make deploy`, and then reload it in QGIS to see how it works. If all goes well, the toolbar icon will be highlighted when you click on it, and the "Canvas Click" message should appear when you click on the map canvas.

Now, let's replace the `GeometryInfoMapTool.canvasReleaseEvent()` method with code to identify the feature the user clicked on. Here's the necessary code:

```
def canvasReleaseEvent(self, event):
    found_features = self.identify(event.x(), event.y(),
                    self.TopDownStopAtFirst,
                    self.VectorLayer)
    if len(found_features) > 0:
      layer = found_features[0].mLayer
      feature = found_features[0].mFeature
      geometry = feature.geometry()
```

As you can see, we call `QgsMapToolIdentify.identify()` to see which feature the user clicked on. The parameters we're using tell the method to only return the top-most vector feature at the point where the user clicked; the `identify()` method can also return all features at a given point or the pixel value if the user clicked on a raster layer, but in our case, we only want the top-most vector feature.

Once we've found the clicked-on feature, we identify which map layer the feature is on, and extract the feature's geometry. With this information, we can analyze the geometry and display the calculated statistics, which is the whole purpose of our plugin.

A `QGSGeometry` object can represent a point, a line, a polygon, a number of points, a number of lines, a number of polygons, or a collection of different types of geometries. To analyze the statistics for any `QGSGeometry` object, we have to be ready to handle all these different types of geometries. Fortunately, the basic logic is quite straightforward:

- If the geometry has multiple parts, we split the geometry into its component parts, and process each part in turn
- For point geometries, we count the number of points
- For line geometries, we count the number of lines and calculate their total length
- For polygon geometries, we count the number of polygons and calculate their total area and perimeter

Let's add two methods to our `GeometryInfoMapTool` class to analyze a geometry:

```
def analyzeGeometry(self, geometry, layer, info):
  crs = layer.dataProvider().crs()
  calculator = QgsDistanceArea()
  calculator.setSourceCrs(crs)
  calculator.setEllipsoid(crs.ellipsoidAcronym())
```

```
calculator.setEllipsoidalMode(crs.geographicFlag())

if geometry.isMultipart():
  self.add(info, 'num_multi', 1)
  parts = geometry.asGeometryCollection()
  for sub_geometry in parts:
    self.analyzeGeometry(sub_geometry, layer, info)
elif geometry.type() == QGis.Point:
  self.add(info, 'num_points', 1)
elif geometry.type() == QGis.Line:
  self.add(info, 'num_lines', 1)
  self.add(info, 'tot_line_length',
      calculator.measure(geometry))
elif geometry.type() == QGis.Polygon:
  self.add(info, 'num_polygons', 1)
  self.add(info, 'tot_poly_area',
      calculator.measure(geometry))
  self.add(info, 'tot_poly_perimeter',
      calculator.measurePerimeter(geometry))

def add(self, info, key, n):
  if key in info:
    info[key] = info[key] + n
  else:
    info[key] = n
```

The `add()` method is just a helper method that adds a number to a dictionary entry if it exists, and creates that entry if it doesn't. This allows us to use the `info` dictionary to store the results as we calculate them.

As you can see, the `analyzeGeometry()` method makes use of a `QgsDistanceArea` object to calculate the lengths and areas of a geometry. Note that our `analyzeGeometry()` method is recursive; if a geometry has multiple parts, each subgeometry might also have multiple parts, so we call `analyzeGeometry()` recursively on each part to allow these nested geometries to be handled correctly.

When we call `analyzeGeometry()` on a given `QGSGeometry`, the results of the analysis will be stored in the `info` dictionary. Let's add some code to the end of our `canvasReleaseEvent()` method to analyze the clicked-on geometry and display the results:

```
info = {}
self.analyzeGeometry(geometry, layer, info)
QMessageBox.information(self.iface.mainWindow(), "debug",
        repr(info))
```

If you now do a `make deploy` and reload the plugin, you should be able to click on a feature and display information about that feature's geometry. The plugin's output should look like the following:

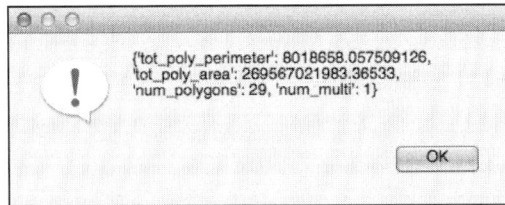

This is certainly telling us something useful, but it's not very readable. Let's look at how we can improve the way we display the statistics.

Firstly, notice that the area and perimeter values are not particularly useful; the `QgsDistanceArea` object returns lengths and areas in meters, but for most geometries, these values are too precise and too big. Let's make it more readable by converting the calculated lengths and areas into a whole number of kilometers. To do this, make the following highlighted changes to your `analyzeGeometry()` method:

```
...
elif geometry.type() == QGis.Line:
    self.add(info, 'num_lines', 1)
    self.add(info, 'tot_line_length',
        int(calculator.measure(geometry)/1000))
elif geometry.type() == QGis.Polygon:
    self.add(info, 'num_polygons', 1)
    self.add(info, 'tot_poly_area',
        int(calculator.measure(geometry)/1000000))
    self.add(info, 'tot_poly_perimeter',
        int(calculator.measurePerimeter(geometry)/1000))
```

As you can see, we're simply dividing the calculated lengths by a thousand to get the length in kilometers, and dividing the calculated area by a million to get the area in square kilometers.

The final thing we want to do is display those calculated statistics in a more friendly way. To do this, replace the `QMessageBox.information()` call at the end of your `canvasReleaseEvent()` method with the following:

```
fields = [("num_multi",
        "Number of multipart geometries", ""),
    ("num_points",
        "Number of point geometries", ""),
    ("num_lines",
```

```
              "Number of line geometries", ""),
            ("tot_line_length",
              "Total length of line geometries",
              "km"),
            ("num_polygons",
              "Number of polygon geometries", ""),
            ("tot_poly_area",
              "Total area of polygon geometries",
              "square km"),
            ("tot_poly_perimeter",
              "Total perimeter of polygon geometries",
              "km")]

    results = []
    for field,label,suffix in fields:
      if field in info:
        results.append("%s = %s %s" %
                (label, str(info[field]),
                suffix))

    QMessageBox.information(self.iface.mainWindow(),
                "Geometry Info",
                "\n".join(results))
```

Your plugin will now display the statistics in a more readable format, for example:

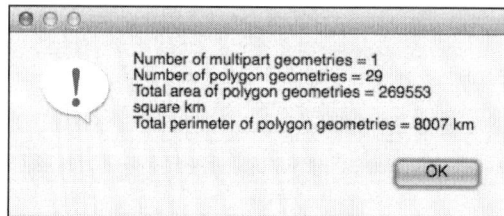

We've now completed our plugin, and can use it to display information about any geometry within QGIS. More importantly, we've learned how to create a complete and useful QGIS plugin, and you can build on this knowledge to create your own plugins.

Possibilities and limitations of plugins

As we have seen, it's quite possible to write a plugin that acts as a sophisticated mapping tool integrated directly into the QGIS user interface, interacting with the map canvas and responding in various ways to the user's actions. Some of the other things you can do with a QGIS plugin include:

- Creating your own subclass of `QgsMapCanvasItem`, so your plugin can draw items directly onto the QGIS map canvas.

- Creating a custom map layer by subclassing `QgsPluginLayer`. This allows your plugin to act as a completely separate map layer.

- Using signal handlers to intercept standard QGIS actions, for example, redrawing the canvas and executing your own code when a signal is sent.

- Creating map layers programmatically, setting up the data provider, and creating custom symbols and renderers to control how the map data is displayed.

- Using the QGIS Map Composer tools to combine rendered map layers, labels, legends, tables, and so on, mimicking the layout of a paper map. The resulting map view can be displayed in a window, printed, or saved to disk as an image or a PDF file.

There are, however, some limitations on what a QGIS plugin is able to do:

- By its very nature, a plugin sits inside the running QGIS application. Your plugin runs alongside all the other plugins that the user has installed, and shares the same user interface and menu structure. This means that you can't implement turnkey mapping applications as QGIS plugins. The full complexity of QGIS is shown to the user, which can be daunting for the user who might be looking for a custom application that performs just one task. In this situation, it might be better to write your code as an external application that uses the PyQGIS library, rather than attempt to write it as a plugin.

- Since the plugin runs within QGIS itself, there are many points of contact between the plugin code and the QGIS environment. As QGIS is constantly evolving, this means that a plugin can stop working when a new version of QGIS is released. This is far more likely to happen with a plugin than with code written as an external application using the PyQGIS library.

- Since the plugin uses the Python interpreter built into QGIS itself, you can't make use of third-party Python libraries that aren't included in QGIS's Python interpreter. While you can get around this for pure Python libraries (by including the Python source code as part of your plugin), if the library you want makes use of extensions written in C, you simply won't be able to use that library in your plugin.

Ultimately, it is up to you to decide if plugins are a suitable way of implementing your mapping application. For some applications, they are ideal; they are certainly a lot easier to develop and distribute than external applications, and if your application is aimed at people who are already using QGIS, then the plugin scheme is a logical approach to take. In other situations, an external application built on top of PyQGIS might be more suitable.

Summary

In this chapter, we delved into the topic of QGIS plugin programming. We created two separate plugins, a simple one to get started with, and a more complex and useful plugin that displays information about a clicked-on feature's geometry. We also looked at the QGIS plugin architecture, the plugin development process, and some of the possibilities and limitations of QGIS plugins. Along the way, we learned about the tools needed to develop QGIS plugins, discovered that plugins are simply Python packages with certain special files in them, and saw how the PyQt command-line tools can be used to compile user-interface templates and resource description files into Python modules so that they can be used within a plugin.

We also looked at how your plugin is integrated into the QGIS user interface using icons and menu items, how to run your plugin, and what happens when your plugin crashes. We also looked briefly at the Plugin Builder, and how it can be useful.

Next, we looked at how to use a Makefile to automate plugin compilation and deployment, and the typical write-make-reload-test cycle used to develop plugins. We saw how to write and use HTML help files within your plugin, how unit tests can be used for QGIS plugins, and how to distribute your plugin, both to the official QGIS plugin repository and to a repository that you set up yourself.

We learned that there are many things you can do with plugins, including drawing into the map canvas, creating custom layers, intercepting QGIS actions, programmatically creating map layers, and composing complex maps. At the same time, we saw that there are some constraints in what a QGIS plugin can do, including the need to share the QGIS user interface with all other plugins, the inability to create turnkey mapping applications, compatibility issues, and difficulties in using some third-party Python libraries.

In the next chapter, we will look at the process of using the PyQGIS libraries within your own external Python programs. This gets around many of the limitations of a QGIS Plugin, at the cost of some additional complexity.

5
Using QGIS in an External Application

In *Chapter 1*, *Getting Started with QGIS*, we looked briefly at a standalone Python program built using PyQt and the PyQGIS library. In this chapter, we will use the same technique to build a complete turnkey mapping application using PyQGIS. Along the way, we will:

- Design and build a simple but complete standalone mapping application

- Learn how to use a wrapper script to handle the platform-specific dependencies before our Python program is run

- Define our application's user interface in a separate Python module so that we keep our UI separate from the application's business logic

- Dynamically show and hide map layers based on the user's preference

- Learn how to use a rule-based renderer to selectively display features based on the map's current zoom level

- See how data-defined properties can be used to calculate the font size to use for a label based on the feature's attributes

- Implement Google Maps style panning and zooming

Introducing Lex

Our mapping application will display a world map, allowing the user to zoom and pan, and display various landmarks on the map. If the user clicks on a landmark, information about that landmark will be displayed.

We'll call our application **Lex**, which is short for **L**andmark **ex**plorer. Lex will make use of two freely available geospatial datasets: a high-resolution shaded-relief basemap, and a comprehensive database of place names, which we will use as the list of landmarks to display:

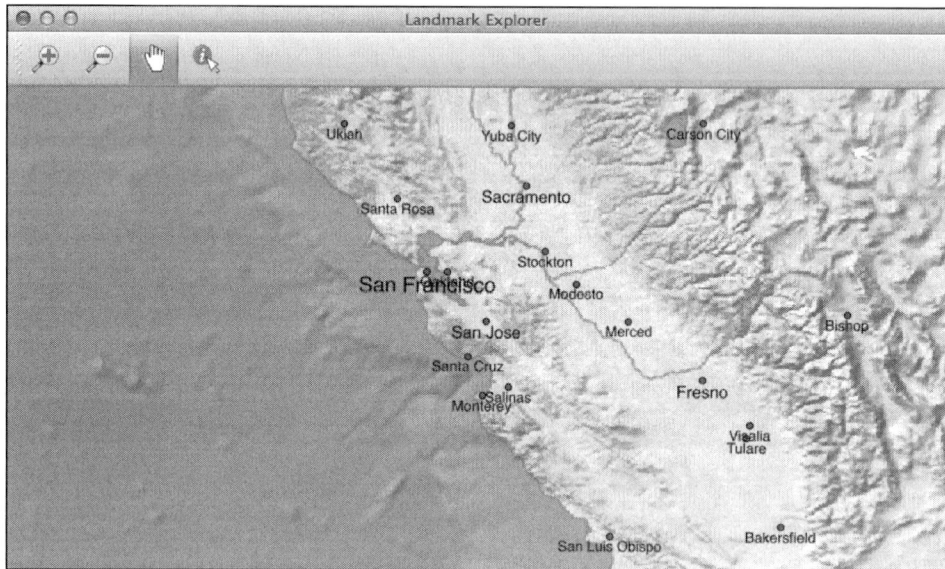

We will build our Lex application using PyQt, and make use of the PyQGIS libraries built into QGIS to do most of the hard work.

Our requirements for the Lex application are as follows:

- It must run as a turnkey application. Double-clicking on the launcher script must start the PyQt program, load all the data, and present a complete working application to the user.

- The user interface must be as professional as possible, with keyboard shortcuts and good-looking toolbar icons.

- When the user clicks on a landmark, the name and jurisdiction, time zone, and latitude/longitude for that landmark should be displayed.

- The look and feel should be as similar as possible to Google Maps.

This last requirement is an important point, as the zooming and panning tools built into QGIS are more complicated than what we would like to have in a turnkey mapping application. Most users are already familiar with the behavior of Google Maps, and we want to mimic this behavior rather than using the default panning and zooming tools supplied by QGIS.

Without further delay, let's start building our application. Our first step will be to download the geospatial data the application will be based on.

Getting the data

Lex will make use of two map layers: a **basemap layer** that displays a shaded-relief raster image, and a **landmark layer** that shows the individual landmarks based on a set of place names. Both of these datasets can be downloaded from the Natural Earth Data website. Visit http://www.naturalearthdata.com and click on the **Get the Data** link to jump to the **Downloads** page.

The basemap data can be found by clicking on the **Raster** link. We'll want the highest-resolution data available, so use the link in the **Large scale data, 1:10m** section.

While you could use any of these datasets as a basemap, we will download the **Natural Earth I with Shaded Relief, Water, and Drainages** dataset. Make sure you download the high-resolution version of this dataset so that the raster image will still look good when the user has zoomed in.

For the landmarks, we'll be using the "populated places" dataset. Go back to the main downloads page and click on the **Cultural** link in the **Large scale data, 1:10m** section. Scroll down to the **Populated Places** section and click on the **Download Populated Places** link.

Once you have finished downloading, you should have two ZIP archives on your computer:

NE1_HR_LC_SR_W_DR.zip

ne_10m_populated_places.zip

Create a folder named `data`, decompress the preceding two ZIP archives, and place the resulting directories into your `data` folder.

Designing the application

We now have a list of requirements for our mapping application, together with the geospatial data we want to display. Before we start coding, however, it's a good idea to step back and think about our application's user interface.

Our application will have one main window, which we will call **Landmark Explorer**. To make it easy to use, we'll display a map canvas along with a simple toolbar. Our basic window layout will look like the following:

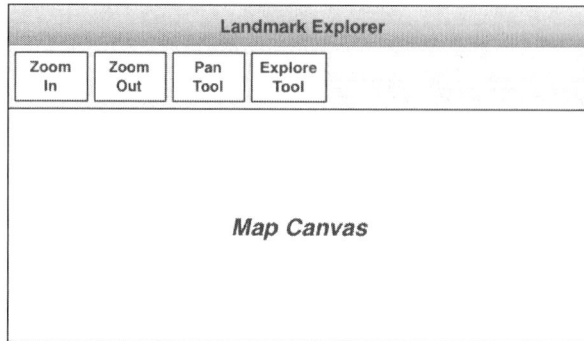

Along with the main window, our Lex application will have a menu bar with the following menus:

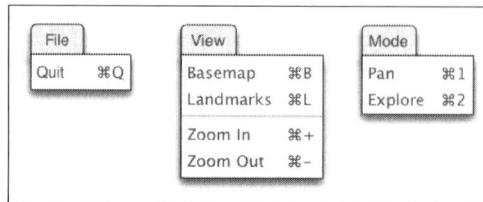

The toolbar will make it easy for new users to work with Lex by pointing and clicking on the toolbar icons, while experienced users can make use of the extensive keyboard shortcuts to access the program's features.

With this design in mind, let's start coding.

Creating the application's framework

Start by creating a folder to hold your application's source code, and move the data folder you created earlier into it. Next, we want to create the basic framework for our application using the techniques we learned in *Chapter 1, Getting Started with QGIS*. Create a module named `lex.py`, and enter the following into this file:

```python
import os, os.path, sys

from qgis.core import *
from qgis.gui import *
from PyQt4.QtGui import *
from PyQt4.QtCore import *

class MapExplorer(QMainWindow):
    def __init__(self):
        QMainWindow.__init__(self)
        self.setWindowTitle("Landmark Explorer")
        self.resize(800, 400)

def main():
    QgsApplication.setPrefixPath(os.environ['QGIS_PREFIX'], True)
    QgsApplication.initQgis()

    app = QApplication(sys.argv)

    window = MapExplorer()
    window.show()
    window.raise_()

    app.exec_()
    app.deleteLater()
    QgsApplication.exitQgis()

if __name__ == "__main__":
    main()
```

We're simply importing the various libraries we'll need and setting up an external PyQGIS application using the techniques we learned earlier. We then create and display a blank window so that the application will do something when it starts up.

Since we want the Lex application to work on any operating system, we're not going to hard-wire the path to QGIS into our source code. Instead, we'll write a **wrapper script** that sets up the required environment variables before launching our Python program. As these wrapper scripts are operating-system dependent, you will need to create an appropriate wrapper script for your operating system.

> Notice that we use `os.environ['QGIS_PREFIX']` in our `lex.py` module to avoid hard-wiring the path to the QGIS application into our source code. Our wrapper script will take care of setting this environment variable before the application is run.

If you are using a computer with Microsoft Windows, your wrapper script will look something like the following:

```
SET OSGEO4W_ROOT=C:\OSGeo4W
SET QGIS_PREFIX=%OSGEO4W_ROOT%\apps\qgis
SET PATH=%QGIS_PREFIX%\bin;%OSGWO4W_ROOT\bin;%PATH%
SET PYTHONPATH=%QGIS_PREFIX%\python;%OSEO4W_ROOT%\apps\
Python27;%PYTHONPATH%
SET PYTHONHOME=%OSGEO4W_ROOT%\apps\Python27
python lex.py
```

Name this script something sensible, for example, `run.bat`, and put it in the same directory as your `lex.py` module.

If you are using a computer that runs Linux, your wrapper script will be named something like `run.sh`, and will look like the following:

```
export PYTHONPATH="/path/to/qgis/build/output/python/"
export LD_LIBRARY_PATH="/path/to/qgis/build/output/lib/"
export QGIS_PREFIX="/path/to/qgis/build/output/"
python lex.py
```

You will need to modify the paths to refer to the directory where QGIS has been installed.

For those running Mac OS X, your wrapper script will also be called `run.sh`, and will contain the following:

```
export PYTHONPATH="$PYTHONPATH:/Applications/QGIS.app/Contents/
Resources/python"
export DYLD_FRAMEWORK_PATH="/Applications/QGIS.app/Contents/
Frameworks"
export QGIS_PREFIX="/Applications/QGIS.app/Contents/Resources"
python lex.py
```

Notice that for Mac OS X and Linux, we have to set the framework or library paths. This allows the PyQGIS Python wrappers to find the underlying C++ shared libraries that they are based on.

> If you are running under Linux or Mac OS X, you'll also have to make your wrapper script executable. To do this, type `chmod +x run.sh` into the bash shell or terminal window.

Once you have created your shell script, try running it. If all goes well, your PyQt application should start up and display a blank window, like the following:

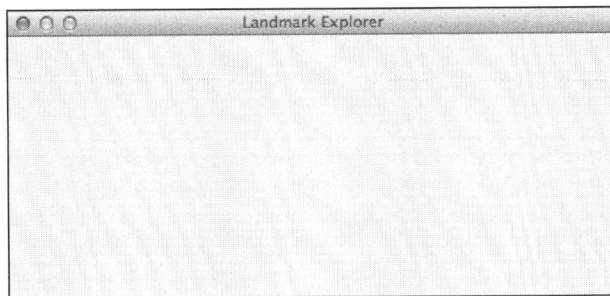

If it doesn't work, you will need to check your wrapper script and/or your `lex.py` module. You might need to modify the directory paths to match your QGIS and Python installations.

Adding the user interface

Now that our program is running, we can start implementing the user interface (UI). A typical PyQt application will make use of Qt Designer to store the application's UI in a template file, which is then compiled into a Python module for use within your application.

As it would take many pages to describe how to use Qt Designer to lay out our window with its toolbar and menus, we're going to cheat and create our user interface directly within Python. At the same time, however, we'll create our UI module as if it was created using Qt Designer; this keeps our application's UI separate, and also shows how our application would work if we were to use Qt Designer to design our user interface.

Create a new module called `ui_explorerWindow.py`, and type the following code into this module:

```python
from PyQt4 import QtGui, QtCore

import resources

class Ui_ExplorerWindow(object):
    def setupUi(self, window):
        window.setWindowTitle("Landmark Explorer")

        self.centralWidget = QtGui.QWidget(window)
        self.centralWidget.setMinimumSize(800, 400)
        window.setCentralWidget(self.centralWidget)

        self.menubar = window.menuBar()
        self.fileMenu = self.menubar.addMenu("File")
        self.viewMenu = self.menubar.addMenu("View")
        self.modeMenu = self.menubar.addMenu("Mode")

        self.toolBar = QtGui.QToolBar(window)
        window.addToolBar(QtCore.Qt.TopToolBarArea, self.toolBar)

        self.actionQuit = QtGui.QAction("Quit", window)
        self.actionQuit.setShortcut(QtGui.QKeySequence.Quit)

        self.actionShowBasemapLayer = QtGui.QAction("Basemap",
            window)
        self.actionShowBasemapLayer.setShortcut("Ctrl+B")
        self.actionShowBasemapLayer.setCheckable(True)

        self.actionShowLandmarkLayer = QtGui.QAction("Landmarks",
            window)
        self.actionShowLandmarkLayer.setShortcut("Ctrl+L")
        self.actionShowLandmarkLayer.setCheckable(True)

        icon = QtGui.QIcon(":/icons/mActionZoomIn.png")
        self.actionZoomIn = QtGui.QAction(icon, "Zoom In", window)
        self.actionZoomIn.setShortcut(QtGui.QKeySequence.ZoomIn)

        icon = QtGui.QIcon(":/icons/mActionZoomOut.png")
        self.actionZoomOut = QtGui.QAction(icon, "Zoom Out",
            window)
        self.actionZoomOut.setShortcut(QtGui.QKeySequence.ZoomOut)

        icon = QtGui.QIcon(":/icons/mActionPan.png")
```

```
self.actionPan = QtGui.QAction(icon, "Pan", window)
self.actionPan.setShortcut("Ctrl+1")
self.actionPan.setCheckable(True)

icon = QtGui.QIcon(":/icons/mActionExplore.png")
self.actionExplore = QtGui.QAction(icon, "Explore",
    window)
self.actionExplore.setShortcut("Ctrl+2")
self.actionExplore.setCheckable(True)

self.fileMenu.addAction(self.actionQuit)

self.viewMenu.addAction(self.actionShowBasemapLayer)
self.viewMenu.addAction(self.actionShowLandmarkLayer)
self.viewMenu.addSeparator()
self.viewMenu.addAction(self.actionZoomIn)
self.viewMenu.addAction(self.actionZoomOut)

self.modeMenu.addAction(self.actionPan)
self.modeMenu.addAction(self.actionExplore)

self.toolBar.addAction(self.actionZoomIn)
self.toolBar.addAction(self.actionZoomOut)
self.toolBar.addAction(self.actionPan)
self.toolBar.addAction(self.actionExplore)

window.resize(window.sizeHint())
```

This module implements our Lex application's user interface, defining a `QtAction` object for each toolbar and menu item, creating a widget to hold our map canvas, and laying everything out within a `QtMainWindow` object. The structure of this module is identical to the way Qt Designer and the `pyuic4` command-line tool make a user interface template available to Python code.

Notice that the `Ui_ExplorerWindow` class makes use of several toolbar icons. We will need to create these icon images and define them in a resource description file, in the same way we created a `resources.py` module in the previous chapter.

We are going to need the following icon images:

- `mActionZoomIn.png`
- `mActionZoomOut.png`
- `mActionPan.png`
- `mActionExplore.png`

If you want, you can download these image files in SVG format from the QGIS source code repository (`https://github.com/qgis/QGIS/tree/master/images/themes/default`), though you will need to convert them from `.svg` to `.png` in order to avoid issues with image file formats. If you don't want to convert the icons yourself, the images are available as part of the source code available with this book. Once you are done, place these four files in the main directory of your Lex application.

> Note that the `mActionExplore.png` icon file is a converted copy of the `mActionIdentify.svg` image in the source code repository. We renamed the image file to match the name of the tool in our Lex application.

Next, we need to create our `resources.qrc` file so that PyQt can use these images. Create this file and enter the following into it:

```
<RCC>
    <qresource prefix="/icons">
        <file>mActionZoomIn.png</file>
        <file>mActionZoomOut.png</file>
        <file>mActionPan.png</file>
        <file>mActionExplore.png</file>
    </qresource>
</RCC>
```

You will need to compile this file using `pyrcc4`. This will give you the `resources.py` module required by your user interface.

Now that we've defined our user interface, let's modify the `lex.py` module to use it. Add the following `import` statements to the top of your module:

```
from ui_explorerWindow import Ui_ExplorerWindow
import resources
```

Next, we want to replace our dummy implementation of the `MapExplorer` window with one that uses our new UI. This is what the `MapExplorer` class definition should look like:

```
class MapExplorer(QMainWindow, Ui_ExplorerWindow):
    def __init__(self):
        QMainWindow.__init__(self)

        self.setupUi(self)
```

If all goes well, our application should now run with a complete user interface—a toolbar, menus, and room for our map canvas:

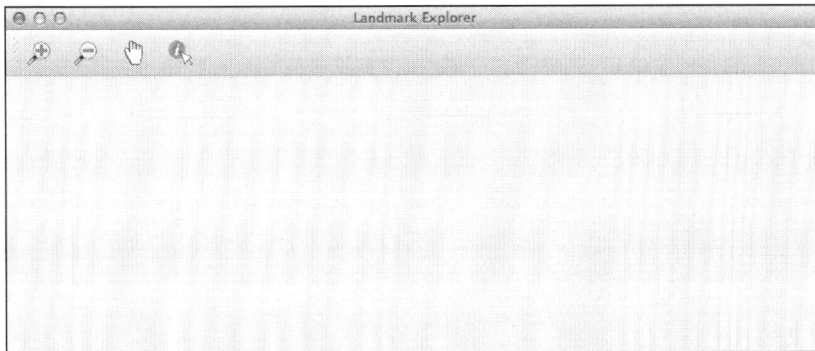

Of course, our user interface doesn't do anything yet, but our Lex application is starting to look like a real program. Now, let's implement the behavior behind our UI.

Connecting the actions

You might have noticed that none of the menu commands and toolbar icons do anything yet—even the **Quit** command doesn't work. Before our actions do anything, we have to connect them to the appropriate method. To do this, add the following to your `MapExplorer.__init__()` method, immediately after the call to `setupUi()`:

```
self.connect(self.actionQuit,
            SIGNAL("triggered()"), qApp.quit)
self.connect(self.actionShowBasemapLayer,
            SIGNAL("triggered()"), self.showBasemapLayer)
self.connect(self.actionShowLandmarkLayer,
            SIGNAL("triggered()"),
            self.showLandmarkLayer)
self.connect(self.actionZoomIn,
            SIGNAL("triggered()"), self.zoomIn)
self.connect(self.actionZoomOut,
            SIGNAL("triggered()"), self.zoomOut)
self.connect(self.actionPan,
            SIGNAL("triggered()"), self.setPanMode)
self.connect(self.actionExplore,
            SIGNAL("triggered()"), self.setExploreMode)
```

We're connecting our **Quit** action to the `qApp.quit()` method. For the other actions, we'll be calling methods within our `MapExplorer` class itself. Let's define some placeholders for these methods:

```
def showBasemapLayer(self):
    pass

def showLandmarkLayer(self):
    pass

def zoomIn(self):
    pass

def zoomOut(self):
    pass

def setPanMode(self):
    pass

def setExploreMode(self):
    pass
```

We'll implement these methods later on, once we have the map canvas up and running.

Creating the map canvas

Our `Ui_ExplorerWindow` class defines an instance variable named `centralWidget`, which acts as a placeholder for our window's contents. Since we want to place a QGIS map canvas into our window, let's implement the code to create our map canvas and place it into this central widget. Add the following to the end of your `MapExplorer` window's `__init__()` method (in `lex.py`):

```
self.mapCanvas = QgsMapCanvas()
self.mapCanvas.useImageToRender(False)
self.mapCanvas.setCanvasColor(Qt.white)
self.mapCanvas.show()

layout = QVBoxLayout()
layout.setContentsMargins(0, 0, 0, 0)
layout.addWidget(self.mapCanvas)
self.centralWidget.setLayout(layout)
```

Next, we want to fill our map canvas with the basemap and landmark map layers. To do this, we'll define a new method called `loadMap()`, and call this at the appropriate time. Add the following method to your `MapExplorer` class:

```
def loadMap(self):
    cur_dir = os.path.dirname(os.path.realpath(__file__))
    filename = os.path.join(cur_dir, "data",
                            "NE1_HR_LC_SR_W_DR",
                            "NE1_HR_LC_SR_W_DR.tif")
    self.basemap_layer = QgsRasterLayer(filename, "basemap")
    QgsMapLayerRegistry.instance().addMapLayer(
            self.basemap_layer)

    filename = os.path.join(cur_dir, "data",
                            "ne_10m_populated_places",
                            "ne_10m_populated_places.shp")
    self.landmark_layer = QgsVectorLayer(filename,
                                         "landmarks", "ogr")
    QgsMapLayerRegistry.instance().addMapLayer(
            self.landmark_layer)

    self.showVisibleMapLayers()
    self.mapCanvas.setExtent(QgsRectangle(-127.7, 24.4, -79.3,
      49.1))
```

This method loads the raster and vector datasets we placed in our `data` directory. We then call a new method, `showVisibleMapLayers()`, to make those layers visible, and then set the extent of the map canvas to show the continental USA when the application first starts up.

Let's implement the `showVisibleMapLayers()` method:

```
def showVisibleMapLayers(self):
    layers = []
    if self.actionShowLandmarkLayer.isChecked():
        layers.append(QgsMapCanvasLayer(self.landmark_layer))
    if self.actionShowBasemapLayer.isChecked():
        layers.append(QgsMapCanvasLayer(self.basemap_layer))
    self.mapCanvas.setLayerSet(layers)
```

As the user can choose to show or hide the basemap and landmark layers individually, we only display the layers that the user has selected to display. We also put this into a separate method so that we can call it when the user toggles the visibility of a layer.

There are a few more things to do before our map can be displayed. First off, add the following line to your `main()` function immediately after the call to `window.raise_()`:

```
window.loadMap()
```

This loads the map once the window has been displayed. Next, add the following to the end of your main window's `__init__()` method:

```
self.actionShowBasemapLayer.setChecked(True)
self.actionShowLandmarkLayer.setChecked(True)
```

This makes the two layers visible when the program starts up. Finally, let's implement the two methods we defined earlier so that the user can choose which layers are shown:

```
def showBasemapLayer(self):
    self.showVisibleMapLayers()

def showLandmarkLayer(self):
    self.showVisibleMapLayers()
```

Running the program should show the two map layers, and you can show or hide each layer using the commands in the **View** menu:

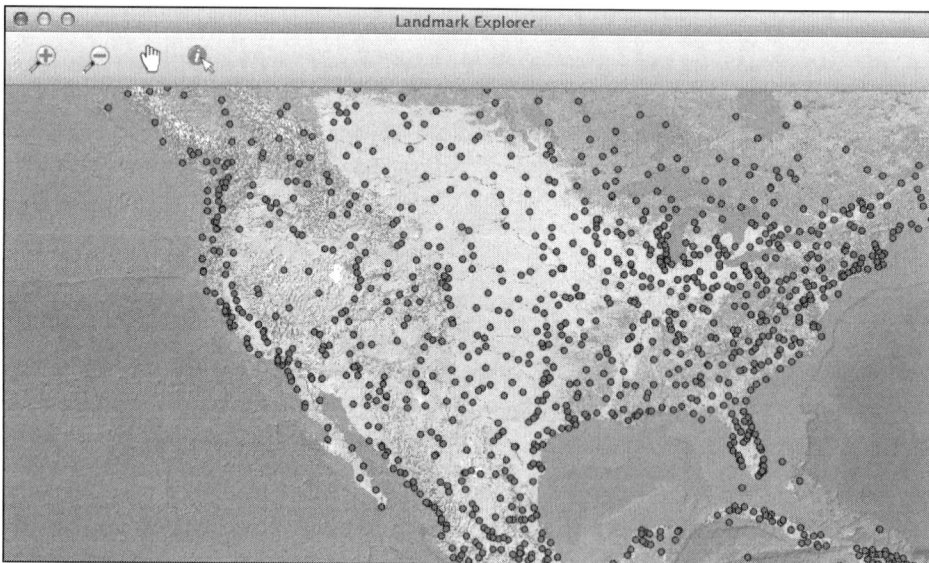

Labeling the points

As you can see from the preceding image, each landmark is simply represented by a colored dot. To make the program more useful, we'll want to display the name of each landmark. This can be done by using the "PAL" labeling engine built into QGIS. Add the following code to your `loadMap()` method, immediately before the call to `self.showVisibleMapLayers()`:

```
p = QgsPalLayerSettings()
p.readFromLayer(self.landmark_layer)
p.enabled = True
p.fieldName = "NAME"
p.placement = QgsPalLayerSettings.OverPoint
p.displayAll = True
p.setDataDefinedProperty(QgsPalLayerSettings.Size,
                         True, True, "12", "")
p.quadOffset = QgsPalLayerSettings.QuadrantBelow
p.yOffset = 1
p.labelOffsetInMapUnits = False
p.writeToLayer(self.landmark_layer)

labelingEngine = QgsPalLabeling()
self.mapCanvas.mapRenderer().setLabelingEngine(labelingEngine)
```

This will label each point on the map. Unfortunately, there are a lot of points, and the resulting map is completely unreadable:

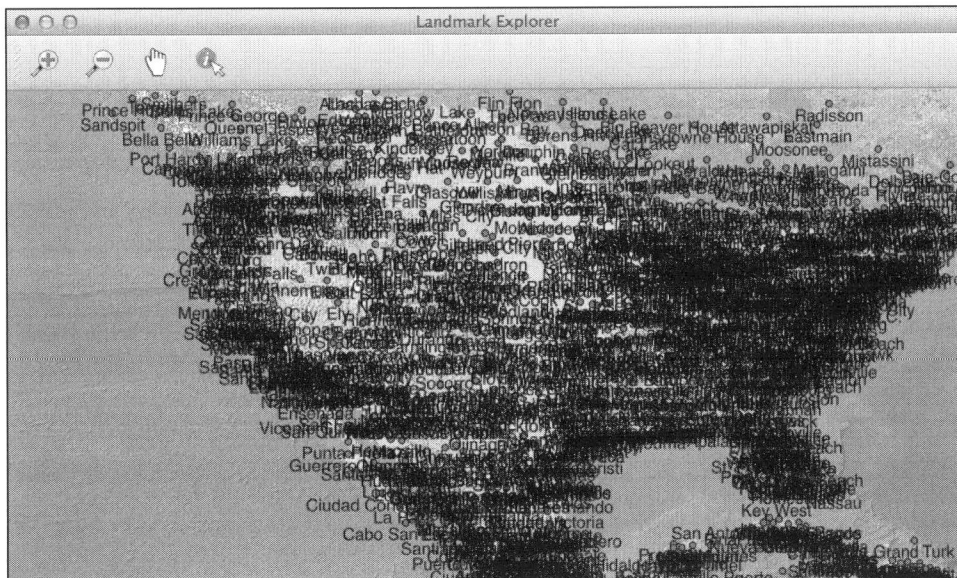

Filtering the landmarks

The reason our labels are unreadable is because there are too many landmarks being displayed. However, not all landmarks are relevant at all zoom levels—we want to hide landmarks that are too small to be useful when the map is zoomed out, while still showing these landmarks when the user zooms in. To do this, we'll use a `QgsRuleBasedRendererV2` object and make use of the SCALERANK attribute to selectively hide features that are too small for the current zoom level.

Add the following code to your `loadMap()` method, before the call to `self.showVisibleMapLayers()`:

```
        symbol = QgsSymbolV2.defaultSymbol(self.landmark_layer.
geometryType())
        renderer = QgsRuleBasedRendererV2(symbol)
        root_rule = renderer.rootRule()
        default_rule = root_rule.children()[0]

        rule = default_rule.clone()
        rule.setFilterExpression("(SCALERANK >= 0) and (SCALERANK <=
1)")
        rule.setScaleMinDenom(0)
        rule.setScaleMaxDenom(99999999)
        root_rule.appendChild(rule)

        rule = default_rule.clone()
        rule.setFilterExpression("(SCALERANK >= 2) and (SCALERANK <=
4)")
        rule.setScaleMinDenom(0)
        rule.setScaleMaxDenom(10000000)
        root_rule.appendChild(rule)

        rule = default_rule.clone()
        rule.setFilterExpression("(SCALERANK >= 5) and (SCALERANK <=
7)")
        rule.setScaleMinDenom(0)
        rule.setScaleMaxDenom(5000000)
        root_rule.appendChild(rule)

        rule = default_rule.clone()
        rule.setFilterExpression("(SCALERANK >= 7) and (SCALERANK <=
10)")
        rule.setScaleMinDenom(0)
        rule.setScaleMaxDenom(2000000)
```

```
root_rule.appendChild(rule)

root_rule.removeChildAt(0)
self.landmark_layer.setRendererV2(renderer)
```

This will have the effect of hiding landmarks that are too small (that is, which have too large a SCALERANK value) when the map is zoomed out. Now, our map looks much more reasonable:

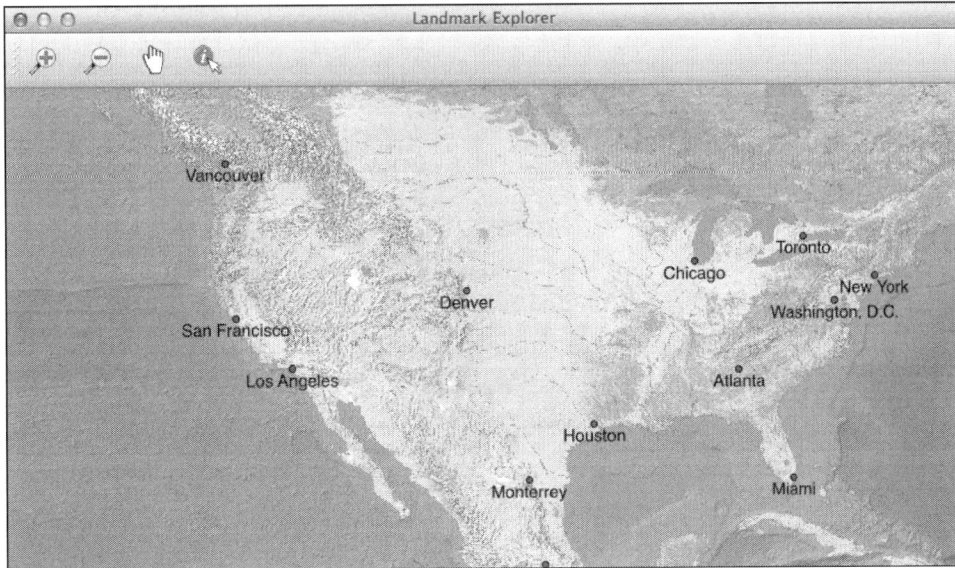

There's just one more feature we'd like to add here; at the moment, all the labels are of the same size. However, we'd like the larger landmarks to be shown with a larger label. To do this, replace the p.setDataDefinedProperty(...) line in your program with the following:

```
expr = ("CASE WHEN SCALERANK IN (0,1) THEN 18" +
        "WHEN SCALERANK IN (2,3,4) THEN 14 " +
        "WHEN SCALERANK IN (5,6,7) THEN 12 " +
        "WHEN SCALERANK IN (8,9,10) THEN 10 " +
        "ELSE 9 END")
p.setDataDefinedProperty(QgsPalLayerSettings.Size, True,
                         True, expr, "")
```

This calculates the font size based on the feature's SCALERANK attribute value. As you can imagine, using data-defined properties in this way can be extremely useful.

Implementing the zoom tool

Next, we want to support zooming in and out. As mentioned earlier, one of the requirements for our Lex application is that it must work like Google Maps rather than QGIS, and this is an example of where we have to support this. QGIS has a zoom tool, which the user clicks on and then clicks or drags on the map to zoom in or out. In Lex, the user will click on the toolbar icons directly to do the zooming. Fortunately, this is easy to do; simply implement the `zoomIn()` and `zoomOut()` methods in the following way:

```
def zoomIn(self):
    self.mapCanvas.zoomIn()

def zoomOut(self):
    self.mapCanvas.zoomOut()
```

Now, try to run your program. As you zoom in and out, you can see the various landmarks appear and disappear, and you should also be able to see the different font sizes used for the labels based on each feature's SCALERANK value.

Implementing the pan tool

Panning (that is, clicking and dragging on the map to move around) is another area where the QGIS default behavior isn't quite what we want. QGIS includes a `classQgsMapToolPan` class, which implements panning; however, it also includes some features that could be quite confusing for users coming from Google Maps. In particular, if the user clicks without dragging, the map is re-centered over the clicked-on point. Instead of using `classQgsMapToolPan`, we will implement our own panning map tool. Fortunately, this is simple to do: simply add the following class definition to your `lex.py` module after the end of your `MapExplorer` class definition:

```
class PanTool(QgsMapTool):
    def __init__(self, mapCanvas):
        QgsMapTool.__init__(self, mapCanvas)
        self.setCursor(Qt.OpenHandCursor)
        self.dragging = False

    def canvasMoveEvent(self, event):
        if event.buttons() == Qt.LeftButton:
            self.dragging = True
            self.canvas().panAction(event)

    def canvasReleaseEvent(self, event):
        if event.button() == Qt.LeftButton and self.dragging:
            self.canvas().panActionEnd(event.pos())
            self.dragging = False
```

We then need to add the following to the end of our main window's __init__()
method to create an instance of our panning tool:

```
self.panTool = PanTool(self.mapCanvas)
self.panTool.setAction(self.actionPan)
```

We can now implement our setPanMode() method to use this map tool:

```
def setPanMode(self):
    self.actionPan.setChecked(True)
    self.mapCanvas.setMapTool(self.panTool)
```

Finally, we'll want to select the panning mode when the application starts up. To do
this, add the following to your main() function after the call to window.loadMap():

```
window.setPanMode()
```

Implementing the explore mode

So far, the user can choose which map layers are displayed, and can zoom and pan
the map view. The only thing missing is the entire point of the application: exploring
landmarks. To do this, we'll have to implement our application's **explore** mode.

In the previous chapter, we saw how we can use a QgsMapToolIdentify subclass to
respond when the user clicks on a vector feature. We're going to use the same logic
here to implement a new map tool, which we'll call ExploreTool. Add the following
class definition to your lex.py module after the PanTool class definition:

```
class ExploreTool(QgsMapToolIdentify):
    def __init__(self, window):
        QgsMapToolIdentify.__init__(self, window.mapCanvas)
        self.window = window

    def canvasReleaseEvent(self, event):
        found_features = self.identify(event.x(), event.y(),
                                       self.TopDownStopAtFirst,
                                       self.VectorLayer)
        if len(found_features) > 0:
            layer = found_features[0].mLayer
            feature = found_features[0].mFeature
            geometry = feature.geometry()

            info = []

            name = feature.attribute("NAME")
```

```
        if name != None: info.append(name)

        admin_0 = feature.attribute("ADM0NAME")
        admin_1 = feature.attribute("ADM1NAME")
        if admin_0 and admin_1:
            info.append(admin_1 + ", " + admin_0)

        timezone = feature.attribute("TIMEZONE")
        if timezone != None:
            info.append("Timezone: " + timezone)

        longitude = geometry.asPoint().x()
        latitude  = geometry.asPoint().y()
        info.append("Lat/Long: %0.4f, %0.4f" % (latitude,
                                                 longitude))

        QMessageBox.information(self.window,
                               "Feature Info",
                               "\n".join(info))
```

This tool identifies the landmark feature the user clicked on, extracts the relevant attributes for that feature, and displays the results in a message box. To use our new map tool, we'll have to add the following to the end of our `MapExplorer` window's `__init__()` method:

```
        self.exploreTool = ExploreTool(self)
        self.exploreTool.setAction(self.actionExplore)
```

We'll then need to implement our `setExploreMode()` method to use this tool:

```
        def setExploreMode(self):
        self.actionPan.setChecked(False)
        self.actionExplore.setChecked(True)
        self.mapCanvas.setMapTool(self.exploreTool)
```

Notice that when the user switches to the explore mode, we have to uncheck the panning mode action. This ensures that the two modes are mutually exclusive. The final step we have to take is to modify our `setPanMode()` method so that it unchecks the explore mode action when the user switches back to the panning mode. To do this, add the following highlighted line to your `setPanMode()` method:

```
    def setPanMode(self):
        self.actionPan.setChecked(True)
        self.actionExplore.setChecked(False)
        self.mapCanvas.setMapTool(self.panTool)
```

This completes our Lex program. The user can now zoom in and out, pan around, and click on a feature to get more information about that landmark:

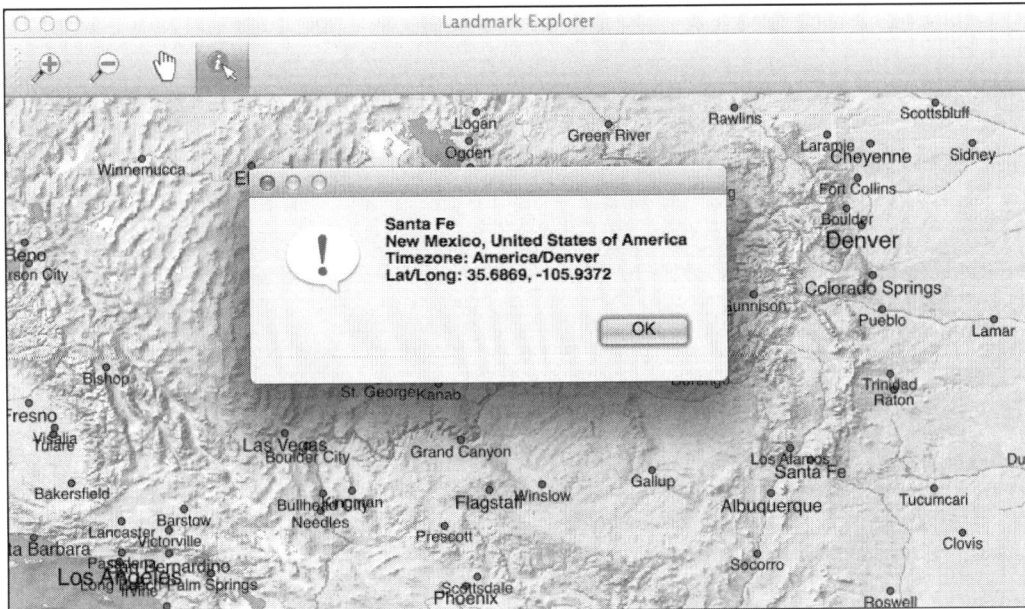

Further improvements and enhancements

Of course, while Lex is a useful and complete mapping application, it is really only a starting point. The information provided in the freely available populated places dataset doesn't make for a particularly interesting set of landmarks, and our application is still quite basic. Here are some suggested improvements you could make to the Lex application:

- Add a **Search** action, where the user can type in the name of a feature and Lex will zoom and pan the map to show that feature.

- Let the user choose any two landmarks, and display the distance between those two points in both kilometers and miles.

- Allow the user to load their own set of landmarks, either from a shapefile or an Excel spreadsheet. When loading from a shapefile, the user could be prompted to select the attribute(s) to display for each feature. When loading data from a spreadsheet (using, for example, the xlrd library), the various columns would contain the latitude and longitude values as well as the label and other data to display for each landmark.

- See what is involved in bundling the Lex application and QGIS itself into a double-clickable installer for your operating system. The *PyQGIS Developer cookbook* has some tips on how to do this, and there are various tools such as **py2exe** and **py2app**, which you can use as a starting point.

Implementing these extra features would be a great way of learning more about PyQGIS and how to use it within your own standalone mapping programs.

Summary

In this chapter, we designed and implemented a simple but complete turnkey mapping application using PyQGIS. In doing this, we learned how a wrapper script can be used to keep platform-specific settings out of your Python program. We also saw how we can define our application's UI in a separate module even if we don't use Qt Designer to create our user interface templates.

We learned how to use the "PAL" labeling engine built into QGIS to display a label for each feature within a vector map layer. We saw that a `QgsRuleBasedRendererV2` object can be used to show or hide certain features based on the map's scale factor, and that data-defined properties allow us to calculate values such as the label's font size; we also saw how the `CASE...WHEN` expression can be used to calculate data-defined properties in sophisticated ways.

Finally, we saw how to implement Google Maps style panning and zooming within a mapping application.

In the next chapter, we will learn about some of the more advanced features of the QGIS Python API and how we can use them within our mapping applications.

6
Mastering the QGIS Python API

In this chapter, we will look at a number of more advanced aspects of the PyQGIS library, as well as various techniques for working with QGIS using Python. In particular, we will learn:

- How to work with symbol layers
- More advanced ways of using symbols to draw vector data onto a map
- How to implement your own symbols and renderers in Python
- How to create a custom map layer using Python
- How to implement your own custom map canvas items
- How to use memory data providers

Working with symbol layers

In the previous chapters, we created symbols to display vector features by instantiating one of the three basic subclasses of `QgsSymbolV2`:

- `QgsMarkerSymbolV2` for point geometries
- `QgsLineSymbolV2` for line geometries
- `QgsFillSymbolV2` for polygon geometries

We did this either by calling one of the preceding class's static `createSimple()` methods, or by asking the `QgsSymbolV2` class to provide us with the default symbol for a given type of geometry. Irrespective of how we did it, the result was a ready-to-use symbol object that displays a given type of vector geometry.

Internally, symbols consist of one or more symbol layers that are displayed one on top of the other, to draw the vector feature:

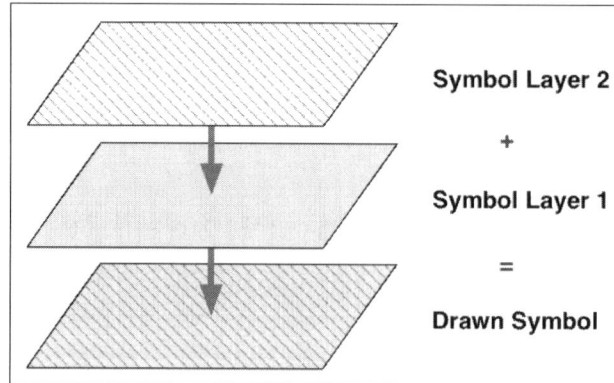

> The symbol layers are drawn in the order in which they are added to the symbol. So, in this example, **Symbol Layer 1** will be drawn *before* **Symbol Layer 2**. This has the effect of drawing the second symbol layer on top of the first. Make sure you get the order of your symbol layers correct, or you might find a symbol layer completely obscured by another layer.

While the symbols we have been working with so far have had only one layer, there are some clever tricks you can perform with multilayer symbols. We will look at multilayer symbols in the section *Combining symbol layers*.

When you create a symbol, it will automatically be initialized with a default symbol layer. For example, a line symbol (an instance of QgsLineSymbolV2) will be created with a single layer of type QgsSimpleLineSymbolLayerV2. This layer is used to draw the line feature onto the map.

To work with symbol layers, you need to remove this default layer and replace it with your own symbol layer or layers. For example:

```
symbol = QgsSymbolV2.defaultSymbol(layer.geometryType())
symbol.deleteSymbolLayer(0) # Remove default symbol layer.
```

```
symbol_layer_1 = QgsSimpleFillSymbolLayerV2()
symbol_layer_1.setFillColor(QColor("yellow"))

symbol_layer_2 = QgsLinePatternFillSymbolLayer()
symbol_layer_2.setLineAngle(30)
symbol_layer_2.setDistance(2.0)
symbol_layer_2.setLineWidth(0.5)
symbol_layer_2.setColor(QColor("green"))

symbol.appendSymbolLayer(symbol_layer_1)
symbol.appendSymbolLayer(symbol_layer_2)
```

The following methods can be used to manipulate the layers within a symbol:

- `symbol.symbolLayerCount()`: This returns the number of symbol layers within this symbol.

- `symbol.symbolLayer(index)`: This returns the given symbol layer within the symbol. Note that the first symbol layer has an index of zero.

- `symbol.changeSymbolLayer(index, symbol_layer)`: This replaces a given symbol layer within the symbol.

- `symbol.appendSymbolLayer(symbol_layer)`: This appends a new symbol layer to the symbol.

- `symbol.insertSymbolLayer(index, symbol_layer)`: This inserts a symbol layer at a given index.

- `symbol.deleteSymbolLayer(index)`: This removes the symbol layer at the given index.

> Remember that to use the symbol once you've created it, you create an appropriate renderer and then assign that renderer to your map layer. For example:
>
> ```
> renderer = QgsSingleSymbolRendererV2(symbol)
> layer.setRendererV2(renderer)
> ```

The following symbol layer classes are available for you to use:

PyQGIS class	Description	Example
QgsSimpleMarkerSymbolLayerV2	This displays a point geometry as a small colored circle.	
QgsEllipseSymbolLayerV2	This displays a point geometry as an ellipse.	
QgsFontMarkerSymbolLayerV2	This displays a point geometry as a single character. You can choose the font and character to be displayed.	
QgsSvgMarkerSymbolLayerV2	This displays a point geometry using a single SVG format image.	
QgsVectorFieldSymbolLayer	This displays a point geometry by drawing a **displacement line**. One end of the line is the coordinate of the point, while the other end is calculated using attributes of the feature.	
QgsSimpleLineSymbolLayerV2	This displays a line geometry or the outline of a polygon geometry using a line of a given color, width, and style.	
QgsMarkerLineSymbolLayerV2	This displays a line geometry or the outline of a polygon geometry by repeatedly drawing a marker symbol along the length of the line.	

`QgsSimpleFillSymbolLayerV2`	This displays a polygon geometry by filling the interior with a given solid color and then drawing a line around the perimeter.	
`QgsGradientFillSymbolLayerV2`	This fills the interior of a polygon geometry using a color or grayscale gradient.	
`QgsCentroidFillSymbolLayerV2`	This draws a simple dot at the centroid of a polygon geometry.	
`QgsLinePatternFillSymbolLayer`	This draws the interior of a polygon geometry using a repeated line. You can choose the angle, width, and color to use for the line.	
`QgsPointPatternFillSymbolLayer`	This draws the interior of a polygon geometry using a repeated point.	
`QgsSVGFillSymbolLayer`	This draws the interior of a polygon geometry using a repeated SVG format image.	

These predefined symbol layers, either individually or in various combinations, give you enormous flexibility in how features are to be displayed. However, if these aren't enough for you, you can also implement your own symbol layers using Python. We will look at how this can be done later in this chapter.

Combining symbol layers

By combining symbol layers, you can achieve a range of complex visual effects. For example, you can combine an instance of `QgsSimpleMarkerSymbolLayerV2` with an instance of `QgsVectorFieldSymbolLayer` to display a point geometry using two symbols at once:

One of the main uses of symbol layers is to draw different LineString or PolyLine symbols to represent different types of roads. For example, you can draw a complex road symbol by combining multiple symbol layers, like this:

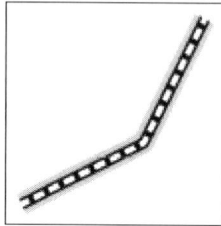

This effect is achieved by using three separate symbol layers:

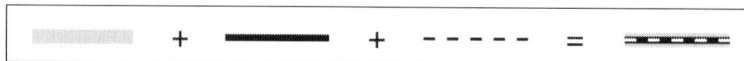

Here is the Python code used to generate the preceding map symbol:

```
symbol =QgsLineSymbolV2.createSimple({})
symbol.deleteSymbolLayer(0) # Remove default symbol layer.

symbol_layer = QgsSimpleLineSymbolLayerV2()
symbol_layer.setWidth(4)
symbol_layer.setColor(QColor("light gray"))
symbol_layer.setPenCapStyle(Qt.FlatCap)
symbol.appendSymbolLayer(symbol_layer)

symbol_layer = QgsSimpleLineSymbolLayerV2()
symbol_layer.setColor(QColor("black"))
symbol_layer.setWidth(2)
symbol_layer.setPenCapStyle(Qt.FlatCap)
symbol.appendSymbolLayer(symbol_layer)
```

```
symbol_layer = QgsSimpleLineSymbolLayerV2()
symbol_layer.setWidth(1)
symbol_layer.setColor(QColor("white"))
symbol_layer.setPenStyle(Qt.DotLine)
symbol.appendSymbolLayer(symbol_layer)
```

As you can see, you can set the line width, color, and style to create whatever effect you want. As always, you have to define the layers in the correct order, with the back-most symbol layer defined first. By combining line symbol layers in this way, you can create almost any type of road symbol that you want.

You can also use symbol layers when displaying polygon geometries. For example, you can draw QgsPointPatternFillSymbolLayer on top of QgsSimpleFillSymbolLayerV2 to have repeated points on top of a simple filled polygon, like this:

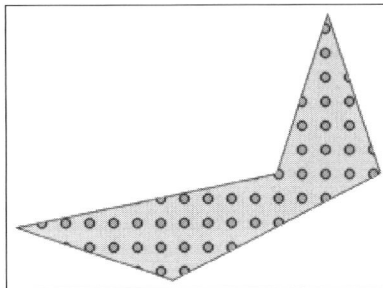

Finally, you can make use of **transparency** to allow the various symbol layers (or entire symbols) to blend into each other. For example, you can create a pinstripe effect by combining two symbol layers, like this:

```
symbol = QgsFillSymbolV2.createSimple({})
symbol.deleteSymbolLayer(0) # Remove default symbol layer.

symbol_layer = QgsGradientFillSymbolLayerV2()
symbol_layer.setColor2(QColor("dark gray"))
symbol_layer.setColor(QColor("white"))
symbol.appendSymbolLayer(symbol_layer)

symbol_layer = QgsLinePatternFillSymbolLayer()
symbol_layer.setColor(QColor(0, 0, 0, 20))
symbol_layer.setLineWidth(2)
symbol_layer.setDistance(4)
symbol_layer.setLineAngle(70)
symbol.appendSymbolLayer(symbol_layer)
```

The result is quite subtle and visually pleasing:

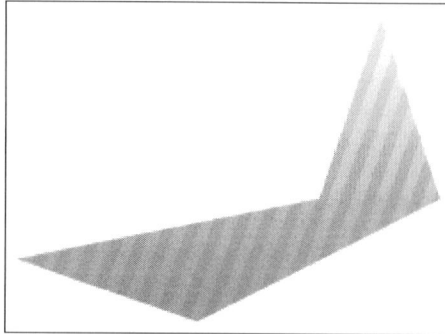

In addition to changing the transparency for a symbol layer, you can also change the transparency for the symbol as a whole. This is done by using the `setAlpha()` method, like this:

```
symbol.setAlpha(0.3)
```

The result looks like this:

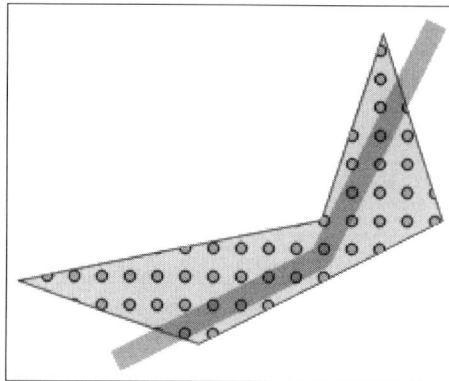

> Note that `setAlpha()` takes a floating point number between 0.0 and 1.0, while the transparency of a `QColor` object, like the ones we used earlier, is specified using an alpha value between 0 and 255.

Implementing symbol layers in Python

If the built-in symbol layers aren't flexible enough for your needs, you can implement your own symbol layers using Python. To do this, you create a subclass of the appropriate type of symbol layer (QgsMarkerSymbolLayerV2, QgsLineSymbolV2, or QgsFillSymbolV2) and implement the various drawing methods yourself. For example, here is a simple marker symbol layer that draws a cross for a Point geometry:

```
class CrossSymbolLayer(QgsMarkerSymbolLayerV2):
    def __init__(self, length=10.0, width=2.0):
        QgsMarkerSymbolLayerV2.__init__(self)
        self.length = length
        self.width  = width

    def layerType(self):
        return "Cross"

    def properties(self):
        return {'length' : self.length,
                'width' : self.width}

    def clone(self):
        return CrossSymbolLayer(self.length, self.width)

    def startRender(self, context):
        self.pen = QPen()
        self.pen.setColor(self.color())
        self.pen.setWidth(self.width)

    def stopRender(self, context):
        self.pen = None

    def renderPoint(self, point, context):
        left = point.x() - self.length
        right = point.x() + self.length
        bottom = point.y() - self.length
        top = point.y() + self.length

        painter = context.renderContext().painter()
        painter.setPen(self.pen)
        painter.drawLine(left, bottom, right, top)
        painter.drawLine(right, bottom, left, top)
```

Using this custom symbol layer in your code is straightforward:

```
symbol = QgsMarkerSymbolV2.createSimple({})
symbol.deleteSymbolLayer(0)

symbol_layer = CrossSymbolLayer()
symbol_layer.setColor(QColor("gray"))

symbol.appendSymbolLayer(symbol_layer)
```

Running this code will draw a cross at the location of each point geometry, as follows:

Of course, this is a simple example, but it shows you how to use custom symbol layers implemented in Python. Let's now take a closer look at the implementation of the CrossSymbolLayer class, and see what each method does:

- __init__(): Notice how the __init__ method accepts parameters that customize the way the symbol layer works. These parameters, which should always have default values assigned to them, are the **properties** associated with the symbol layer. If you want to make your custom symbol available within the **QGIS Layer Properties** window, you will need to register your custom symbol layer and tell QGIS how to edit the symbol layer's properties. We will look at this shortly.

- layerType(): This method returns a unique name for your symbol layer.

- properties(): This should return a dictionary that contains the various properties used by this symbol layer. The properties returned by this method will be stored in the QGIS project file, and used later to restore the symbol layer.

- clone(): This method should return a copy of the symbol layer. Since we have defined our properties as parameters to the __init__ method, implementing this method simply involves creating a new instance of the class and copying the properties from the current symbol layer to the new instance.

- `startRender()`: This method is called before the first feature in the map layer is rendered. This can be used to define any objects that will be required to draw the feature. Rather than creating these objects each time, it is more efficient (and therefore faster) to create them only once to render all the features. In this example, we create the `QPen` object that we will use to draw the Point geometries.

- `stopRender()`: This method is called after the last feature has been rendered. This can be used to release the objects created by the `startRender()` method.

- `renderPoint()`: This is where all the work is done for drawing point geometries. As you can see, this method takes two parameters: the point at which to draw the symbol, and the **rendering context** (an instance of `QgsSymbolV2RenderContext`) to use for drawing the symbol.

- The rendering context provides various methods to access the feature being displayed, as well as information about the rendering operation, the current scale factor, and so on. Most importantly, it allows you to access the PyQt `QPainter` object required to actually draw the symbol on the screen.

The `renderPoint()` method is only used for symbol layers that draw point geometries. For line geometries, you should implement the `renderPolyline()` method, which has the following signature:

```
def renderPolyline(self, points, context):
```

The `points` parameter will be a `QPolygonF` object that contains the various points that make up the LineString, and `context` will be the rendering context to use to draw the geometry.

If your symbol layer is intended to work with polygons, you should implement the `renderPolygon()` method, which looks like this:

```
def renderPolygon(self, outline, rings, context):
```

Here, `outline` is a `QPolygonF` object that contains the points that make up the exterior of the polygon, and `rings` is a list of `QPolygonF` objects that define the interior rings or "holes" within the polygon. As always, `context` is the rendering context to use when drawing the geometry.

A custom symbol layer created in this way will work fine if you just want to use it within your own external PyQGIS application. However, if you want to use a custom symbol layer within a running copy of QGIS, and in particular, if you want to allow end users to work with the symbol layer using the **Layer Properties** window, there are some extra steps you will have to take, which are as follows:

- If you want the symbol to be visually highlighted when the user clicks on it, you will need to change your symbol layer's `renderXXX()` method to see if the feature being drawn has been selected by the user, and if so, change the way it is drawn. The easiest way to do this is to change the geometry's color. For example:

```
if context.selected():
    color = context.selectionColor()
else:
    color = self.color
```

- To allow the user to edit the symbol layer's properties, you should create a subclass of `QgsSymbolLayerV2Widget`, which defines the user interface to edit the properties. For example, a simple widget for the purpose of editing the length and width of a `CrossSymbolLayer` can be defined as follows:

```
class CrossSymbolLayerWidget(QgsSymbolLayerV2Widget):
    def __init__(self, parent=None):
        QgsSymbolLayerV2Widget.__init__(self, parent)
        self.layer = None

        self.lengthField = QSpinBox(self)
        self.lengthField.setMinimum(1)
        self.lengthField.setMaximum(100)
        self.connect(self.lengthField,
                     SIGNAL("valueChanged(int)"),
                     self.lengthChanged)

        self.widthField = QSpinBox(self)
        self.widthField.setMinimum(1)
        self.widthField.setMaximum(100)
        self.connect(self.widthField,
                     SIGNAL("valueChanged(int)"),
                     self.widthChanged)

        self.form = QFormLayout()
        self.form.addRow('Length', self.lengthField)
        self.form.addRow('Width', self.widthField)
```

```
        self.setLayout(self.form)

    def setSymbolLayer(self, layer):
        if layer.layerType() == "Cross":
            self.layer = layer
            self.lengthField.setValue(layer.length)
            self.widthField.setValue(layer.width)

    def symbolLayer(self):
        return self.layer

    def lengthChanged(self, n):
        self.layer.length = n
        self.emit(SIGNAL("changed()"))

    def widthChanged(self, n):
        self.layer.width = n
        self.emit(SIGNAL("changed()"))
```

We define the contents of our widget using the standard __init__()
initializer. As you can see, we define two fields, lengthField and
widthField, which let the user change the length and width properties
respectively for our symbol layer.

The setSymbolLayer() method tells the widget which QgsSymbolLayerV2
object to use, while the symbolLayer() method returns the
QgsSymbolLayerV2 object this widget is editing. Finally, the two
XXXChanged() methods are called when the user changes the value of the
fields, allowing us to update the symbol layer's properties to match the
value set by the user.

- Finally, you will need to register your symbol layer. To do this, create
  a subclass of QgsSymbolLayerV2AbstractMetadata and pass it to the
  QgsSymbolLayerV2Registry object's addSymbolLayerType() method. Here
  is an example implementation of the metadata for our CrossSymbolLayer
  class, along with the code to register it within QGIS:

```
class CrossSymbolLayerMetadata(QgsSymbolLayerV2AbstractMetadata):
    def __init__(self):
        QgsSymbolLayerV2AbstractMetadata.__init__(self, "Cross",
"Cross marker", QgsSymbolV2.Marker)

    def createSymbolLayer(self, properties):
        if "length" in properties:
```

```
            length = int(properties['length'])
        else:
            length = 10
        if "width" in properties:
            width = int(properties['width'])
        else:
            width = 2
        return CrossSymbolLayer(length, width)

    def createSymbolLayerWidget(self, layer):
        return CrossSymbolLayerWidget()

registry = QgsSymbolLayerV2Registry.instance()
registry.addSymbolLayerType(CrossSymbolLayerMetadata())
```

Note that the parameters for the `QgsSymbolLayerV2AbstractMetadata.__init__` `()` method are as follows:

- `name`: The unique name for the symbol layer, which must match the name returned by the symbol layer's `layerType()` method.

- `visibleName`: A display name for this symbol layer, as shown to the user within the **Layer Properties** window.

- `type`: The type of symbol that this symbol layer will be used for.

The `createSymbolLayer()` method is used to restore the symbol layer based on the properties stored in the QGIS project file when the project was saved. The `createSymbolLayerWidget()` method is called to create the user interface widget that lets the user view and edit the symbol layer's properties.

Implementing renderers in Python

If you need to choose symbols based on more complicated criteria than the built-in renderers will provide, you can write your own custom `QgsFeatureRendererV2` subclass using Python. For example, the following Python code implements a simple renderer that alternates between odd and even symbols as point features are displayed:

```
class OddEvenRenderer(QgsFeatureRendererV2):
    def __init__(self):
        QgsFeatureRendererV2.__init__(self, "OddEvenRenderer")
        self.evenSymbol = QgsMarkerSymbolV2.createSimple({})
        self.evenSymbol.setColor(QColor("light gray"))
```

```
        self.oddSymbol = QgsMarkerSymbolV2.createSimple({})
        self.oddSymbol.setColor(QColor("black"))
        self.n = 0

    def clone(self):
        return OddEvenRenderer()

    def symbolForFeature(self, feature):
        self.n = self.n + 1
        if self.n % 2 == 0:
            return self.evenSymbol
        else:
            return self.oddSymbol

    def startRender(self, context, layer):
        self.n = 0
        self.oddSymbol.startRender(context)
        self.evenSymbol.startRender(context)

    def stopRender(self, context):
        self.oddSymbol.stopRender(context)
        self.evenSymbol.stopRender(context)

    def usedAttributes(self):
        return []
```

Using this renderer will cause the various point geometries to be displayed in alternating colors, for example:

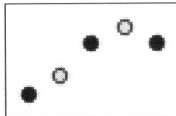

Let's take a closer look at how this class was implemented, and what the various methods do:

- `__init__()`: This is your standard Python initializer. Notice how we have to provide a unique name for the renderer when calling the `QgsFeatureRendererV2.__init__()` method; this is used to keep track of the various renderers within QGIS itself.

- `clone()`: This creates a copy of this renderer. If your renderer uses properties to control how it works, this method should copy those properties into the new renderer object.

- `symbolForFeature()`: This returns the symbol to use for drawing the given feature.

- `startRender()`: This gives you the opportunity to prepare your renderer and any symbols you use before the features are rendered. Note that you must call the `startRender()` method on each symbol that your renderer uses; as the renderer can make use of multiple symbols, you need to implement this so that your symbols are also given a chance to prepare for rendering.

- `stopRender()`: This finishes rendering the features. Once again, you need to implement this so that your symbols can have a chance to clean up once the rendering process has finished.

- `usedAttributes()`: This method should be implemented to return the list of feature attributes that the renderer makes use of. If your renderer does not use attributes to choose between the various symbols, then you do not need to implement this method.

If you wish, you can also implement your own widget that lets the user change the way the renderer works. This is done by subclassing `QgsRendererV2Widget` and setting up the widget to edit the renderer's various properties in the same way that we implemented a subclass of `QgsSymbolLayerV2Widget` to edit the properties for a symbol layer. You will also need to provide metadata for your new renderer (by subclassing `QgsRendererV2AbstractMetadata`) and use the `QgsRendererV2Registry` object to register your new renderer. If you do this, the user will be able to select your custom renderer for new map layers, and change the way your renderer works by editing the renderer's properties.

Working with custom map layers

Instead of using a standard map layer with a data provider, features, symbols, and so on, you can implement your own **custom map layer** entirely in Python. Custom map layers are generally used to draw specific data that is too complicated to represent as vector format data, or to draw special visual features such as a grid or a watermark onto the map.

Custom map layers are implemented by subclassing the `QgsPluginLayer` class. The process is actually very simple, though you will need to translate between map and device coordinates so that the items you draw in your Python layer match up with the features drawn in the other layers within your canvas.

> Don't get confused by the name; you don't have to write a QGIS plugin to create your own `QgsPluginLayer` subclass.

Let's see how we can create our own subclass of `QgsPluginLayer`. We're going to create a simple grid that can appear as a layer within the map. Let's start by defining the `QgsPluginLayer` subclass itself:

```
class GridLayer(QgsPluginLayer):
    def __init__(self):
        QgsPluginLayer.__init__(self, "GridLayer", "Grid Layer")
        self.setValid(True)
```

In our `__init__()` method, we give the plugin layer a unique name (`"GridLayer"`) and a user-visible name (`"Grid Layer"`), and then tell QGIS that the layer is valid.

Next, we need to set up the coordinate reference system and extent of our layer. Since we're creating a grid that covers the entire Earth, we'll use the standard EPSG 4236 coordinate system (that is, latitude/longitude coordinates), and set the extent of the layer to cover the entire surface of the Earth:

```
self.setCrs(QgsCoordinateReferenceSystem(4326))
self.setExtent(QgsRectangle(-180, 90, 180, 90))
```

We're now ready to define the method that draws the contents of the layer. As you might imagine, this method is called `draw()`. Let's start by obtaining the `QPainter` object we'll use to do the actual drawing:

```
def draw(self, renderContext):
    painter = renderContext.painter()
```

Next, we want to find the portion of the Earth's surface that is currently visible:

```
extent = renderContext.extent()
```

This gives us the portion of the grid that we want to draw. To make sure the grid lines are on whole degrees of latitude and longitude, we round the extent up and down to the nearest whole number, like this:

```
xMin = int(math.floor(extent.xMinimum()))
xMax = int(math.ceil(extent.xMaximum()))
yMin = int(math.floor(extent.yMinimum()))
yMax = int(math.ceil(extent.yMaximum()))
```

Next, we need to set up the painter to draw the grid lines:

```
pen = QPen()
pen.setColor(QColor("light gray"))
pen.setWidth(1.0)
painter.setPen(pen)
```

Now, we're almost ready to start drawing the grid. To draw the grid lines, though, we'll need some way of translating between latitude/longitude values and pixel coordinates on the computer screen. We'll do this using a `QgsMapToPixel` object, which we can get from the rendering context:

```
mapToPixel = renderContext.mapToPixel()
```

Now, we're finally ready to draw the grid lines. Let's start by drawing a vertical grid line on each whole degree of longitude:

```
for x in range(xMin, xMax+1):
    coord1 = mapToPixel.transform(x, yMin)
    coord2 = mapToPixel.transform(x, yMax)
    painter.drawLine(coord1.x(), coord1.y(),
                     coord2.x(), coord2.y())
```

We can then do the same for the horizontal grid lines:

```
for y in range(yMin, yMax+1):
    coord1 = mapToPixel.transform(xMin, y)
    coord2 = mapToPixel.transform(xMax, y)
    painter.drawLine(coord1.x(), coord1.y(),
                     coord2.x(), coord2.y())
```

The last thing we need to do is tell QGIS that our layer was drawn successfully. We do this by having our `draw()` method return `True`:

```
return True
```

This completes our implementation of the `GridLayer` class. If you want to use this class within a QGIS script or plugin, you will need to register the class so that QGIS knows about it. Fortunately, doing this is straightforward:

```
class GridLayerType(QgsPluginLayerType):
    def __init__(self):
        QgsPluginLayerType.__init__(self, "GridLayer")

    def createLayer(self):
        return GridLayer()

registry = QgsPluginLayerRegistry.instance()
registry.addPluginLayerType(GridLayerType())
```

If you run this program within QGIS and add the `GridLayer` to your project, you'll see the grid lines drawn on the map:

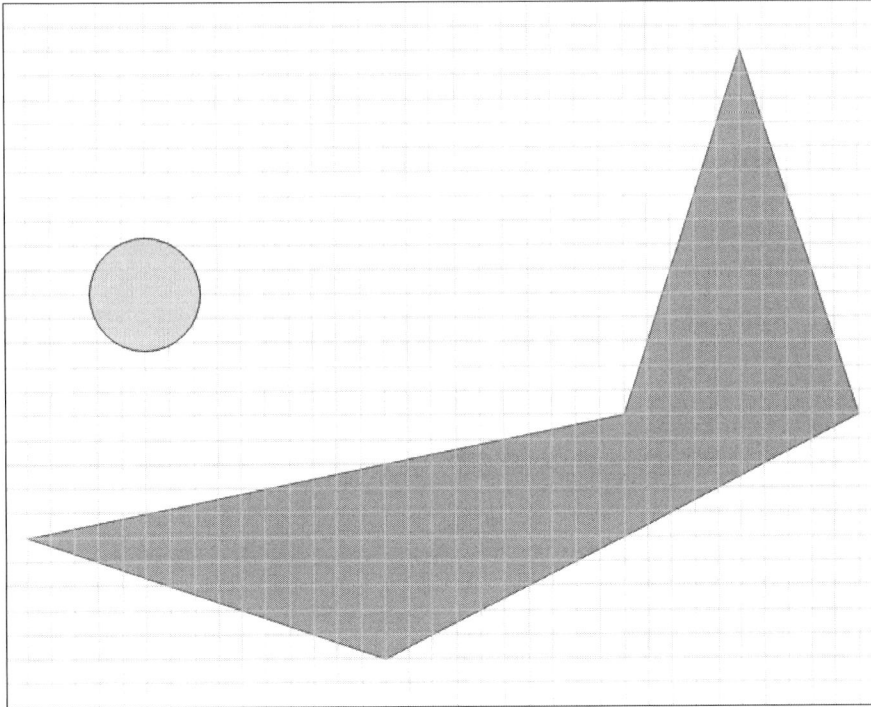

Look carefully at the preceding image; you'll see that the grid lines are drawn in front of the polygon, but behind the circle. This is one of the main benefits of implementing your own map layer, as opposed to using a map canvas item; you can choose which layers appear in front or behind your custom map layer.

Creating custom map canvas items

A map canvas item is an item that is placed on top of the map canvas. Standard map canvas items include text annotations, vertex markers, and the visual highlighting of a feature. It is also possible to create your own custom map canvas items by subclassing QgsMapCanvasItem. To see how this works, let's create a map canvas item that draws a compass rose onto the map:

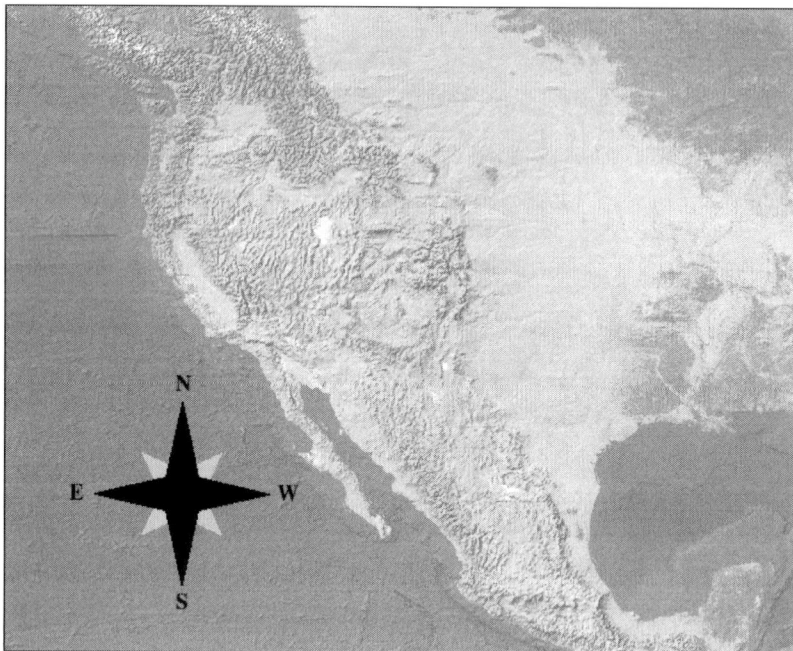

We'll start by creating the basic QgsMapCanvasItem subclass:

```
class CompassRoseItem(QgsMapCanvasItem):
    def __init__(self, canvas):
        QgsMapCanvasItem.__init__(self, canvas)
        self.center = QgsPoint(0, 0)
        self.size   = 100

    def setCenter(self, center):
        self.center = center

    def center(self):
        return self.center
```

```
def setSize(self, size):
    self.size = size

def size(self):
    return self.size

def boundingRect(self):
    return QRectF(self.center.x() - self.size/2,
                  self.center.y() - self.size/2,
                  self.center.x() + self.size/2,
                  self.center.y() + self.size/2)

def paint(self, painter, option, widget):
    # ...
```

As you can see, we position the compass rose onto the map canvas by defining `center` and `size` instance variables, and provide methods to retrieve and set these values. We also implement the required `boundingRect()` method, which returns the overall bounding rectangle for the canvas item, in screen coordinates.

This leaves us with the `paint()` method, which does the job of drawing the compass rose. While this method takes three parameters, the only parameter we'll be using is the first one, which is the `QPainter` object we will use to draw the compass rose.

The compass rose might look quite complicated, but the code needed to implement it is quite straightforward. The most complicated part is figuring out the dimensions of the `"N"`, `"S"`, `"E"`, and `"W"` labels so that we have enough room left for the compass rose itself. Let's start by calculating some basic information about the labels that we are going to display:

```
def paint(self, painter, option, widget):
    fontSize = int(18 * self.size/100)
    painter.setFont(QFont("Times", pointSize=fontSize,
                          weight=75))
    metrics = painter.fontMetrics()
    labelSize = metrics.height()
    margin    = 5
```

We calculate the size of the font to use for the labels (in points), and then set our painter to use a boldfaced `"Times"` font of that size. We then get a `QFontMetrics` object that we will use to calculate the labels' dimensions, and define a hardwired pixel margin so that we leave a gap between the label and the compass rose itself.

Next, we want to draw the two central parts of the compass rose in light gray and black respectively. To do this, we'll use a `QPainterPath` object to define the area to be filled in:

```
x = self.center.x()
y = self.center.y()
size = self.size - labelSize - margin

path = QPainterPath()
path.moveTo(x, y - size * 0.23)
path.lineTo(x - size * 0.45, y - size * 0.45)
path.lineTo(x - size * 0.23, y)
path.lineTo(x - size * 0.45, y + size * 0.45)
path.lineTo(x, y + size * 0.23)
path.lineTo(x + size * 0.45, y + size * 0.45)
path.lineTo(x + size * 0.23, y)
path.lineTo(x + size * 0.45, y - size * 0.45)
path.closeSubpath()

painter.fillPath(path, QColor("light gray"))

path = QPainterPath()
path.moveTo(x, y - size)
path.lineTo(x - size * 0.18, y - size * 0.18)
path.lineTo(x - size, y)
path.lineTo(x - size * 0.18, y + size * 0.18)
path.lineTo(x, y + size)
path.lineTo(x + size * 0.18, y + size * 0.18)
path.lineTo(x + size, y)
path.lineTo(x + size * 0.18, y - size * 0.18)
path.closeSubpath()

painter.fillPath(path, QColor("black"))
```

Finally, we want to draw the labels at each of the four compass points:

```
labelX = x - metrics.width("N")/2
labelY = y - self.size + labelSize - metrics.descent()
painter.drawText(QPoint(labelX, labelY), "N")

labelX = x - metrics.width("S")/2
labelY = y + self.size - labelSize + metrics.ascent()
painter.drawText(QPoint(labelX, labelY), "S")
```

```
labelX = x - self.size + labelSize/2 - metrics.width("E")/2
labelY = y - metrics.height()/2 + metrics.ascent()
painter.drawText(QPoint(labelX, labelY), "E")

labelX = x + self.size - labelSize/2 - metrics.width("W")/2
labelY = y - metrics.height()/2 + metrics.ascent()
painter.drawText(QPoint(labelX, labelY), "W")
```

This completes the implementation of our `QgsMapCanvasItem` subclass. To use it, we simply have to create and initialize a new `CompassRoseItem`. Here is an example of how we can display a `CompassRoseItem` within the map canvas:

```
rose = CompassRoseItem(iface.mapCanvas())
rose.setCenter(QPointF(150, 400))
rose.setSize(80)
```

Your new `QgsMapCanvasItem` will automatically be added to the map canvas when the object is initialized—you don't need to explicitly add it to the canvas. To remove the compass rose from the map canvas, you can do the following:

```
iface.mapCanvas().scene().removeItem(rose)
```

Note that map canvas items float above the map layers, and unfortunately, cannot directly interact with the user—you can't intercept and respond to mouse events using a map canvas item.

Using memory-based layers

While a map layer would normally display geospatial data taken from an external data source such as a shapefile, a raster DEM file, or a database, it is also possible to create geospatial features directly from your Python code. For example, imagine that you write a program to display the halfway point along a road. This halfway point could be represented as a `QgsPoint` geometry, which would be displayed on the map using an appropriate marker symbol. Since you are calculating the point, this isn't a feature you would want to store in a shapefile or database. Rather, the feature is calculated and displayed when your program is run.

This is an ideal application for a memory-based layer. This type of layer stores geospatial features in memory, allowing you to create new features on the fly and display them within a map layer.

To create a memory-based map layer, instantiate a new `QgsVectorLayer` object, just like normal. The initializer for this class looks like the following:

```
layer = QgsVectorLayer(path, baseName, providerLib)
```

> This is slightly simplified — there is another parameter, `loadDefaultStyleFlag`, which doesn't apply to memory-based layers. Fortunately, there's a default value for this parameter, so we can ignore it.

Let's take a look at the three parameters needed to create a memory-based map layer:

- `path`: This string provides information that is needed to create the memory-based layer, including the type of information that the layer will store. We will look at this parameter in more detail shortly.

- `baseName`: This is the name used for the memory-based layer. The name can be anything you like, though the user will see it in the QGIS layer legend.

- `providerLib`: This should be set to `"memory"` for memory-based layers.

To create a simple memory-based layer, you can do the following:

```
layer = QgsVectorLayer("Polygon", "My Layer", "memory")
```

This will create a memory-based layer named `"My Layer"`, which stores polygon features with no attributes.

The `path` parameter will let us do much more than simply define the type of geometry to be stored in the layer. The `path` parameter has the following overall syntax:

```
geometryType?key=value&key=value...
```

This URL-like syntax starts with the type of geometry, and can have any number of key/value pairs that provide additional information about the memory layer. The following geometry types are currently supported:

- `Point`
- `LineString`
- `Polygon`
- `MultiPoint`
- `MultiLineString`
- `MultiPolygon`

Using the key/value pairs, you can also define:

- The coordinate reference system that the layer should use. For example:

  ```
  crs=IGNF:WGS84G
  ```

  The coordinate reference system can be defined using a CRS authority code, as in the preceding example, or you can specify the CRS in WKT format, for example: `crs=+proj=longlat +a=69000 +b=55000 +no_defs`.

> If you don't define the coordinate reference system in this way, QGIS will prompt the user to select a CRS when your program is run. This could be very confusing for the user, so you should always specify a CRS when you create a memory layer.

- Attributes to store for each feature within the layer. Here is an example of an attribute definition:

  ```
  field=phone_number:string
  ```

  The following types of fields are currently supported:

    ◦ `integer`
    ◦ `double`
    ◦ `string`

  You can also specify the field length and precision by listing these in parentheses, for example, `field=height:double(10,2)` or `field=name:string(50)`.

  If you want to have multiple attributes, you simply have one `field=...` entry for each of the attributes you want to define.

> The memory layer's data provider has an `addAttributes()` method, which you might assume you'd use to define the attributes. However, the `addAttributes()` method only adds the attributes to the data provider, not the map layer, which can cause QGIS to crash. To avoid this, it is better to define your attributes within the path when you set up your map layer, rather than trying to add them later.

- A spatial index for this layer's features:

  ```
  index=yes
  ```

Let's use this to create a more complex memory layer that stores point geometries using a specified coordinate reference system, a spatial index, and some attributes. Here is how we might do this:

```
layer = QgsVectorLayer(
"Point?crs=EPSG:4326&field=height:double&field=name:string(255)&index=
yes", "Point Layer", "memory")
```

Once we've instantiated our memory layer, we can create the various features we want to display, and then add them to the layer. The following pseudocode shows how this is done:

```
provider = layer.dataProvider()

feature1 = ...
feature2 = ...

provider.addFeatures([feature1, feature2, ...])
```

As you can see, we define the various features (which are instances of `QgsFeature`), and then add them all at once to the memory layer. You can add the features one at a time, of course, but it's generally more efficient to define a list of features and add them all at once.

Let's now see how we can create a feature. We start by defining the underlying geometry that the feature will display. There are various ways of creating geometries, including:

- Instantiating a `QgsPoint`, `QgsPolyLine`, `QgsPolygon`, or related object, and then using this to create a `QgsGeometry` object using one of the `QgsGeometry.fromXXX()` methods. For example:

  ```
  point = QgsPoint(x, y)
  geometry = QgsGeometry.fromPoint(point)
  ```

- Creating a WKT-format string that represents the geometry, and then creating the `QgsGeometry` object using this string. For example:

  ```
  geometry = QgsGeometry.fromWkt("POINT (10 10)")
  ```

- Creating a new `QgsGeometry` object out of an existing geometry by using one of the geometry manipulation methods. For example:

  ```
  new_geometry = old_geometry.buffer(10)
  ```

Once we have the geometry, we're ready to create the `QgsFeature` object itself:

```
feature = QgsFeature()
feature.setGeometry(geometry)
```

Next, we want to set the attributes for this feature. Before we can do this though, we need to tell the feature which attributes it will store. This is done in the following way:

```
fields = provider.fields()
feature.setFields(fields)
```

Finally, we can set the attribute values. For example:

```
feature.setAttribute("height", 301)
feature.setAttribute("name", "Eiffel Tower")
```

Putting all this together, let's build a complete example program that creates a memory layer, populates it with a few `QgsPoint` features, and updates the map canvas to show those points. Here is this example program:

```
layer =
  QgsVectorLayer("Point?crs=EPSG:4326&field=height:double&field
  =name:string(255)", "Point Layer", "memory")
provider = layer.dataProvider()
QgsMapLayerRegistry.instance().addMapLayer(layer)

fields = provider.fields()
features = []

feature = QgsFeature()
feature.setGeometry(QgsGeometry.fromWkt("POINT (2.2945 48.8582)"))
feature.setFields(fields)
feature.setAttribute("height", 301)
feature.setAttribute("name", "Eiffel Tower")
features.append(feature)

feature = QgsFeature()
feature.setGeometry(QgsGeometry.fromWkt("POINT (0.0761 51.5081)"))
feature.setFields(fields)
feature.setAttribute("height", 27)
feature.setAttribute("name", "Tower of London")
features.append(feature)

feature = QgsFeature()
feature.setGeometry(QgsGeometry.fromWkt("POINT (10.3964
  43.7231)"))
feature.setFields(fields)
feature.setAttribute("height", 56)
feature.setAttribute("name", "Leaning Tower of Pisa")
features.append(feature)

provider.addFeatures(features)
layer.updateExtents()
iface.mapCanvas().zoomToFullExtent()
```

Running this program from within QGIS will create a new memory-based map layer named `"Point Layer"` with three features in it, which represent the location of three famous towers in Western Europe:

To make this example useful, we would add symbols to draw the towers in a more meaningful way, and probably also display the name and height as a label beside each point. However, you can see how a memory layer can be used to create spatial data from within your program and include it as a layer within the map.

Note that you aren't limited to using memory layers to represent actual geospatial data. You could just as easily use the memory layer to display information that doesn't represent a location. For example, you can use a memory layer to draw arrows onto a map, or to shade certain areas of the map using a semi-transparent polygon. Memory-based map layers are an extremely powerful tool, and one that you will often use when writing your own programs based on QGIS.

Summary

In this chapter, we looked at many of the more advanced features of the QGIS Python API. We learned how the various built-in symbol layers can be used to draw geometries on the map, how to combine symbol layers in useful ways, and how to implement your own symbol layers using Python. We then looked at writing your own custom renderer to choose which symbol to use for each feature, and how to create your own custom map layer using Python code. We investigated the creation of custom map canvas items, and then saw how memory-based map layers can be used to programmatically add features to your map.

With this, we complete our tour of the more advanced aspects of PyQGIS. In the next chapter, we will learn how to create custom map tools that let the user select, add, edit, and delete features within a PyQGIS application.

7
Selecting and Editing Features in a PyQGIS Application

When running the QGIS application, the user has a range of tools available to create and manipulate geospatial features. For example, the **Add Feature** tool lets the user create a new feature, while the **Move Feature** tool and the **Node** tool allow the user to move and edit existing geospatial features. However, these tools are only available within QGIS itself — if you want to write an external application on top of the PyQGIS library, these built-in tools aren't available, and you will have to implement these features yourself.

In this chapter, we will look at what is involved in adding functionality to a PyQGIS application so that the user can select and edit geospatial features. In particular, we will examine:

- How to work with selections
- How the layer editing mode can be used to save or undo the changes the user has made to a map layer
- How to create map tools that will allow the user to add and edit Point geometries
- How to let the user remove a geometry from a map layer
- How to implement custom map tools that allow the user to add LineString and Polygon geometries to a map layer
- How to let the user edit a LineString or Polygon geometry

Working with selections

The vector layer class, `QgsVectorLayer`, includes support for keeping track of the user's current selection. Doing this is relatively straightforward: there are methods that set and alter the selection, as well as retrieve the selected features. When features are selected, they are visually highlighted on the screen so that the user can see what has been selected.

> If you create your own custom symbol layer, you will need to handle the highlighting of the selected features yourself. We saw how to do this in *Chapter 6, Mastering the QGIS Python API*, in the section titled *Implementing symbol layers in Python*.

While there are several ways in which the user can select features, the most straightforward way is to click on them. This can be implemented by using a simple map tool, for example:

```
class SelectTool(QgsMapToolIdentify):
    def __init__(self, window):
        QgsMapToolIdentify.__init__(self, window.mapCanvas)
        self.window = window
        self.setCursor(Qt.ArrowCursor)

    def canvasReleaseEvent(self, event):
        found_features = self.identify(event.x(), event.y(),
                        self.TopDownStopAtFirst,
                        self.VectorLayer)
        if len(found_features) > 0:
            layer = found_features[0].mLayer
            feature = found_features[0].mFeature

            if event.modifiers() & Qt.ShiftModifier:
                layer.select(feature.id())
            else:
                layer.setSelectedFeatures([feature.id()])
        else:
            self.window.layer.removeSelection()
```

This is very similar to the `ExploreTool` we implemented in the previous chapter as part of the Lex application. The only difference is that, instead of displaying information about the clicked-on feature, we tell the map layer to select it.

Note that we check to see if the *Shift* key is held down. If so, the clicked-on feature is added to the current selection; otherwise, the current selection will be replaced with the newly selected feature. Also, if the user clicks on the background of the map, the current selection will be removed. These are all standard user interface conventions the user will be familiar with.

Once we have a selection, it is quite straightforward to get the selected features from the map layer. For example:

```
if layer.selectedFeatureCount() == 0:
    QMessageBox.information(self, "Info",
                           "There is nothing selected.")
else:
    msg = []
    msg.append("Selected Features:")
    for feature in layer.selectedFeatures():
        msg.append("    " + feature.attribute("NAME"))
    QMessageBox.information(self, "Info", "\n".join(msg))
```

If you want to see all this in action, you can download and run the **SelectionExplorer** program, which is included in the sample code of this chapter.

Using the layer editing mode

To let the user change the contents of a map layer, you first have to turn on the **editing mode** for that layer. The layer editing mode is similar to the way transactions are handled in a database:

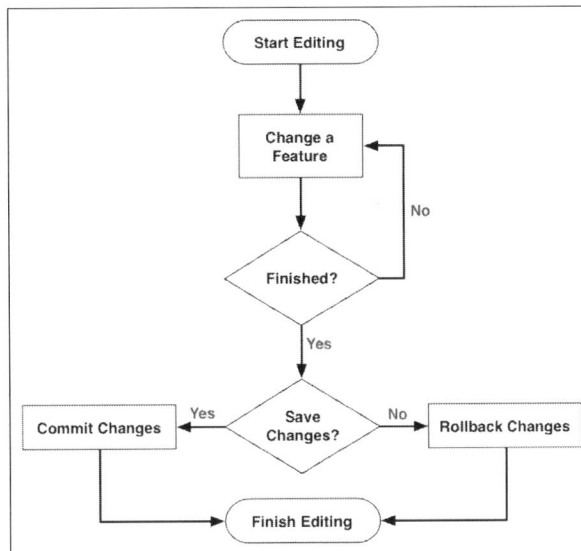

The changes you make to the layer are held in memory until you decide to either **commit** the changes to the layer, or **roll back** the changes to discard them. The following pseudocode is an example of how to implement this using PyQGIS:

```
layer.startEditing()

# ...make changes...

if modified:
    reply = QMessageBox.question(window, "Confirm",
                                 "Save changes to layer?",
                                 QMessageBox.Yes | QMessageBox.No,
                                 QMessageBox.Yes)
    if reply == QMessageBox.Yes:
        layer.commitChanges()
    else:
        line.rollBack()
else:
    layer.rollBack()
```

As you can see, we turn on the editing mode for a given map layer by calling `layer.startEditing()`. As well as set up an internal *editing buffer* to hold the changes you make, this tells the layer to visually highlight the layer's features by drawing small vertex markers on each of the vertices, as shown in the following image:

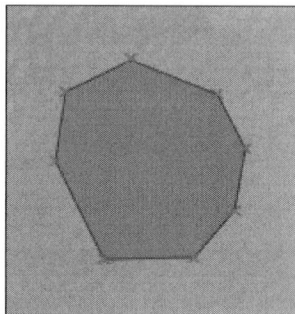

We then allow the user to make changes to the layer's features. We will learn how this is done in the following sections of this chapter. When the user turns off the editing mode, we check whether any changes have been made, and if so, display a confirmation message box to the user. Depending on the user's response, we either save the changes by calling `layer.commitChanges()` or discard them by calling `layer.rollBack()`.

Both `commitChanges()` and `rollBack()` turn off the editing mode, hiding the vertex markers and erasing the contents of the editing buffer.

When you use the layer's editing mode, you *must* use the various methods in `QgsVectorLayer` to modify the features, rather than using the equivalent methods in the data provider. For example, you should call `layer.addFeature(feature)` instead of `layer.dataProvider().addFeatures([feature])`.

The layer's editing methods only work when the layer is in the editing mode. These methods add the changes to the internal editing buffer so that they can be committed or rolled back at the appropriate time. If you make your changes directly to the data provider, you will bypass the editing buffer, so the rollback feature won't work.

Now that we have seen the overall process used to edit the contents of a map layer, let's create some map tools that will let the user add and edit geospatial data.

Adding Points

The following map tool allows the user to add a new Point feature to the given layer:

```
class AddPointTool(QgsMapTool):
    def __init__(self, canvas, layer):
        QgsMapTool.__init__(self, canvas)
        self.canvas = canvas
        self.layer  = layer
        self.setCursor(Qt.CrossCursor)

    def canvasReleaseEvent(self, event):
        point = self.toLayerCoordinates(self.layer, event.pos())

        feature = QgsFeature()
        feature.setGeometry(QgsGeometry.fromPoint(point))
        self.layer.addFeature(feature)
        self.layer.updateExtents()
```

As you can see, this straightforward map tool sets the mouse cursor to a cross shape, and when the user releases the mouse over the map canvas, a new `QgsGeometry` object is created that represents a point at the current mouse position. This point is then added to the layer using `layer.addFeature()`, and the layer's extent is updated in case the newly added point is outside the layer's current extent.

Of course, this map tool is only a starting point—you would typically add code to set the feature's attributes and to notify the application that a point has been added. However, as you can see, allowing the user to create a new Point feature is quite straightforward.

Editing Points

Editing a Point feature is also quite straightforward: since the geometry consists of only one point, the user can simply click-and-drag to move the point around within the map layer. The following is a map tool that implements this behavior:

```python
class MovePointTool(QgsMapToolIdentify):
    def __init__(self, mapCanvas, layer):
        QgsMapToolIdentify.__init__(self, mapCanvas)
        self.setCursor(Qt.CrossCursor)
        self.layer    = layer
        self.dragging = False
        self.feature  = None

    def canvasPressEvent(self, event):
        found_features = self.identify(event.x(), event.y(),
                                       [self.layer],
                                       self.TopDownAll)
        if len(found_features) > 0:
            self.dragging = True
            self.feature  = found_features[0].mFeature
        else:
            self.dragging = False
            self.feature  = None

    def canvasMoveEvent(self, event):
        if self.dragging:
            point = self.toLayerCoordinates(self.layer,
                                            event.pos())

            geometry = QgsGeometry.fromPoint(point)

            self.layer.changeGeometry(self.feature.id(), geometry)
            self.canvas().refresh()

    def canvasReleaseEvent(self, event):
        self.dragging = False
        self.feature  = None
```

As you can see, we subclass `QgsMapToolIdentify` for this map tool. This lets us use the `identify()` method to find the geometry that the user clicked on, just like we did in the `SelectTool`, which we implemented earlier in this chapter.

Notice that our `canvasMoveEvent()` method keeps track of the user's current mouse position. It also updates the feature's geometry by calling `layer.changeGeometry()` to remember the changed mouse position as the user moves the point around. The `canvasPressEvent()` enables dragging if and only if the user clicked on a Point, and the `canvasReleaseEvent()` method tidies up so that the user can move another point by clicking on it.

If you are writing a standalone PyQGIS application that includes a point-based `QgsVectorLayer`, you can use the `AddPointTool` and `MovePointTool` classes we defined here to allow the user to add and edit Point features within your vector layer. The only thing missing (for Point geometries) is the ability to remove points. Let's implement this now.

Deleting Points and other features

Fortunately, the code required to delete a Point feature will also work for other types of geometries, so we don't need to implement separate `DeletePointTool`, `DeleteLineTool`, and `DeletePolygonTool` classes. Instead, we only need a generic `DeleteTool`. The following code implements this map tool:

```
class DeleteTool(QgsMapToolIdentify):
    def __init__(self, mapCanvas, layer):
        QgsMapToolIdentify.__init__(self, mapCanvas)
        self.setCursor(Qt.CrossCursor)
        self.layer   = layer
        self.feature = None


    def canvasPressEvent(self, event):
        found_features = self.identify(event.x(), event.y(),
                                       [self.layer],
                                       self.TopDownAll)
        if len(found_features) > 0:
            self.feature = found_features[0].mFeature
        else:
            self.feature = None


    def canvasReleaseEvent(self, event):
        found_features = self.identify(event.x(), event.y(),
                                       [self.layer],
                                       self.TopDownAll)
        if len(found_features) > 0:
            if self.feature.id() == found_features[0].mFeature.id():
                self.layer.deleteFeature(self.feature.id())
```

Once again, we are using the `QgsMapToolIdentify` class to let us quickly find the feature the user clicked on. We use the `canvasPressEvent()` and `canvasReleaseEvent()` methods to ensure that the user clicked and released the mouse over the same feature; this ensures that the map tool works in a more user-friendly way than simply deleting the feature when the user clicks on it. If both the mouse click and the mouse release were over the same feature, we would delete it.

With the help of these map tools, it is quite straightforward to implement a PyQGIS application that allows the user to add, edit, and delete Point features within a map layer. These, however, are the "low hanging fruit"—our next task, where we have to let the user add and edit LineString and Polygon geometries, is more complex.

Adding lines and polygons

To add a LineString or a Polygon geometry, the user will *draw* the desired shape by clicking on each vertex in turn. Appropriate feedback will be displayed as the user clicks on each vertex. For example, a LineString geometry would be displayed in the following way:

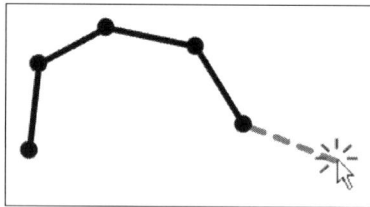

To draw the outline of a Polygon geometry, the user will once again click on each vertex in turn. This time, however, the polygon itself will be displayed to make the resulting shape clear, as the following image shows:

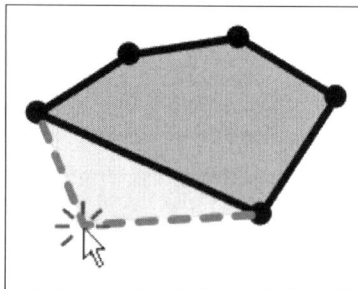

In both cases, the basic logic of clicking on each vertex and displaying appropriate feedback is the same.

QGIS includes a map tool named `QgsMapToolCapture`, which handles exactly this behavior: it allows the user to draw a LineString or the outline of a Polygon geometry by clicking on each vertex in turn. Unfortunately, `QgsMapToolCapture` is not available as part of the PyQGIS library, so we will have to re-implement it ourselves using Python.

Let's start by looking at the design of our `QgsMapToolCapture` port, which we will call `CaptureTool`. This will be a standard map tool, derived from `QgsMapTool`, which makes use of `QgsRubberBand` objects to draw the visual highlighting of the LineString or Polygon as it is drawn.

A `QgsRubberBand` is a map canvas item that draws a geometry on top of the map. Since a rubber band draws its entire geometry in a single color and style, we have to use two rubber bands in our capture tool: one that draws the already captured part of the geometry and a second temporary rubber band that extends the geometry out to the current mouse position. The following illustration shows how this works for both LineString and Polygon geometries:

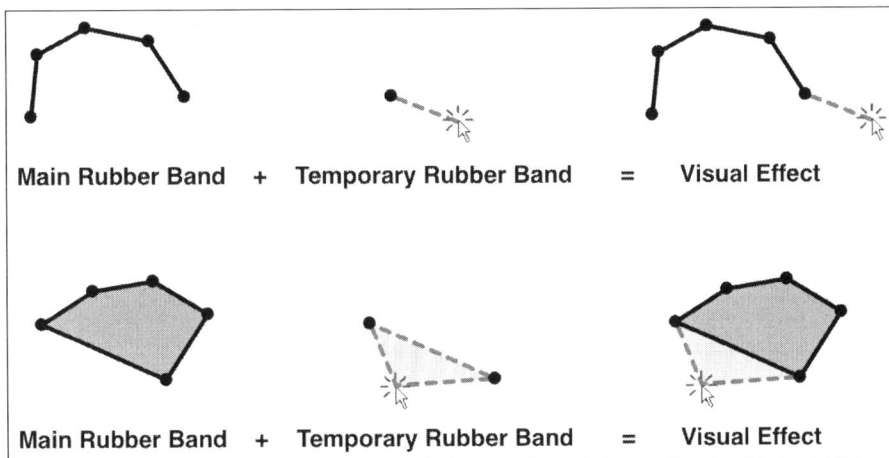

Here are some additional features that we will include in `CaptureTool`:

- It will have a *capture mode* that indicates whether the user is creating a LineString or a Polygon geometry.
- The user can press the *Backspace* or *Delete* key to remove the last vertex added.
- The user can press the *Enter* or *Return* key to finish the capturing process.
- If we are capturing a Polygon, the geometry will be *closed* when the user finishes capturing. This means that we add an extra point to the geometry so that the outline begins and ends at the same point.

- When the user finishes capturing a geometry, the geometry will be added to the layer, and a callback function will be used to tell the application that a new geometry has been added.

Now that we know what we're doing, let's start implementing the `CaptureTool` class. The first part of our class definition will look like the following:

```
class CaptureTool(QgsMapTool):
    CAPTURE_LINE    = 1
    CAPTURE_POLYGON = 2

    def __init__(self, canvas, layer, onGeometryAdded,
                 captureMode):
        QgsMapTool.__init__(self, canvas)
        self.canvas          = canvas
        self.layer           = layer
        self.onGeometryAdded = onGeometryAdded
        self.captureMode     = captureMode
        self.rubberBand      = None
        self.tempRubberBand  = None
        self.capturedPoints  = []
        self.capturing       = False
        self.setCursor(Qt.CrossCursor)
```

At the top of our class, we define two constants, `CAPTURE_LINE` and `CAPTURE_POLYGON`, which define the available capture modes. We then have the class initializer, which will accept the following parameters:

- `canvas`: This is the `QgsMapCanvas` this map tool will be part of.
- `layer`: This is the `QgsVectorLayer` the geometry will be added to.
- `onGeometryAdded`: This is a Python-callable object (that is, a method or function) that will be called when a new geometry has been added to the map layer.
- `captureMode`: This indicates whether we are capturing a LineString or a Polygon geometry.

We then set the various instance variables to their initial state, and tell the map tool to use a cross cursor, which makes it easier for the user to see exactly where they are clicking.

Our next task is to implement the various `XXXEvent()` methods to respond to the user's actions. We'll start with `canvasReleaseEvent()`, which responds to a left-click by adding a new vertex to the geometry, and to a right-click by finishing off the capture process and then adding the geometry to the map layer.

> We implement this behavior in the `canvasReleaseEvent()` method, rather than `canvasPressEvent()`, because we want the vertex to be added when the user releases the mouse button, rather than when they initially press it.

Here is the implementation of the `canvasReleaseEvent()` method. Note that we make use of several helper methods, which we will define shortly:

```
def canvasReleaseEvent(self, event):
    if event.button() == Qt.LeftButton:
        if not self.capturing:
            self.startCapturing()
        self.addVertex(event.pos())
    elif event.button() == Qt.RightButton:
        points = self.getCapturedGeometry()
        self.stopCapturing()
        if points != None:
            self.geometryCaptured(points)
```

Next, we have the `canvasMoveEvent()` method, which responds to the action of the user moving the mouse by updating the temporary rubber band to reflect the current mouse position:

```
def canvasMoveEvent(self, event):
    if self.tempRubberBand != None and self.capturing:
        mapPt,layerPt = self.transformCoordinates(event.pos())
        self.tempRubberBand.movePoint(mapPt)
```

The interesting part here is the call to `tempRubberBand.movePoint()`. The `QgsRubberBand` class works in map coordinates, so we first have to convert from the current mouse position, which is in pixels, to map coordinates. We then call `movePoint()`, which moves the current vertex in the rubber band to the new position.

There is one more event handling method to define: `onKeyEvent()`. This responds to the user pressing the *Backspace* or *Delete* keys by removing the last added vertex, and to the user pressing *Return* or *Enter* by closing and saving the current geometry. Here is the code for this method:

```
def keyPressEvent(self, event):
    if event.key() == Qt.Key_Backspace or \
        event.key() == Qt.Key_Delete:
        self.removeLastVertex()
        event.ignore()
```

```
if event.key() == Qt.Key_Return or event.key() ==
   Qt.Key_Enter:
      points = self.getCapturedGeometry()
      self.stopCapturing()
      if points != None:
          self.geometryCaptured(points)
```

Now that we've defined our event handling methods, let's now define the various helper methods that these event handlers rely on. We'll start with the `transformCoordinates()` method, which converts from a mouse position, which is in canvas coordinates, to map and layer coordinates:

```
def transformCoordinates(self, canvasPt):
    return (self.toMapCoordinates(canvasPt),
            self.toLayerCoordinates(self.layer, canvasPt))
```

If, for example, the mouse is currently at position (17,53) on the canvas, this may translate to a map and layer coordinate of `lat=37.234` and `long=-112.472`. As the map and layer might use different coordinate reference systems, we calculate and return the coordinates for both.

Let's now define the `startCapturing()` method, which prepares our two rubber bands and sets `self.capturing` to `True`, so we know that we are currently capturing a geometry:

```
def startCapturing(self):
    color = QColor("red")
    color.setAlphaF(0.78)

    self.rubberBand = QgsRubberBand(self.canvas,
                                    self.bandType())
    self.rubberBand.setWidth(2)
    self.rubberBand.setColor(color)
    self.rubberBand.show()

    self.tempRubberBand = QgsRubberBand(self.canvas,
                                        self.bandType())
    self.tempRubberBand.setWidth(2)
    self.tempRubberBand.setColor(color)
    self.tempRubberBand.setLineStyle(Qt.DotLine)
    self.tempRubberBand.show()

    self.capturing = True
```

Notice that we use another helper method, `bandType()`, to decide on the type of geometry that the rubber band should draw. Let's define that method now:

```
def bandType(self):
    if self.captureMode == CaptureTool.CAPTURE_POLYGON:
        return QGis.Polygon
    else:
        return QGis.Line
```

Next up is the `stopCapturing()` method, which removes our two rubber bands from the map canvas, resets our instance variables back to their initial state, and tells the map canvas to refresh itself so that the rubber bands are hidden:

```
def stopCapturing(self):
    if self.rubberBand:
        self.canvas.scene().removeItem(self.rubberBand)
        self.rubberBand = None
    if self.tempRubberBand:
        self.canvas.scene().removeItem(self.tempRubberBand)
        self.tempRubberBand = None
    self.capturing = False
    self.capturedPoints = []
    self.canvas.refresh()
```

We now come to the `addVertex()` method. This adds a new vertex to the current geometry at the clicked-on mouse position, and updates the rubber bands to match:

```
def addVertex(self, canvasPoint):
    mapPt,layerPt = self.transformCoordinates(canvasPoint)

    self.rubberBand.addPoint(mapPt)
    self.capturedPoints.append(layerPt)

    self.tempRubberBand.reset(self.bandType())
    if self.captureMode == CaptureTool.CAPTURE_LINE:
        self.tempRubberBand.addPoint(mapPt)
    elif self.captureMode == CaptureTool.CAPTURE_POLYGON:
        firstPoint = self.rubberBand.getPoint(0, 0)
        self.tempRubberBand.addPoint(firstPoint)
        self.tempRubberBand.movePoint(mapPt)
        self.tempRubberBand.addPoint(mapPt)
```

Note that we add the captured point to the `self.capturedPoints` list. This is the list of points that will define the geometry when we finish capturing. Setting up the temporary rubber band is a bit convoluted, but the basic idea is to define LineString or Polygon so that it covers the currently highlighted portion of the new geometry.

Let's now define the `removeLastVertex()` method, which is called when the user presses *Backspace* or *Delete* to undo their last click. This method is slightly complicated because we have to update both rubber bands to remove the last vertex, as well as the `self.capturedPoints` list:

```
def removeLastVertex(self):
    if not self.capturing: return

    bandSize     = self.rubberBand.numberOfVertices()
    tempBandSize = self.tempRubberBand.numberOfVertices()
    numPoints    = len(self.capturedPoints)

    if bandSize < 1 or numPoints < 1:
        return

    self.rubberBand.removePoint(-1)

    if bandSize > 1:
        if tempBandSize > 1:
            point = self.rubberBand.getPoint(0, bandSize-2)
            self.tempRubberBand.movePoint(tempBandSize-2,
                                          point)
    else:
        self.tempRubberBand.reset(self.bandType())

    del self.capturedPoints[-1]
```

We've now defined quite a few methods for our `CaptureTool`. Fortunately, there are only two methods left. Let's now define the `getCapturedGeometry()` method. This method checks whether a LineString geometry has at least two points, and whether a Polygon geometry has at least three points. It then closes the polygon and returns the list of points that make up the captured geometry:

```
def getCapturedGeometry(self):
    points = self.capturedPoints
    if self.captureMode == CaptureTool.CAPTURE_LINE:
        if len(points) < 2:
            return None
    if self.captureMode == CaptureTool.CAPTURE_POLYGON:
```

```
        if len(points) < 3:
            return None
    if self.captureMode == CaptureTool.CAPTURE_POLYGON:
        points.append(points[0]) # Close polygon.
    return points
```

Finally, we have the `geometryCaptured()` method, which responds to the geometry that is captured. This method creates a new geometry of the given type, adds it as a feature to the map layer, and uses the `onGeometryAdded` callable object passed to the initializer of our `CaptureTool`, to tell the rest of the application that a new geometry has been added to the layer:

```
def geometryCaptured(self, layerCoords):
    if self.captureMode == CaptureTool.CAPTURE_LINE:
        geometry = QgsGeometry.fromPolyline(layerCoords)
    elif self.captureMode == CaptureTool.CAPTURE_POLYGON:
        geometry = QgsGeometry.fromPolygon([layerCoords])

    feature = QgsFeature()
    feature.setGeometry(geometry)
    self.layer.addFeature(feature)
    self.layer.updateExtents()
    self.onGeometryAdded()
```

While `CaptureTool` is complicated, it is a very powerful class that allows the user to add new lines and polygons to a map layer. There are a few features we haven't implemented here (coordinate snapping, checking whether the resulting geometry is valid, and adding support for inner rings that form "holes" within a polygon), but even as is, this is a useful tool for adding new features to a map.

Editing lines and polygons

The last major functionality we will examine is the ability to edit LineString and Polygon features. Just as the `CaptureTool` allowed the user to click and drag to create new lines and polygons, we will implement `EditTool`, which lets the user click and drag to move the existing feature's vertices. The following image shows what the user will see when they use this tool to move a vertex:

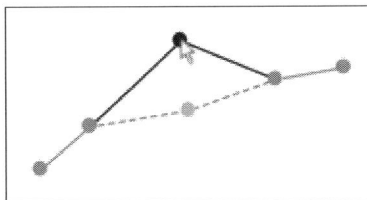

Our editing tool will also let the user add new vertices by double-clicking on a line segment, and delete vertices by right-clicking on the same line segment.

Let's define our `EditTool` class:

```
class EditTool(QgsMapTool):
    def __init__(self, mapCanvas, layer, onGeometryChanged):
        QgsMapTool.__init__(self, mapCanvas)
        self.setCursor(Qt.CrossCursor)
        self.layer              = layer
        self.onGeometryChanged  = onGeometryChanged
        self.dragging           = False
        self.feature            = None
        self.vertex             = None
```

As you can see, `EditTool` is a subclass of `QgsMapTool`, and the initializer accepts three parameters: the map canvas, the layer to be edited, and an `onGeometryChanged` callable object, which will be called when the user makes a change to a geometry.

Next, we want to define the `canvasPressEvent()` method. We'll start by identifying the feature that the user clicked on:

```
    def canvasPressEvent(self, event):
        feature = self.findFeatureAt(event.pos())
        if feature == None:
            return
```

We'll implement the `findFeatureAt()` method shortly. Now that we know which feature the user clicked on, we want to identify the vertex within that feature that is closest to the click point, and how far away from the vertex the user clicked. Here is the relevant code:

```
        mapPt, layerPt = self.transformCoordinates(event.pos())
        geometry = feature.geometry()

        vertexCoord, vertex, prevVertex, nextVertex, distSquared = \
            geometry.closestVertex(layerPt)

        distance = math.sqrt(distSquared)
```

As you can see, we're using a copy of the `transformCoordinates()` method (borrowed from our `CaptureTool` class) to convert from canvas coordinates to map and layer coordinates. We then use the `QgsGeometry.closestVertex()` method to identify the closest vertex to the mouse click. This method returns a number of values, including the square of the distance from the closest vertex to the mouse position. We use the `math.sqrt()` function to convert this into a regular distance value, which will be in layer coordinates.

Now that we know how far away the mouse click was from the vertex, we have to decide whether the distance was too much. If the user didn't click anywhere near a vertex, we'll want to ignore the mouse click. To do this, we'll calculate a **tolerance** value. The tolerance is determined by how far the click point can be from a vertex while still considering it to be a click on that vertex. As with the distance value we calculated earlier, the tolerance is measured in layer coordinates. We'll use a helper method, `calcTolerance()`, to calculate this value. Here is the relevant code to add at the end of our `canvasPressEvent()` method:

```
tolerance = self.calcTolerance(event.pos())
if distance > tolerance: return
```

As you can see, we ignore the mouse click if it is too far away from the vertex, that is, if the distance is greater than the tolerance. Now that we know that the user did click near the vertex, we want to respond to that mouse click. How we do this depends on whether the user pressed the left or the right mouse button:

```
if event.button() == Qt.LeftButton:
    # Left click -> move vertex.
    self.dragging = True
    self.feature  = feature
    self.vertex   = vertex
    self.moveVertexTo(event.pos())
    self.canvas().refresh()
elif event.button() == Qt.RightButton:
    # Right click -> delete vertex.
    self.deleteVertex(feature, vertex)
    self.canvas().refresh()
```

As you can see, we're relying on a number of helper methods to do most of the work. We'll define these methods shortly, but first, let's finish implementing our event handling methods, starting with `canvasMoveEvent()`. This method responds as the user moves the mouse over the canvas. It does this by moving the dragged vertex (if any) to the current mouse position:

```
def canvasMoveEvent(self, event):
    if self.dragging:
        self.moveVertexTo(event.pos())
        self.canvas().refresh()
```

Next, we have `canvasReleaseEvent()`, which moves the vertex to its final position, refreshes the map canvas, and updates our instance variables to reflect the fact that we are no longer dragging a vertex:

```
def canvasReleaseEvent(self, event):
    if self.dragging:
        self.moveVertexTo(event.pos())
        self.layer.updateExtents()
        self.canvas().refresh()
        self.dragging = False
        self.feature  = None
        self.vertex   = None
```

Our final event-handling method is `canvasDoubleClickEvent()`, which responds to a double-click by adding a new vertex to the feature. This method is similar to the `canvasPressEvent()` method; we have to identify the clicked-on feature, and then identify which line segment the user double-clicked on:

```
def canvasDoubleClickEvent(self, event):
    feature = self.findFeatureAt(event.pos())
    if feature == None:
        return

    mapPt,layerPt = self.transformCoordinates(event.pos())
    geometry      = feature.geometry()

    distSquared,closestPt,beforeVertex = \
        geometry.closestSegmentWithContext(layerPt)

    distance = math.sqrt(distSquared)
    tolerance = self.calcTolerance(event.pos())
    if distance > tolerance: return
```

As you can see, we ignore the double-click if the mouse position is too far away from the line segment. Next, we want to add the new vertex to the geometry, and update the map layer and the map canvas to reflect this change:

```
geometry.insertVertex(closestPt.x(), closestPt.y(),
                      beforeVertex)
self.layer.changeGeometry(feature.id(), geometry)
self.canvas().refresh()
```

This completes all of the event-handling methods for our `EditTool`. Let's now implement our various helper methods, starting with the `findFeatureAt()` method that identifies the clicked-on feature:

```
def findFeatureAt(self, pos):
    mapPt,layerPt = self.transformCoordinates(pos)
    tolerance = self.calcTolerance(pos)
    searchRect = QgsRectangle(layerPt.x() - tolerance,
                              layerPt.y() - tolerance,
                              layerPt.x() + tolerance,
                              layerPt.y() + tolerance)

    request = QgsFeatureRequest()
    request.setFilterRect(searchRect)
    request.setFlags(QgsFeatureRequest.ExactIntersect)

    for feature in self.layer.getFeatures(request):
        return feature

    return None
```

We use the tolerance value to define a search rectangle centered around the click point, and identify the first feature that intersects that rectangle:

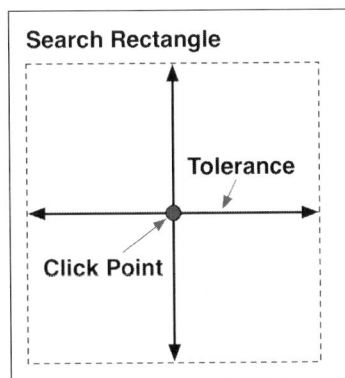

Next up is the `calcTolerance()` method, which calculates how much distance we can tolerate before a click is considered to be too far away from a vertex or geometry:

```
def calcTolerance(self, pos):
    pt1 = QPoint(pos.x(), pos.y())
    pt2 = QPoint(pos.x() + 10, pos.y())

    mapPt1,layerPt1 = self.transformCoordinates(pt1)
    mapPt2,layerPt2 = self.transformCoordinates(pt2)
    tolerance = layerPt2.x() - layerPt1.x()

    return tolerance
```

We calculate this by identifying two points on the map canvas that are ten pixels apart, and converting both of these coordinates into layer coordinates. We then return the distance between these two points, which will be the tolerance in the layer coordinate system.

We now get to the interesting part: moving and deleting vertices. Let's start with the method to move a vertex to a new location:

```
def moveVertexTo(self, pos):
    geometry = self.feature.geometry()
    layerPt = self.toLayerCoordinates(self.layer, pos)
    geometry.moveVertex(layerPt.x(), layerPt.y(), self.vertex)
    self.layer.changeGeometry(self.feature.id(), geometry)
    self.onGeometryChanged()
```

As you can see, we convert the position into layer coordinates, tell the `QgsGeometry` object to move the vertex to this location, and then tell the layer to save the updated geometry. Finally, we use the `onGeometryChanged` callable object to tell the rest of the application that the geometry has been changed.

Deleting a vertex is slightly more complicated, as we have to prevent the user from deleting a vertex if there aren't enough vertices left to make a valid geometry — LineString must have a minimum of two vertices, while a polygon must have at least three. Here is the implementation of our `deleteVertex()` method:

```
def deleteVertex(self, feature, vertex):
    geometry = feature.geometry()

    if geometry.wkbType() == QGis.WKBLineString:
        lineString = geometry.asPolyline()
        if len(lineString) <= 2:
            return
```

```
elif geometry.wkbType() == QGis.WKBPolygon:
    polygon = geometry.asPolygon()
    exterior = polygon[0]
    if len(exterior) <= 4:
        return

if geometry.deleteVertex(vertex):
    self.layer.changeGeometry(feature.id(), geometry)
    self.onGeometryChanged()
```

Note that the polygon check has to allow for the fact that the first and last points on the polygon's exterior are the same. This is why we check to see whether a polygon has at least four coordinates rather than three.

This completes our implementation of the `EditTool` class for editing LineString and Polygon geometries. To see this map tool in action along with the other geometry-editing map tools we defined in this chapter, check out the **GeometryEditor** program, which is included in the sample code of this chapter.

Summary

In this chapter, we learned how to write a PyQGIS application that lets the user select and edit features. We created a map tool that uses the selection-handling methods in `QgsVectorLayer` to let the user select features, and learned how to work with the currently selected features within your program. We then looked at how the layer's editing mode allows the user to make changes and then either commit those changes or discard them. Finally, we created a series of map tools that allow the user to add, edit, and delete Point, LineString, and Polygon geometries within a map layer.

Putting all these tools together, your PyQGIS application can sport a complete range of selection- and geometry-editing features. In the final two chapters of this book, we will use these tools together with the knowledge we gained in the previous chapters, to build a complete standalone mapping application using Python and QGIS.

8
Building a Complete Mapping Application using Python and QGIS

In this chapter, we will design and start building a complete turnkey mapping application. While our example application might seem somewhat specialized, the process of designing and implementing this application, and much of the code that we use, will apply to all sorts of mapping applications that you might like to write yourself.

Due to the complexity of the application we're creating, we will split the implementation across two chapters. In this chapter, we will lay the groundwork for the mapping application by:

- Designing the application
- Building the high-resolution basemap on which our vector data will be displayed
- Implementing the overall structure of the application
- Defining the application's user interface

In the following chapter, we will implement the map tools that let the user enter and manipulate map data, edit attributes, and calculate the shortest path between two points.

Introducing ForestTrails

Imagine that you work for a company responsible for developing and maintaining a large recreational forest. People use the various access roads and purpose-built trails in the forest for walking, biking and horse riding. Your task is to write a computer program that lets the user create a database of access roads and trails to assist with the ongoing maintenance of the forest. For simplicity, we will use the term **track** to refer to either an access road or a trail. Each track will have the following:

- **Type**: Whether the track is a walking trail, a bike trail, a horse trail, or an access road
- **Name**: Not all trails and access roads are named, though some are
- **Direction**: Some trails and access roads are one-way, while others can be travelled in both directions
- **Status**: Whether the track is currently open or closed

Since the recreational forest is continually being developed, new tracks are being regularly added, while existing tracks are sometimes modified or even removed if they are no longer needed. This means that you can't hardwire the set of tracks into your program; you will need to include a *track editing* mode so that the user can add, edit, and remove tracks.

A specific request you have been given is to produce a set of directions that the track maintenance team can follow in order to go from a given starting point to any place in the forest. To implement this, the program will have to let the user choose the starting and ending points, and calculate and display the **shortest available path** between those two points.

Designing the ForestTrails application

Based on our set of requirements, it seems clear that tracks can be represented by LineString geometries. We will also need an appropriate basemap on which these geometries will be displayed. This means that our application will have at least the following two map layers:

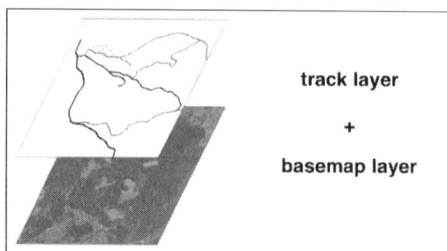

Since we want the data to be persistent, we will use a SpatiaLite database to hold our track data, while the basemap is simply a GeoTIFF raster image that we load and display.

Along with these two main map layers, we will make use of memory-based layers to display the following temporary information on top of the map:

- The currently selected starting point
- The currently selected ending point
- The shortest available path between these two points

To keep things easier, we're going to display each of these in a separate map layer. This means that our application is going to have a total of five map layers:

- `basemapLayer`
- `trackLayer`
- `startPointLayer`
- `endPointLayer`
- `shortestPathLayer`

Along with the map itself, our application will sport a toolbar and a menu bar, both of which let the user access the various features of the system. The following actions will be available in the toolbar and menu bar:

- **Zoom in**: This will let the user zoom in on the map.
- **Zoom out**: This lets the user zoom out.
- **Pan**: This is the pan mode we implemented earlier, which allows the user to move around on the map.
- **Edit**: Clicking on this item will turn on the track editing mode. If we are already in the track editing mode, clicking on it again will prompt the user to save their changes before turning off the editing mode.
- **Add track**: This lets the user add a new track. Note that this item is only available while in the track editing mode.
- **Edit track**: This lets the user edit an existing track. This is only enabled if the user is in the track editing mode.
- **Delete track**: This lets the user delete a track. This is only available in the track editing mode.
- **Get info**: This enables the Get Info map tool. When the user clicks on a track, this tool will display the attributes for that track, and allow the user to make changes to those attributes.

- **Set start point**: This lets the user set the current starting point for the shortest path calculation.

- **Set end point**: This item lets the user click on the map to set the ending point for the shortest path calculation.

- **Find the shortest path**: This displays the shortest available path between the current starting and ending points. Clicking on this item again will hide the path.

This gives us a good idea of what our application should look like, and how it will work. Let's now start writing our ForestTrails program by implementing the basic logic for the application and its main window.

Creating the application

Our application is going to be a standalone Python program built using PyQt and the PyQGIS library. Taking the Lex application we implemented in *Chapter 5, Using QGIS in an External Application*, as a starting point, let's see how we can organize the source files for the ForestTrails system. We'll start with the following basic structure:

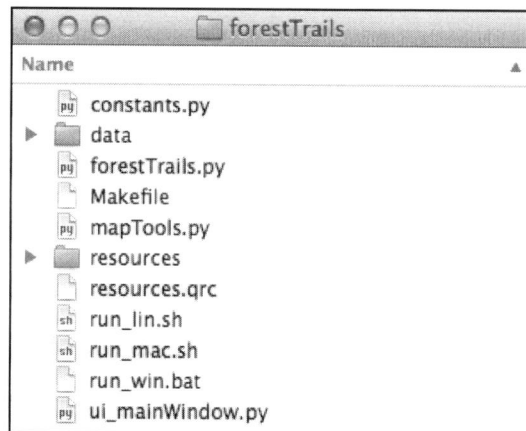

This is very similar to the structure we used for the Lex application, so most of this should be familiar to you. The main difference is that we're using two subdirectories to hold additional files. Let's take a look at what each of these files and directories will be used for:

- `constants.py`: This module will hold various constants used throughout the ForestTrails system.

- `data`: This is a directory that we will use to hold our raster basemap as well as the SpatiaLite database that holds our tracks.

- `forestTrails.py`: This is the main program for our application.

- `Makefile`: This file tells the make tool how to compile the `resources.qrc` file into a `resources.py` module that our application can use.

- `mapTools.py`: This module implements our various map tools.

- `resources`: This is a directory where we will place our various icons and other resources. Since we have so many icon files, it makes sense to put these into a subdirectory rather than cluttering up the main directory with all these files.

- `resources.qrc`: This is the resource description file for our application.

- `run_lin.sh`: This bash shell script is used to run our application on Linux systems.

- `run_mac.sh`: This bash shell script is used to run our application on Mac OS X systems.

- `run_win.bat`: This batch file is used to run our application on MS Windows machines.

- `ui_mainWindow.py`: This Python module defines the user interface for our main window.

Laying out the application

Let's implement the ForestTrails system one small step at a time. Create a directory to hold the source code for the ForestTrails system, and then create the `data` and `resources` subdirectories within it. As many of the files in the main directory are straightforward, let's just go ahead and create the following files:

- The `Makefile` should look like this:

```
RESOURCE_FILES = resources.py

default: compile

compile: $(RESOURCE_FILES)

%.py : %.qrc
  pyrcc4 -o $@ $<

%.py : %.ui
  pyuic4 -o $@ $<

clean:
  rm $(RESOURCE_FILES)
  rm *.pyc
```

> Note that if your `pyrcc4` command is in a nonstandard location, you might need to modify this file so that `make` can find it.

- Create the `resources.qrc` file as follows:

```
<RCC>
<qresource>
<file>resources/mActionZoomIn.png</file>
<file>resources/mActionZoomOut.png</file>
<file>resources/mActionPan.png</file>
<file>resources/mActionEdit.svg</file>
<file>resources/mActionAddTrack.svg</file>
<file>resources/mActionEditTrack.png</file>
<file>resources/mActionDeleteTrack.svg</file>
<file>resources/mActionGetInfo.svg</file>
<file>resources/mActionSetStartPoint.svg</file>
<file>resources/mActionSetEndPoint.svg</file>
<file>resources/mActionFindShortestPath.svg</file>
</qresource>
</RCC>
```

Note that we've included various image files that will be used for our toolbar actions. All these files are in our `resources` subdirectory. We'll look at how to obtain these image files shortly.

- The `run-lin.sh` file should look like this:

```
#!/bin/sh
export PYTHONPATH="/path/to/qgis/build/output/python/"
export LD_LIBRARY_PATH="/path/to/qgis/build/output/lib/"
export QGIS_PREFIX="/path/to/qgis/build/output/"
python forestTrails.py
```

- Similarly, `run-mac.sh` should contain the following:

```
export PYTHONPATH="$PYTHONPATH:/Applications/QGIS.app/Contents/
Resources/python"
export DYLD_FRAMEWORK_PATH="/Applications/QGIS.app/Contents/
Frameworks"
export QGIS_PREFIX="/Applications/QGIS.app/Contents/Resources"
python forestTrails.py
```

- The `run-win.bat` file should contain:

```
SET OSGEO4W_ROOT=C:\OSGeo4W
SET QGIS_PREFIX=%OSGEO4W_ROOT%\apps\qgis
```

```
SET PATH=%PATH%;%QGIS_PREFIX%\bin
SET PYTHONPATH=%QGIS_PREFIX%\python;%PYTHONPATH%
python forestTrails.py
```

> If your QGIS installation is in a nonstandard place, you might need to modify the appropriate script so that the required libraries can be found.

Since the `resources.qrc` file imports our various toolbar icons and makes them available to the application, we'll want to set up those icon files. Let's do that now.

Defining the toolbar icons

There are a total of 11 toolbar actions that we will want to display icons for:

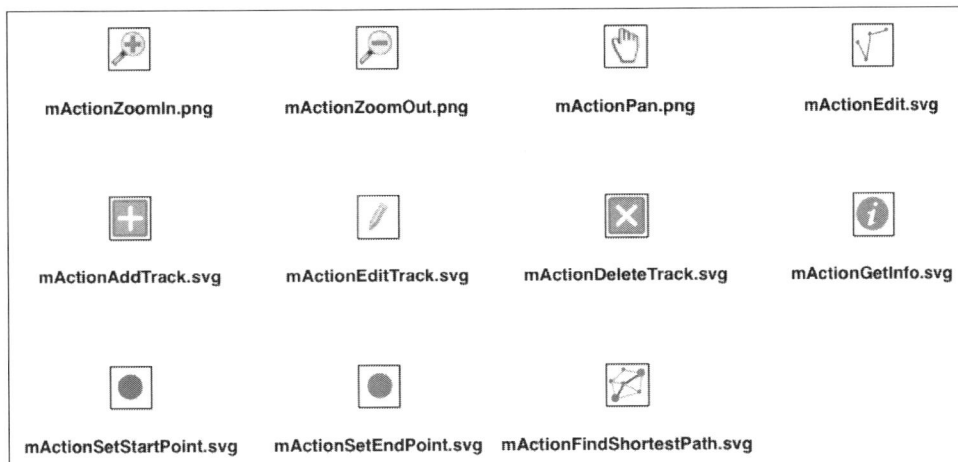

mActionZoomIn.png   mActionZoomOut.png   mActionPan.png   mActionEdit.svg

mActionAddTrack.svg   mActionEditTrack.svg   mActionDeleteTrack.svg   mActionGetInfo.svg

mActionSetStartPoint.svg   mActionSetEndPoint.svg   mActionFindShortestPath.svg

Feel free to create or download your own icons for these toolbar actions, or you can use the icon files included in the source code provided with this chapter. The file format isn't important, just as long as you include the right suffix in the `resoures. qrc` file, and in `ui_mainWindow.py` when the toolbar action is initialized.

Make sure you place these files into the `resources` subdirectory, and run `make` to build the `resources.py` module so that these icons are available for your application to use.

With this groundwork done, we're ready to start defining the application code itself. Let's start with the `constants.py` module.

The constants.py module

This module will hold various constants that we use to represent the track attribute values; by defining them in one place, we make sure that the attribute values are used consistently, and we don't have to remember exactly what the values are. For example, the type attribute for the tracks layer can have the following values:

- ROAD
- WALKING
- BIKE
- HORSE

Rather than hardwiring these values every time we need them, we're going to define these values in the constants.py module. Create this module and enter the following code into it:

```
TRACK_TYPE_ROAD    = "ROAD"
TRACK_TYPE_WALKING = "WALKING"
TRACK_TYPE_BIKE    = "BIKE"
TRACK_TYPE_HORSE   = "HORSE"

TRACK_DIRECTION_BOTH     = "BOTH"
TRACK_DIRECTION_FORWARD  = "FORWARD"
TRACK_DIRECTION_BACKWARD = "BACKWARD"

TRACK_STATUS_OPEN   = "OPEN"
TRACK_STATUS_CLOSED = "CLOSED"
```

We'll be adding a few more constants as we go along, but this is enough to get us started.

The forestTrails.py module

This module defines the main program for the ForestTrails application. It looks very similar to the lex.py module we defined in *Chapter 5, Using QGIS in an External Application*. Create your forestTrails.py file, and enter the following import statements into it:

```
import os, os.path, sys

from qgis.core import *
from qgis.gui import *
from PyQt4.QtGui import *
from PyQt4.QtCore import *

from ui_mainWindow import Ui_MainWindow

import resources
from constants import *
from mapTools import *
```

Next, we want to define the main window for our application in a class, which we will call `ForestTrailsWindow`. This is where the bulk of the application code will be implemented; this class will get quite complicated, but we're going to start easy and just define the window itself, and have empty placeholder methods for all the toolbar actions.

Let's define the class itself and the `__init__()` method to initialize a new window:

```
class ForestTrailsWindow(QMainWindow, Ui_MainWindow):
    def __init__(self):
        QMainWindow.__init__(self)

        self.setupUi(self)

        self.connect(self.actionQuit, SIGNAL("triggered()"),
                     self.quit)
        self.connect(self.actionZoomIn, SIGNAL("triggered()"),
                     self.zoomIn)
        self.connect(self.actionZoomOut, SIGNAL("triggered()"),
                     self.zoomOut)
        self.connect(self.actionPan, SIGNAL("triggered()"),
                     self.setPanMode)
        self.connect(self.actionEdit, SIGNAL("triggered()"),
                     self.setEditMode)
        self.connect(self.actionAddTrack, SIGNAL("triggered()"),
                     self.addTrack)
        self.connect(self.actionEditTrack, SIGNAL("triggered()"),
                     self.editTrack)
        self.connect(self.actionDeleteTrack,SIGNAL("triggered()"),
                     self.deleteTrack)
        self.connect(self.actionGetInfo, SIGNAL("triggered()"),
                     self.getInfo)
```

```
        self.connect(self.actionSetStartPoint,
                     SIGNAL("triggered()"),
              self.setStartPoint)
        self.connect(self.actionSetEndPoint,
                     SIGNAL("triggered()"),
                self.setEndPoint)
        self.connect(self.actionFindShortestPath,
                     SIGNAL("triggered()"),
                  self.findShortestPath)

        self.mapCanvas = QgsMapCanvas()
        self.mapCanvas.useImageToRender(False)
        self.mapCanvas.setCanvasColor(Qt.white)
        self.mapCanvas.show()

        layout = QVBoxLayout()
        layout.setContentsMargins(0, 0, 0, 0)
        layout.addWidget(self.mapCanvas)
        self.centralWidget.setLayout(layout)
```

This is very similar to the __init__() method for the Lex application; we'll define the Ui_MainWindow class in the ui_mainWindow.py module to set up the application's user interface. This is where all those actionXXX instance variables will be defined. In our __init__() method, we're connecting these actions to various methods, which will respond when the user selects the action from the toolbar or menu bar.

The rest of the __init__() method simply sets up a map canvas and lays it out within the window. With this method behind us, we can now define all those action-handling methods. We can borrow two of these directly from lex.py:

```
    def zoomIn(self):
        self.mapCanvas.zoomIn()

    def zoomOut(self):
        self.mapCanvas.zoomOut()
```

For the rest, we'll hold off on implementing them until the application is a bit more complete. To allow our program to run, we'll set up empty placeholder methods for the remaining action handlers:

```
    def quit(self):
        pass
```

```
    def setPanMode(self):
        pass

    def setEditMode(self):
        pass

    def addTrack(self):
        pass

    def editTrack(self):
        pass

    def deleteTrack(self):
        pass

    def getInfo(self):
        pass

    def setStartingPoint(self):
        pass

    def setEndingPoint(self):
        pass

    def findShortestPath(self):
        pass
```

The last part of the `forestTrails.py` module is the `main()` function, which is called when the program is run:

```
def main():
    QgsApplication.setPrefixPath(os.environ['QGIS_PREFIX'], True)
    QgsApplication.initQgis()

    app = QApplication(sys.argv)

    window = ForestTrailsWindow()
    window.show()
    window.raise_()
    window.setPanMode()

    app.exec_()
    app.deleteLater()
    QgsApplication.exitQgis()
```

```
if __name__ == "__main__":
    main()
```

Once again, this is almost identical to the code we saw earlier in the Lex application.

This completes our initial implementation of the `forestTrails.py` module. Our next step is to create the module that will hold all our map tools.

The mapTools.py module

We used `mapTools.py` in the Lex application to define our various map tools separately from the main program. We're going to do the same here. For now, though, our `mapTools.py` module is almost empty:

```
from qgis.core import *
from qgis.gui import *
from PyQt4.QtGui import *
from PyQt4.QtCore import *
from constants import *
```

Obviously, we'll be adding to this as we start to implement our various map tools, but for now, this is enough.

The ui_mainWindow.py module

This is the last module we need to define for our initial implementation of the ForestTrails system. As in the Lex application, this module defines a `Ui_MainWindow` class, which implements the application's user interface, and defines `QAction` objects for the various menu and toolbar items. We'll start by importing the modules that our class will need:

```
from PyQt4.QtGui import *
from PyQt4.QtCore import *
import resources
```

Next, we'll define the `Ui_MainWindow` class and the `setupUi()` method that will do all the work:

```
class Ui_MainWindow(object):
    def setupUi(self, window):
```

The first part of the `setupUi()` method sets the title for the window, creates a `centralWidget` instance variable to hold the map view, and initializes the application's menus and toolbar:

```
window.setWindowTitle("Forest Trails")

self.centralWidget = QWidget(window)
self.centralWidget.setMinimumSize(800, 400)
window.setCentralWidget(self.centralWidget)

self.menubar = window.menuBar()
self.fileMenu = self.menubar.addMenu("File")
self.mapMenu = self.menubar.addMenu("Map")
self.editMenu = self.menubar.addMenu("Edit")
self.toolsMenu = self.menubar.addMenu("Tools")

self.toolBar = QToolBar(window)
window.addToolBar(Qt.TopToolBarArea, self.toolBar)
```

Next, we want to define all the `QAction` objects for the various toolbar and menu items. For each action, we'll define the action's icon and keyboard shortcut, and check whether or not the action is **checkable** (that is, stays on when the user clicks on it):

```
self.actionQuit = QAction("Quit", window)
self.actionQuit.setShortcut(QKeySequence.Quit)

icon = QIcon(":/resources/mActionZoomIn.png")
self.actionZoomIn = QAction(icon, "Zoom In", window)
self.actionZoomIn.setShortcut(QKeySequence.ZoomIn)

icon = QIcon(":/resources/mActionZoomOut.png")
self.actionZoomOut = QAction(icon, "Zoom Out", window)
self.actionZoomOut.setShortcut(QKeySequence.ZoomOut)

icon = QIcon(":/resources/mActionPan.png")
self.actionPan = QAction(icon, "Pan", window)
self.actionPan.setShortcut("Ctrl+1")
self.actionPan.setCheckable(True)
```

```python
icon = QIcon(":/resources/mActionEdit.svg")
self.actionEdit = QAction(icon, "Edit", window)
self.actionEdit.setShortcut("Ctrl+2")
self.actionEdit.setCheckable(True)

icon = QIcon(":/resources/mActionAddTrack.svg")
self.actionAddTrack = QAction(icon, "Add Track", window)
self.actionAddTrack.setShortcut("Ctrl+A")
self.actionAddTrack.setCheckable(True)

icon = QIcon(":/resources/mActionEditTrack.png")
self.actionEditTrack = QAction(icon, "Edit", window)
self.actionEditTrack.setShortcut("Ctrl+E")
self.actionEditTrack.setCheckable(True)

icon = QIcon(":/resources/mActionDeleteTrack.svg")
self.actionDeleteTrack = QAction(icon, "Delete", window)
self.actionDeleteTrack.setShortcut("Ctrl+D")
self.actionDeleteTrack.setCheckable(True)

icon = QIcon(":/resources/mActionGetInfo.svg")
self.actionGetInfo = QAction(icon, "Get Info", window)
self.actionGetInfo.setShortcut("Ctrl+I")
self.actionGetInfo.setCheckable(True)

icon = QIcon(":/resources/mActionSetStartPoint.svg")
self.actionSetStartPoint = QAction(
        icon, "Set Start Point", window)
self.actionSetStartPoint.setCheckable(True)

icon = QIcon(":/resources/mActionSetEndPoint.svg")
self.actionSetEndPoint = QAction(
        icon, "Set End Point", window)
self.actionSetEndPoint.setCheckable(True)

icon = QIcon(":/resources/mActionFindShortestPath.svg")
self.actionFindShortestPath = QAction(
        icon, "Find Shortest Path", window)
self.actionFindShortestPath.setCheckable(True)
```

We then add the various actions to our application's menus:

```
self.fileMenu.addAction(self.actionQuit)

self.mapMenu.addAction(self.actionZoomIn)
self.mapMenu.addAction(self.actionZoomOut)
self.mapMenu.addAction(self.actionPan)
self.mapMenu.addAction(self.actionEdit)

self.editMenu.addAction(self.actionAddTrack)
self.editMenu.addAction(self.actionEditTrack)
self.editMenu.addAction(self.actionDeleteTrack)
self.editMenu.addAction(self.actionGetInfo)

self.toolsMenu.addAction(self.actionSetStartPoint)
self.toolsMenu.addAction(self.actionSetEndPoint)
self.toolsMenu.addAction(self.actionFindShortestPath)
```

Finally, we'll add the actions to our toolbar and tell the window to resize itself to fit its contents:

```
self.toolBar.addAction(self.actionZoomIn)
self.toolBar.addAction(self.actionZoomOut)
self.toolBar.addAction(self.actionPan)
self.toolBar.addAction(self.actionEdit)
self.toolBar.addSeparator()
self.toolBar.addAction(self.actionAddTrack)
self.toolBar.addAction(self.actionEditTrack)
self.toolBar.addAction(self.actionDeleteTrack)
self.toolBar.addAction(self.actionGetInfo)
self.toolBar.addSeparator()
self.toolBar.addAction(self.actionSetStartPoint)
self.toolBar.addAction(self.actionSetEndPoint)
self.toolBar.addAction(self.actionFindShortestPath)

window.resize(window.sizeHint())
```

This completes our implementation of the `ui_mainWindow.py` module. We now have a complete mini application that should be able to run. Let's try it out.

Running the application

Now that you've entered all this code, it's time to check whether it works. Let's try to run the application using the appropriate startup script. Open a terminal or command-line window, navigate into the `forestTrails` directory, and run the appropriate startup script.

If all goes well, you should see the application's main window along with the toolbar and menu items:

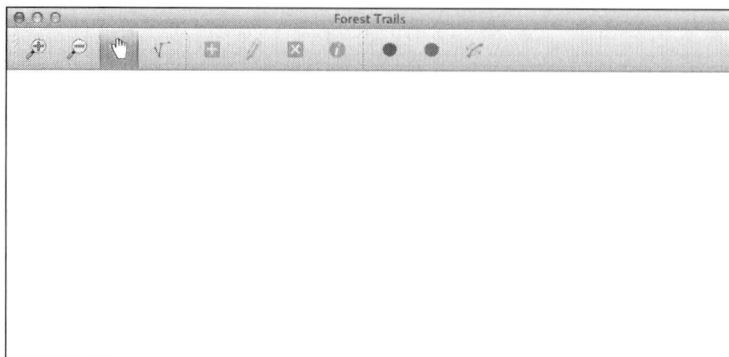

Of course, the main window's map view is empty, and none of the toolbar or menu items do anything yet, but at least we have a working framework for our application. Our next steps are to obtain the basemap for our application, set up our map layers, and then start implementing the various toolbar and menu bar items.

Obtaining the basemap

To follow through this section of the chapter, you are going to need access to the GDAL command-line tools. GDAL is probably already installed on your computer, as QGIS makes use of it. If you don't already have GDAL installed, go to www.gdal.org and click on the **Downloads** link to download and install a copy onto your machine.

One of the challenges of writing a mapping application is to obtain a high-quality basemap on top of which your geospatial data will be displayed. In our case, we want our basemap to show an aerial photograph of the forest. We're going to use the Whakarewarewa Forest in Rotorua, New Zealand, for our ForestTrails application. Fortunately, suitable aerial photographs are available from the *Land Information New Zealand* website.

Go to the following web page, which provides high-resolution aerial photos for the Bay of Plenty, New Zealand:

```
https://data.linz.govt.nz/layer/1760-bay-of-plenty-025m-rural-aerial-
photos-2011-2012/
```

We want to download a basemap that covers the Whakarewarewa forest, which is just south of the city of Rotorua. In the map on the right-hand side of the page, pan and zoom until the following area of the map is visible:

The dark circular area in the center of the map is Lake Rotorua. Zoom in further and pan down to the area just south of Rotorua:

This map shows the Whakarewarewa forest image we want to download. Next, click on the **crop** tool (⬚) in the upper right-hand corner and select the following area of the map:

With the appropriate area of the map selected, click on the **"Download or Order"** link in the upper right-hand corner. The window that appears gives you the option to download the basemap. Make sure you select the following options:

• Map Projection will be NZGD2000

• Image format will be TIFF in the original resolution

> You will need to register to download the file, but the registration process only takes a few seconds, and it doesn't cost anything.

The resulting download should be about 2.8 GB, just under the 3 GB limit for file downloads from this site. If it's too big, you'll have to select a smaller area to download.

Once you've downloaded the file, you will end up with a ZIP archive that contains a number of TIFF format raster image files. Next, we need to combine these images into a single `.tif` file for our basemap. To do this, we'll use the `gdal_merge.py` command that comes with GDAL:

```
gdal_merge.py -o /dst/path/basemap.tif *.tif
```

Choose an appropriate destination for the `basemap.tif` file (by replacing `/dst/path` with a sensible location, for example, the path to your desktop). If the current directory is not set to the folder that contains the downloaded `.tif` files, you'll need to also specify the source path in the command.

It will take a while for this command to stitch together the various images, but the result should be a single large file named `basemap.tif`. This is a TIFF-format raster image that contains the aerial photograph you selected, geo referenced to the appropriate portion of the Earth's surface.

Unfortunately, we can't use this file directly. To see why, run the `gdalinfo` command on the downloaded file:

```
gdalinfo basemap.tif
```

Among other things, this tells us which coordinate reference system the file is using:

```
Coordinate System is:
PROJCS["NZGD2000 / New Zealand Transverse Mercator 2000",
    GEOGCS["NZGD2000",
        DATUM["New_Zealand_Geodetic_Datum_2000",
            SPHEROID["GRS 1980",6378137,298.2572221010002,
                AUTHORITY["EPSG","7019"]],
            AUTHORITY["EPSG","6167"]],
        PRIMEM["Greenwich",0],
        UNIT["degree",0.0174532925199433],
        AUTHORITY["EPSG","4167"]],
    . . .
```

As you can see, the downloaded basemap uses the **New Zealand Transverse Mercator 2000** coordinate system. We need to translate this into the WGS84 (geographic latitude/longitude coordinate) coordinate system so that we can use it in the ForestTrails program. To do this, we'll use the `gdalwarp` command, like this:

```
gdalwarp -t_srs EPSG:4326 basemap.tif basemap_wgs84.tif
```

If you look at the resulting image using `gdalinfo`, you'll see that it has been converted into the lat/long coordinate system:

```
Coordinate System is:
GEOGCS["WGS 84",
    DATUM["WGS_1984",
        SPHEROID["WGS 84",6378137,298.257223563,
            AUTHORITY["EPSG","7030"]],
        AUTHORITY["EPSG","6326"]],
    PRIMEM["Greenwich",0],
```

```
UNIT["degree",0.0174532925199433],
AUTHORITY["EPSG","4326"]]
```

> You might wonder why we didn't download the file directly in the WGS84 coordinate system. We downloaded the file in its original CRS because this gives us more control over the final image. Reprojecting the image ourselves also makes it easier to see how the image was changed when it was reprojected.

So far, so good. However, if we look at the resulting image, we'll see another problem:

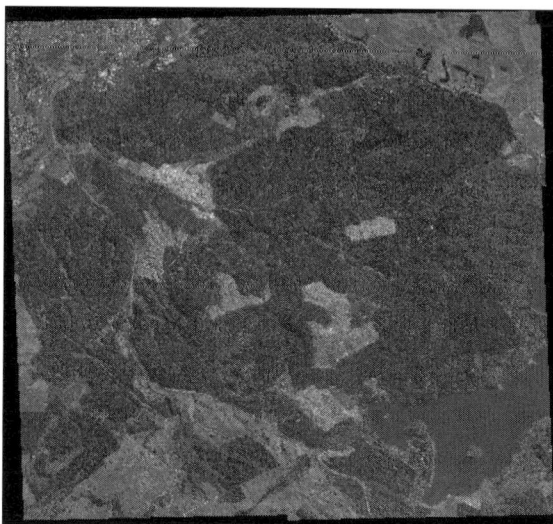

The translation from NZGD2000 into WGS84 rotated the basemap slightly, so the borders of the map don't look good. Now, we need to trim the map to get rid of the unwanted borders. To do this, we'll use the `gdal_warp` command again, this time with a target extent:

```
gdalwarp -te 176.241 -38.2333 176.325 -38.1557 basemap_wgs84.tif
basemap_trimmed.tif
```

> You might need to adjust the lat/long values if you have selected slightly different bounds when downloading the basemap. The corner coordinate values displayed by `gdalinfo` will give you a clue as to what values have to be used.

The resulting file is a good raster basemap for us to use for our ForestTrails program:

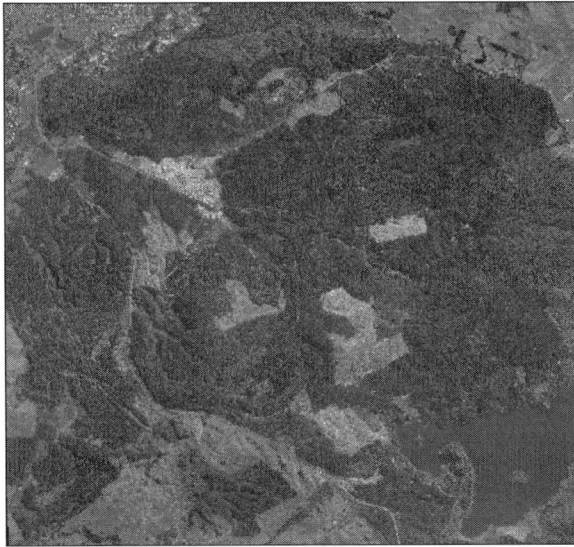

Copy the final image into your `forestTrails/data` directory and rename it back to `basemap.tif`.

Defining the map layers

We know that we want to have a total of five map layers in our application. The basemap layer will display the `basemap.tif` file we just downloaded, while the track layer will use a SpatiaLite database to store and display the track data entered by the user. The remaining map layers will display temporary features held in memory.

Let's start by defining a new method in our `forestTrails.py` module to initialize the SpatiaLite database we will use for the track layer:

```
def setupDatabase(self):
    cur_dir = os.path.dirname(os.path.realpath(__file__))
    dbName = os.path.join(cur_dir, "data", "tracks.sqlite")
    if not os.path.exists(dbName):
        fields = QgsFields()
        fields.append(QgsField("id", QVariant.Int))
        fields.append(QgsField("type", QVariant.String))
        fields.append(QgsField("name", QVariant.String))
        fields.append(QgsField("direction", QVariant.String))
        fields.append(QgsField("status", QVariant.String))
```

```
crs = QgsCoordinateReferenceSystem(4326,
            QgsCoordinateReferenceSystem.EpsgCrsId)

writer = QgsVectorFileWriter(dbName, 'utf-8', fields,
                             QGis.WKBLineString,
                             crs, 'SQLite',
                             ["SPATIALITE=YES"])

if writer.hasError() != QgsVectorFileWriter.NoError:
    print "Error creating tracks database!"

del writer
```

As you can see, we check to see whether the SpatiaLite database file exists in our `data` subdirectory, and create a new database if necessary. We define the various fields that will hold the various track attributes, and use a `QgsVectorFileWriter` object to create the database.

You will also need to modify the `main()` function to call the `setupDatabase()` method. Add the following line to this function after the call to `window.raise_()`:

```
window.setupDatabase()
```

Now that we've set up our database for the track layer, we can define our various map layers. We'll create a new method called `setupMapLayers()` to do this. Let's start by defining a `layers` variable to hold the various map layers, and initialize our base map layer:

```
def setupMapLayers(self):
    cur_dir = os.path.dirname(os.path.realpath(__file__))
    layers = []

    filename = os.path.join(cur_dir, "data", "basemap.tif")
    self.baseLayer = QgsRasterLayer(filename, "basemap")
    QgsMapLayerRegistry.instance().addMapLayer(self.baseLayer)
    layers.append(QgsMapCanvasLayer(self.baseLayer))
```

Next, we want to set up our **tracks** layer. Since this is stored in a SpatiaLite database, we have to use a `QgsDataSourceURI` object to connect the database to the map layer. The following code shows how this is done:

```
uri = QgsDataSourceURI()
uri.setDatabase(os.path.join(cur_dir, "data",
"tracks.sqlite"))
uri.setDataSource('', 'tracks', 'GEOMETRY')
```

```
self.trackLayer = QgsVectorLayer(uri.uri(), "Tracks",
                                 "spatialite")
QgsMapLayerRegistry.instance().addMapLayer(
    self.trackLayer)
layers.append(QgsMapCanvasLayer(self.trackLayer))
```

We can now set up a memory-based map layer to display the shortest path:

```
self.shortestPathLayer = QgsVectorLayer(
    "LineString?crs=EPSG:4326",
    "shortestPathLayer", "memory")
QgsMapLayerRegistry.instance().addMapLayer(
    self.shortestPathLayer)
layers.append(QgsMapCanvasLayer(self.shortestPathLayer))
```

We saw how to create memory-based map layers in *Chapter 6, Mastering the QGIS Python API*, so there shouldn't be any surprises here; we're simply defining the shortest path layer to hold a LineString geometry.

Next, we want to set up another memory-based map layer to show the user's selected starting point:

```
self.startPointLayer = QgsVectorLayer(
                          "Point?crs=EPSG:4326",
                          "startPointLayer", "memory")
QgsMapLayerRegistry.instance().addMapLayer(
    self.startPointLayer)
layers.append(QgsMapCanvasLayer(self.startPointLayer))
```

Also, we want to set another map layer for the ending point:

```
self.endPointLayer = QgsVectorLayer(
    "Point?crs=EPSG:4326",
    "endPointLayer", "memory")
QgsMapLayerRegistry.instance().addMapLayer(
    self.endPointLayer)
layers.append(QgsMapCanvasLayer(self.endPointLayer))
```

This completes all five of our map layers. The final part of the setupMapLayers() method adds these various layers to the map canvas. Note that because we defined the map layers in back-to-front order (in other words, the first entry in layers is the basemap, which should appear at the back), we have to reverse the layers before we add them to the map canvas. Here is the relevant code:

```
layers.reverse()
self.mapCanvas.setLayerSet(layers)
self.mapCanvas.setExtent(self.baseLayer.extent())
```

The last thing we have to do is add a call to `setupMapLayers()` from within our `main()` function. Add the following immediately after the `window.setupDatabase()` line:

```
window.setupMapLayers()
```

Now that our map layers are set up, we can run our program again. There's no vector data yet, but the basemap should be visible, and we can zoom in and out using the toolbar icons:

Defining the map renderers

Now that we have the map layers, we'll want to set up appropriate symbols and renderers to draw the vector data onto the map. Let's start by defining a method called `setupRenderers()`, which creates the renderers for our various map layers. Our first renderer will display the track layer, where we use a `QgsRuleBasedRendererV2` object to display the tracks in different ways depending on the type of track, whether or not the track is open, and whether it is bidirectional or can only be used in one direction. Here is the relevant code:

```
def setupRenderers(self):
    root_rule = QgsRuleBasedRendererV2.Rule(None)

    for track_type in (TRACK_TYPE_ROAD,  TRACK_TYPE_WALKING,
                       TRACK_TYPE_BIKE,  TRACK_TYPE_HORSE):
```

```
        if track_type == TRACK_TYPE_ROAD:
            width = ROAD_WIDTH
        else:
            width = TRAIL_WIDTH

        lineColor = "light gray"
        arrowColor = "dark gray"

        for track_status in (TRACK_STATUS_OPEN,
          TRACK_STATUS_CLOSED):
            for track_direction in (TRACK_DIRECTION_BOTH,
                                    TRACK_DIRECTION_FORWARD,
                                    TRACK_DIRECTION_BACKWARD):
                symbol = self.createTrackSymbol(
                  width, lineColor, arrowColor,
                  track_status, track_direction)
                expression = ("(type='%s') and " +
                              "(status='%s') and " +
                              "(direction='%s')") % (
                                track_type, track_status,
                                track_direction)

                rule = QgsRuleBasedRendererV2.Rule(
                  symbol, filterExp=expression)
                root_rule.appendChild(rule)

    symbol = QgsLineSymbolV2.createSimple({'color' : "black"})
    rule = QgsRuleBasedRendererV2.Rule(symbol, elseRule=True)
    root_rule.appendChild(rule)

    renderer = QgsRuleBasedRendererV2(root_rule)
    self.trackLayer.setRendererV2(renderer)
```

As you can see, we iterate over all the possible track types. Based on the track type, we choose a suitable line width. We also choose a color to use for the line and the arrowheads—for now, we're simply using the same color for every type of track. We then iterate over all the possible status and direction values, and call a helper method named `createTrackSymbol()` to create a suitable symbol for this track type, status, and direction. We then create a `QgsRuleBasedRendererV2.Rule` object that uses that symbol for those tracks with the given type, status, and direction. Finally, we define an "else" rule for the renderer, displaying the track as a simple black line if the track doesn't have any of the expected attribute values.

Our remaining map layers will use straightforward line or marker symbols to display the shortest path, and the starting and ending points. Here's the remainder of the `setupRenderers()` method, which defines these map renderers:

```
symbol = QgsLineSymbolV2.createSimple({'color' : "blue"})
symbol.setWidth(ROAD_WIDTH)
symbol.setOutputUnit(QgsSymbolV2.MapUnit)
renderer = QgsSingleSymbolRendererV2(symbol)
self.shortestPathLayer.setRendererV2(renderer)

symbol = QgsMarkerSymbolV2.createSimple(
                        {'color' : "green"})
symbol.setSize(POINT_SIZE)
symbol.setOutputUnit(QgsSymbolV2.MapUnit)
renderer = QgsSingleSymbolRendererV2(symbol)
self.startPointLayer.setRendererV2(renderer)

symbol = QgsMarkerSymbolV2.createSimple({'color' : "red"})
symbol.setSize(POINT_SIZE)
symbol.setOutputUnit(QgsSymbolV2.MapUnit)
renderer = QgsSingleSymbolRendererV2(symbol)
self.endPointLayer.setRendererV2(renderer)
```

Now that we've defined the `setupRenderers()` method itself, let's modify our `main()` function to call it. Add the following line immediately after the call to `setupMapLayers()`:

```
window.setupRenderers()
```

There are a few more things we need to do to finish implementing our map renderers. Firstly, we need to define the `createTrackSymbol()` helper method that we used to set up the track renderer. Add the following to your `ForestTrailsWindow` class:

```
def createTrackSymbol(self, width, lineColor, arrowColor,
                        status, direction):
    symbol = QgsLineSymbolV2.createSimple({})
    symbol.deleteSymbolLayer(0) # Remove default symbol layer.

    symbolLayer = QgsSimpleLineSymbolLayerV2()
    symbolLayer.setWidth(width)
    symbolLayer.setWidthUnit(QgsSymbolV2.MapUnit)
    symbolLayer.setColor(QColor(lineColor))
    if status == TRACK_STATUS_CLOSED:
        symbolLayer.setPenStyle(Qt.DotLine)
```

```
symbol.appendSymbolLayer(symbolLayer)

if direction == TRACK_DIRECTION_FORWARD:
    registry = QgsSymbolLayerV2Registry.instance()
    markerLineMetadata = registry.symbolLayerMetadata(
        "MarkerLine")
    markerMetadata    = registry.symbolLayerMetadata(
        "SimpleMarker")

    symbolLayer = markerLineMetadata.createSymbolLayer(
                    {'width': '0.26',
                     'color': arrowColor,
                     'rotate': '1',
                     'placement': 'interval',
                     'interval' : '20',
                     'offset': '0'})
    subSymbol = symbolLayer.subSymbol()
    subSymbol.deleteSymbolLayer(0)
    triangle = markerMetadata.createSymbolLayer(
                    {'name': 'filled_arrowhead',
                     'color': arrowColor,
                     'color_border': arrowColor,
                     'offset': '0,0',
                     'size': '3',
                     'outline_width': '0.5',
                     'output_unit': 'mapunit',
                     'angle': '0'})
    subSymbol.appendSymbolLayer(triangle)

    symbol.appendSymbolLayer(symbolLayer)
elif direction == TRACK_DIRECTION_BACKWARD:
    registry = QgsSymbolLayerV2Registry.instance()
    markerLineMetadata = registry.symbolLayerMetadata(
        "MarkerLine")
    markerMetadata    = registry.symbolLayerMetadata(
        "SimpleMarker")

    symbolLayer = markerLineMetadata.createSymbolLayer(
                    {'width': '0.26',
                     'color': arrowColor,
                     'rotate': '1',
                     'placement': 'interval',
                     'interval' : '20',
                     'offset': '0'})
```

```
        subSymbol = symbolLayer.subSymbol()
        subSymbol.deleteSymbolLayer(0)
        triangle = markerMetadata.createSymbolLayer(
                        {'name': 'filled_arrowhead',
                         'color': arrowColor,
                         'color_border': arrowColor,
                         'offset': '0,0',
                         'size': '3',
                         'outline_width': '0.5',
                         'output_unit': 'mapunit',
                         'angle': '180'})
        subSymbol.appendSymbolLayer(triangle)

        symbol.appendSymbolLayer(symbolLayer)

    return symbol
```

The complex part of this method is the code to draw an arrowhead onto the track to indicate the track's direction. Apart from this, we simply draw a line to represent the track using the specified color and width, and if the track is closed, we draw the track as a dotted line.

Our final task here is to add some more entries to our constants.py module to represent the various sizes and line widths used by our renderers. Add the following to the end of this module:

```
ROAD_WIDTH  = 0.0001
TRAIL_WIDTH = 0.00003
POINT_SIZE  = 0.0004
```

All of these values are in map units.

Unfortunately, we can't see these renderers being used yet, as we don't have any vector features to display, but we need to implement them now so that our code will work when the time comes. We won't see these renderers in action until the next chapter, when the user starts adding tracks and selecting start/end points on the map.

The Pan Tool

To let the user move around the map, we'll make use of the `PanTool` class we
implemented in an earlier chapter. Add the following class definition to the
`mapTools.py` module:

```
class PanTool(QgsMapTool):
    def __init__(self, mapCanvas):
        QgsMapTool.__init__(self, mapCanvas)
        self.setCursor(Qt.OpenHandCursor)
        self.dragging = False

    def canvasMoveEvent(self, event):
        if event.buttons() == Qt.LeftButton:
            self.dragging = True
            self.canvas().panAction(event)

    def canvasReleaseEvent(self, event):
        if event.button() == Qt.LeftButton and self.dragging:
            self.canvas().panActionEnd(event.pos())
            self.dragging = False
```

Back in our `forestTrails.py` module, add the following new method:

```
def setupMapTools(self):
    self.panTool = PanTool(self.mapCanvas)
    self.panTool.setAction(self.actionPan)
```

This method will initialize the various map tools that our application will use; we'll
add to this method as we go along. For now, add the following to your `main()`
function, after the call to `window.setupRenderers()`:

```
window.setupMapTools()
```

We can now replace our dummy implementation of `setPanMode()` with the real thing:

```
def setPanMode(self):
    self.mapCanvas.setMapTool(self.panTool)
```

If you run your program now, you'll see that the user can now zoom in and out and
use the pan tool to move around the basemap.

Implementing the track editing mode

Our final task for this chapter is to implement the track editing mode. We learned in the previous chapter how we can turn on the editing mode for a map layer and then use various map tools to let the user add, edit, and delete features. We'll start to implement the actual map tools in *Chapter 9, Completing the Forest Trails Application*, but for now, let's define our track editing mode itself.

The `setEditMode()` method is used to enter and leave the track editing mode. Replace the placeholder method you defined earlier with this new implementation:

```
def setEditMode(self):
    if self.editing:
        if self.modified:
            reply = QMessageBox.question(self, "Confirm",
                                         "Save Changes?",
                                         QMessageBox.Yes |
                                         QMessageBox.No,
                                         QMessageBox.Yes)
            if reply == QMessageBox.Yes:
                self.trackLayer.commitChanges()
            else:
                self.trackLayer.rollBack()
        else:
            self.trackLayer.commitChanges()
        self.trackLayer.triggerRepaint()
        self.editing = False
        self.setPanMode()
    else:
        self.trackLayer.startEditing()
        self.trackLayer.triggerRepaint()
        self.editing  = True
        self.modified = False
        self.setPanMode()
    self.adjustActions()
```

If the user is currently editing the tracks and has made some changes, we ask the user whether they want to save their changes, and either commit the changes or roll them back. If no changes have been made, we roll back (to turn off the vector layer's editing mode) and switch back to the panning mode.

There are a couple of instance variables that we use here to monitor the state of our track editing: `self.editing` will be set to `True` if we're currently editing the tracks, and `self.modified` is set to `True` if the user has changed anything in the track layer. We'll have to add the following to our `ForestTrailsWindow.__init__()` method to initialize these two instance variables:

```
self.editing  = False
self.modified= False
```

There's another method that we haven't seen before: `adjustActions()`. This method will enable/disable and check/uncheck the various actions: depending on the application's current state. For example, when we enter the track editing mode, our `adjustActions()` method will enable the add, edit, and delete tools, and these tools will be disabled again when the user leaves the track-editing mode.

We can't implement all of `adjustActions()` at the moment because we haven't yet defined the various map tools that our application will use. For now, we'll write the first half of this method:

```
def adjustActions(self):
    if self.editing:
        self.actionAddTrack.setEnabled(True)
        self.actionEditTrack.setEnabled(True)
        self.actionDeleteTrack.setEnabled(True)
        self.actionGetInfo.setEnabled(True)
        self.actionSetStartPoint.setEnabled(False)
        self.actionSetEndPoint.setEnabled(False)
        self.actionFindShortestPath.setEnabled(False)
    else:
        self.actionAddTrack.setEnabled(False)
        self.actionEditTrack.setEnabled(False)
        self.actionDeleteTrack.setEnabled(False)
        self.actionGetInfo.setEnabled(False)
        self.actionSetStartPoint.setEnabled(True)
        self.actionSetEndPoint.setEnabled(True)
        self.actionFindShortestPath.setEnabled(True)
```

We'll also need to add a call to `adjustActions()` in our `main()` function after the call to `setPanMode()`:

```
window.adjustActions()
```

With the track editing mode implemented, the user can click on the **Edit** toolbar icon to enter the track editing mode, and click on it again to leave that mode. Of course, we can't make any changes yet, but the code itself is in place.

There's one more feature we'd like to add to our application; if the user makes some changes to the track layer and then tries to quit the application, we'd like to give the user the chance to save their changes. To do this, we'll implement the `quit()` method, which we linked to the `actionQuit` action:

```
def quit(self):
    if self.editing and self.modified:
        reply = QMessageBox.question(self, "Confirm",
                                     "Save Changes?",
                                     QMessageBox.Yes |
                                     QMessageBox.No |
                                     QMessageBox.Cancel,
                                     QMessageBox.Yes)
        if reply == QMessageBox.Yes:
            self.curEditedLayer.commitChanges()
        elif reply == QMessageBox.No:
            self.curEditedLayer.rollBack()

        if reply != QMessageBox.Cancel:
            qApp.quit()
    else:
        qApp.quit()
```

This is very similar to the part of the `setEditMode()` method that lets the user leave the track editing mode, except that we call `qApp.quit()` to quit the application at the end. We have one more method to define, which intercepts an attempt to close the window and calls `self.quit()`. This prompts the user to save their changes if they close the window while editing. Here is the definition for this method:

```
def closeEvent(self, event):
    self.quit()
```

Summary

In this chapter, we designed and started to implement a complete mapping application for maintaining a map of tracks and roads within a recreational forest. We implemented the application itself, defined our map layers, obtained a high-resolution basemap for our application, and implemented zooming, panning, and the code necessary for editing the track layer.

In the next chapter, we will round out the implementation of our ForestTrails system by implementing the map tools to let the user add, edit, and delete tracks. We will also implement the code for editing track attributes and finding the shortest available path between two points.

9

Completing the ForestTrails Application

In this chapter, we will complete our implementation of the ForestTrails application that we started building in the preceding chapter. So far, our application displays the basemap and lets the user zoom and pan across the map. We've also implemented the track editing mode, though the user can't enter or edit track data yet.

In this chapter, we will add the following features to the ForestTrails application:

- Map tools that let the user add, edit, and delete tracks
- A toolbar action that lets the user view and edit the attributes for a track
- The **Set Start Point** and **Set End Point** actions
- Calculating and displaying the shortest available path between the two selected points using a memory-based map layer

The Add Track map tool

Our first task is to let the user add a new track while in the track editing mode. This involves defining a new map tool, which we will call AddTrackTool. Before we start implementing the AddTrackTool class, however, we're going to create a mixin class that provides various helper methods for our map tools. We'll call this mixin class MapToolMixin.

Here is our initial implementation of the `MapToolMixin` class, which should be placed near the top of your `mapTools.py` module:

```
class MapToolMixin
    def setLayer(self, layer):
        self.layer = layer

    def transformCoordinates(self, screenPt):
        return (self.toMapCoordinates(screenPt),
                self.toLayerCoordinates(self.layer, screenPt))

    def calcTolerance(self, pos):
        pt1 = QPoint(pos.x(), pos.y())
        pt2 = QPoint(pos.x() + 10, pos.y())

        mapPt1,layerPt1 = self.transformCoordinates(pt1)
        mapPt2,layerPt2 = self.transformCoordinates(pt2)
        tolerance = layerPt2.x() - layerPt1.x()

        return tolerance
```

We've seen both the `transformCoordinates()` and `calcTolerance()` methods before when we created the geometry editing map tools in *Chapter 7, Selecting and Editing Features in a PyQGIS Application*. The only difference is that we're storing a reference to the edited map layer so that we don't have to supply it as a parameter each time we want to calculate the tolerance or transform coordinates.

We can now start implementing the `AddTrackTool` class. This is very similar to `CaptureTool` we defined in *Chapter 7, Selecting and Editing Features in a PyQGIS Application*, except that it only captures LineString geometries and it creates a new track feature with default attributes when the user finishes defining the track. Here is the class definition with the `__init__()` method for our new map tool, which should be placed in the `mapTools.py` module:

```
class AddTrackTool(QgsMapTool, MapToolMixin):
    def __init__(self, canvas, layer, onTrackAdded):
        QgsMapTool.__init__(self, canvas)
        self.canvas           = canvas
        self.onTrackAdded     = onTrackAdded
        self.rubberBand       = None
        self.tempRubberBand   = None
        self.capturedPoints   = []
        self.capturing        = False
        self.setLayer(layer)
        self.setCursor(Qt.CrossCursor)
```

As you can see, our class inherits from both `QgsMapTool` and `MapToolMixin`. We also call the `setLayer()` method so that our mixin knows which layer to work with. This also makes the currently edited layer available via `self.layer`.

We next define the various event handling methods for our map tool:

```
def canvasReleaseEvent(self, event):
    if event.button() == Qt.LeftButton:
        if not self.capturing:
            self.startCapturing()
        self.addVertex(event.pos())
    elif event.button() == Qt.RightButton:
        points = self.getCapturedPoints()
        self.stopCapturing()
        if points != None:
            self.pointsCaptured(points)


def canvasMoveEvent(self, event):
    if self.tempRubberBand != None and self.capturing:
        mapPt,layerPt = self.transformCoordinates(event.pos())
        self.tempRubberBand.movePoint(mapPt)


def keyPressEvent(self, event):
    if event.key() == Qt.Key_Backspace or \
        event.key() == Qt.Key_Delete:
        self.removeLastVertex()
        event.ignore()
    if event.key() == Qt.Key_Return or \
        event.key() == Qt.Key_Enter:
        points = self.getCapturedPoints()
        self.stopCapturing()
        if points != None:
            self.pointsCaptured(points)
```

Once again, we've seen this logic before in the `CaptureTool` class. The only difference is that we're only capturing LineString geometries, so we don't need to worry about the capture mode.

We now get to the `startCapturing()` and `stopCapturing()` methods. These create and release the rubber bands used by our map tool:

```
def startCapturing(self):
    color = QColor("red")
    color.setAlphaF(0.78)
```

```
        self.rubberBand = QgsRubberBand(self.canvas, QGis.Line)
        self.rubberBand.setWidth(2)
        self.rubberBand.setColor(color)
        self.rubberBand.show()

        self.tempRubberBand = QgsRubberBand(self.canvas,
           QGis.Line)
        self.tempRubberBand.setWidth(2)
        self.tempRubberBand.setColor(color)
        self.tempRubberBand.setLineStyle(Qt.DotLine)
        self.tempRubberBand.show()

        self.capturing = True

    def stopCapturing(self):
        if self.rubberBand:
            self.canvas.scene().removeItem(self.rubberBand)
            self.rubberBand = None
        if self.tempRubberBand:
            self.canvas.scene().removeItem(self.tempRubberBand)
            self.tempRubberBand = None
        self.capturing = False
        self.capturedPoints = []
        self.canvas.refresh()
```

Next, we have the `addVertex()` method, which adds a new vertex to the track:

```
    def addVertex(self, canvasPoint):
        mapPt,layerPt = self.transformCoordinates(canvasPoint)

        self.rubberBand.addPoint(mapPt)
        self.capturedPoints.append(layerPt)

        self.tempRubberBand.reset(QGis.Line)
        self.tempRubberBand.addPoint(mapPt)
```

Note that we call `self.transformCoordinates()`, which is a method defined by our mixin class.

Our next method is `removeLastVertex()`. This deletes the last added vertex when the user presses the *Delete* key:

```
    def removeLastVertex(self):
        if not self.capturing: return
```

```
bandSize     = self.rubberBand.numberOfVertices()
tempBandSize = self.tempRubberBand.numberOfVertices()
numPoints    = len(self.capturedPoints)

if bandSize < 1 or numPoints < 1:
    return

self.rubberBand.removePoint(-1)

if bandSize > 1:
    if tempBandSize > 1:
        point = self.rubberBand.getPoint(0, bandSize-2)
        self.tempRubberBand.movePoint(tempBandSize-2,
                                      point)
else:
    self.tempRubberBand.reset(QGis.Line)

del self.capturedPoints[-1]
```

We now define the `getCapturedPoints()` method, which returns either the set of points the user clicked on or `None` if the user didn't click on enough points to make a LineString:

```
def getCapturedPoints(self):
    points = self.capturedPoints
    if len(points) < 2:
        return None
    else:
        return points
```

Our final method is `pointsCaptured()`, which responds when the user finishes clicking on the points for a new track. Unlike the equivalent method in `CaptureTool`, we have to set the various attributes for the new track:

```
def pointsCaptured(self, points):
    fields = self.layer.dataProvider().fields()

    feature = QgsFeature()
    feature.setGeometry(QgsGeometry.fromPolyline(points))
    feature.setFields(fields)
    feature.setAttribute("type",      TRACK_TYPE_ROAD)
    feature.setAttribute("status",    TRACK_STATUS_OPEN)
    feature.setAttribute("direction", TRACK_DIRECTION_BOTH)
```

```
self.layer.addFeature(feature)
self.layer.updateExtents()
self.onTrackAdded()
```

Now that we've defined our map tool, let's update our application to use this tool. Back in the `forestTrails.py` module, add the following to the end of the `setupMapTools()` method:

```
self.addTrackTool = AddTrackTool(self.mapCanvas,
                                 self.trackLayer,
                                 self.onTrackAdded)
self.addTrackTool.setAction(self.actionAddTrack)
```

We can now define our `addTrack()` method as follows:

```
def addTrack(self):
    if self.actionAddTrack.isChecked():
        self.mapCanvas.setMapTool(self.addTrackTool)
    else:
        self.setPanMode()
```

If the user checks the **Add Track** action, we activate the Add Track tool. If the user unchecks the action by clicking on it again, we will switch back to the pan mode.

Finally, we have to define a helper method called `onTrackAdded()`. This method responds when the user adds a new track to our track layer. Here is the implementation of this method:

```
def onTrackAdded(self):
    self.modified = True
    self.mapCanvas.refresh()
    self.actionAddTrack.setChecked(False)
    self.setPanMode()
```

Testing the application

With all of this code implemented, it's time to test out our application. Run the appropriate startup script, and zoom in slightly on the map. Then click on the **Edit** action, followed by the **Add Track** action. All going well, you should be able to click on the map to define the vertices of a new track. When you're done, press the *Return* key to create the new track. The result should look something like the following screenshot:

If you then click on the Edit Tracks icon again, you'll be asked if you want to save your changes. Go ahead, and your new track should be made permanent.

Now go back to the track editing mode and try creating a second track that connects with the first. For example:

If you then zoom in, you'll quickly discover a major flaw in the design of our application, as shown in the next screenshot:

The tracks aren't connected together. Since the user can click anywhere on the map, there's no way of ensuring that the tracks are connected—and if the tracks aren't connected, the **Find Shortest Path** command won't work.

There are a few ways we can solve this problem, but the easiest one in this case is to implement **vertex snapping**, that is, if the user clicks close to an existing vertex, we snap the click location onto the vertex so that the various tracks are connected.

Vertex snapping

To implement vertex snapping, we're going to add some new methods to `MapToolMixin`. We'll start with the `findFeatureAt()` method. This method finds a feature close to the click location. Here is the implementation of this method:

```
def findFeatureAt(self, pos, excludeFeature=None):
    mapPt,layerPt = self.transformCoordinates(pos)
    tolerance = self.calcTolerance(pos)
    searchRect = QgsRectangle(layerPt.x() - tolerance,
                              layerPt.y() - tolerance,
                              layerPt.x() + tolerance,
                              layerPt.y() + tolerance)

    request = QgsFeatureRequest()
    request.setFilterRect(searchRect)
    request.setFlags(QgsFeatureRequest.ExactIntersect)
```

```
        for feature in self.layer.getFeatures(request):
            if excludeFeature != None:
                if feature.id() == excludeFeature.id():
                    continue
            return feature

        return None
```

> As you can see, this method takes an optional `excludeFeature`
> parameter. This lets us exclude a given feature from the search, which
> will be important later on.

Next up, we'll define the `findVertexAt()` method, which identifies the vertex close
to the given click location (if any). Here is the implementation of this method:

```
    def findVertexAt(self, feature, pos):
        mapPt,layerPt = self.transformCoordinates(pos)
        tolerance     = self.calcTolerance(pos)

        vertexCoord,vertex,prevVertex,nextVertex,distSquared = \
            feature.geometry().closestVertex(layerPt)

        distance = math.sqrt(distSquared)
        if distance > tolerance:
            return None
        else:
            return vertex
```

As you can see, we use the `QgsGeometry.closestVertex()` method to find the
vertex closest to the given position and then see if that vertex is within the tolerance
distance. If so, we return the vertex index for the clicked-on vertex; otherwise, we
return `None`.

Notice that this method uses the `math.sqrt()` function. To be able to use this
function, you'll need to add the following near the top of the module:

```
    import math
```

With these two new methods defined, we're ready to start implementing vertex
snapping. Here is the signature for the method we are going to write:

```
    snapToNearestVertex(pos, trackLayer, excludeFeature=None)
```

In this method, `pos` is the click position (in canvas coordinates), `trackLayer` is a reference to our track layer (which contains the features and vertices we need to check), and `excludeFeature` is an optional feature to exclude when looking for nearby vertices.

> The `excludeFeature` parameter will be useful when we start editing tracks. We'll use it to stop a track from snapping to itself.

Upon completion, our method will return the coordinate of the clicked-on vertex. If the user didn't click anywhere near a feature, or close to a vertex, then this method will return the click position instead, converted to layer coordinates. This lets the user click on the map canvas, away from any vertices, to draw new features, while still snapping to an existing vertex when the user clicks on it.

Here is the implementation of our `snapToNearestVertex()` method:

```
def snapToNearestVertex(self, pos, trackLayer,
                        excludeFeature=None):
    mapPt,layerPt = self.transformCoordinates(pos)
    feature = self.findFeatureAt(pos, excludeFeature)
    if feature == None: return layerPt

    vertex = self.findVertexAt(feature, pos)
    if vertex == None: return layerPt

    return feature.geometry().vertexAt(vertex)
```

As you can see, we use our `findFeatureAt()` method to search for features that are close to the given click point. If we find a feature, we then call `self.findVertexAt()` to find the vertex close to where the user clicked. Finally, if we find a vertex, we return the coordinates of that vertex. Otherwise, we return the original click position converted to layer coordinates.

With these extensions to our mixin class, we can easily add snapping to our `AddTrack` tool. All we have to do is replace our `addVertex()` method with the following:

```
def addVertex(self, canvasPoint):
    snapPt = self.snapToNearestVertex(canvasPoint, self.layer)
    mapPt = self.toMapCoordinates(self.layer, snapPt)

    self.rubberBand.addPoint(mapPt)
    self.capturedPoints.append(snapPt)

    self.tempRubberBand.reset(QGis.Line)
    self.tempRubberBand.addPoint(mapPt)
```

Now that we have vertex snapping enabled, it'll be easy to ensure that our tracks are connected. Note that we'll also use vertex snapping when we edit a track and when the user selects the start and end points for the Shortest Available Path calculation. This is why we've added these methods to our mixin rather than to the `AddTrack` tool.

The Edit Track map tool

Our next task is to implement the Edit Track action. To do this, we'll take `EditTool` we defined in *Chapter 7, Selecting and Editing Features in a PyQGIS Application*, and modify it to work specifically with tracks. Fortunately, we only need to support LineString geometries and can make use of our mixin class, which will simplify the implementation of this new map tool.

Let's start by adding our new class definition to the `mapTools.py` module, along with the `__init__()` method:

```
class EditTrackTool(QgsMapTool, MapToolMixin):
    def __init__(self, canvas, layer, onTrackEdited):
        QgsMapTool.__init__(self, canvas)
        self.onTrackEdited = onTrackEdited
        self.dragging     = False
        self.feature      = None
        self.vertex       = None
        self.setLayer(layer)
        self.setCursor(Qt.CrossCursor)
```

We now define our `canvasPressEvent()` method to respond when the user presses the mouse button over our map canvas:

```
    def canvasPressEvent(self, event):
        feature = self.findFeatureAt(event.pos())
        if feature == None:
            return

        vertex = self.findVertexAt(feature, event.pos())
        if vertex == None: return

        if event.button() == Qt.LeftButton:
            # Left click -> move vertex.
            self.dragging = True
            self.feature  = feature
            self.vertex   = vertex
            self.moveVertexTo(event.pos())
            self.canvas().refresh()
```

```
    elif event.button() == Qt.RightButton:
        # Right click -> delete vertex.
        self.deleteVertex(feature, vertex)
        self.canvas().refresh()
```

As you can see, we're using our mixin's methods to find the clicked-on feature and vertex. This simplifies the implementation of the `canvasPressedEvent()` method.

We now come to the `canvasMoveEvent()` and `canvasReleaseEvent()` methods, which are basically identical to the methods defined in `EditTool` from *Chapter 7, Selecting and Editing Features in a PyQGIS Application*:

```
def canvasMoveEvent(self, event):
    if self.dragging:
        self.moveVertexTo(event.pos())
        self.canvas().refresh()

def canvasReleaseEvent(self, event):
    if self.dragging:
        self.moveVertexTo(event.pos())
        self.layer.updateExtents()
        self.canvas().refresh()
        self.dragging = False
        self.feature  = None
        self.vertex   = None
```

Our `canvasDoubleClickEvent()` method is also very similar, the only difference being that we can use the `findFeatureAt()` method defined by our mixin class:

```
def canvasDoubleClickEvent(self, event):
    feature = self.findFeatureAt(event.pos())
    if feature == None:
        return

    mapPt,layerPt = self.transformCoordinates(event.pos())
    geometry      = feature.geometry()

    distSquared,closestPt,beforeVertex = \
        geometry.closestSegmentWithContext(layerPt)

    distance = math.sqrt(distSquared)
    tolerance = self.calcTolerance(event.pos())
    if distance > tolerance: return

    geometry.insertVertex(closestPt.x(), closestPt.y(),
                          beforeVertex)
```

```
self.layer.changeGeometry(feature.id(), geometry)
self.onTrackEdited()
self.canvas().refresh()
```

We now have the moveVertexTo() method, which moves the clicked-on vertex to the current mouse location. While the logic is very similar to the method with the same name in our EditTool, we also want to support vertex snapping so that the user can click on an existing vertex to connect two tracks together. Here is the implementation of this method:

```
def moveVertexTo(self, pos):
    snappedPt = self.snapToNearestVertex(pos, self.layer,
                                         self.feature)

    geometry = self.feature.geometry()
    layerPt = self.toLayerCoordinates(self.layer, pos)
    geometry.moveVertex(snappedPt.x(), snappedPt.y(),
                        self.vertex)
    self.layer.changeGeometry(self.feature.id(), geometry)
    self.onTrackEdited()
```

Notice that our call to snapToNearestVertex() makes use of the excludeFeature parameter to exclude the clicked-on feature when finding a vertex to snap to. This ensures that we don't snap a feature to itself.

Finally, we have the deleteVertex() method, which is copied almost verbatim from the EditTool class:

```
def deleteVertex(self, feature, vertex):
    geometry = feature.geometry()

    lineString = geometry.asPolyline()
    if len(lineString) <= 2:
        return

    if geometry.deleteVertex(vertex):
        self.layer.changeGeometry(feature.id(), geometry)
        self.onTrackEdited()
```

With this complex map tool implemented, we can now use it to let the user edit a track. Back in the forestTrails.py module, add the following to the end of the setupMapTools() method:

```
self.editTrackTool = EditTrackTool(self.mapCanvas,
                                   self.trackLayer,
```

```
                                            self.onTrackEdited)
        self.editTrackTool.setAction(self.actionEditTrack)
```

We now want to replace our placeholder for the `editTrack()` method with the following:

```
def editTrack(self):
    if self.actionEditTrack.isChecked():
        self.mapCanvas.setMapTool(self.editTrackTool)
    else:
        self.setPanMode()
```

As with the `addTrack()` method, we switch to the edit tool when the user clicks on our action, and switch back to panning mode if the user clicks on the action a second time.

The last thing we need to do is implement the `ForestTrailsWindow.onTrackEdited()` method to respond when the user makes a change to a track. Here is this new method:

```
def onTrackEdited(self):
    self.modified = True
    self.mapCanvas.refresh()
```

We simply need to remember that the track layer has been modified and redraw the map canvas to show the change. Note that we don't switch back to the panning mode, as the user will continue to make changes to the track vertices until he or she explicitly switches off the edit tool by clicking on the toolbar icon a second time, or by choosing a different action from the toolbar.

With this implemented, you can rerun your program, switch to track editing mode, and click on the **Edit Track** action to add, move, or delete vertices. If you look carefully, you'll see that the vertex you're dragging will snap to the vertex of another feature when you move the mouse close to it. As with the `EditTool`, you can double-click on a segment to add a new vertex, or press the *Ctrl* key and click on a vertex to delete it.

The Delete Track map tool

We now want to implement the **Delete Track** action. Fortunately, the map tool for doing is very simple, thanks to our mixin class. Add the following class definition to the `mapTools.py` module:

```
class DeleteTrackTool(QgsMapTool, MapToolMixin):
    def __init__(self, canvas, layer, onTrackDeleted):
        QgsMapTool.__init__(self, canvas)
        self.onTrackDeleted = onTrackDeleted
        self.feature         = None
        self.setLayer(layer)
        self.setCursor(Qt.CrossCursor)

    def canvasPressEvent(self, event):
        self.feature = self.findFeatureAt(event.pos())

    def canvasReleaseEvent(self, event):
        feature = self.findFeatureAt(event.pos())
        if feature != None and feature.id() == self.feature.id():
            self.layer.deleteFeature(self.feature.id())
            self.onTrackDeleted()
```

Then, back in the `forestTrails.py` module, add the following to the end of the `setupMapTools()` method:

```
self.deleteTrackTool = DeleteTrackTool(
    self.mapCanvas, self.trackLayer, self.onTrackDeleted)
self.deleteTrackTool.setAction(self.actionDeleteTrack)
```

Then replace the dummy `deleteTrack()` method with the following:

```
def deleteTrack(self):
    if self.actionDeleteTrack.isChecked():
        self.mapCanvas.setMapTool(self.deleteTrackTool)
    else:
        self.setPanMode()
```

Finally, add a new `onTrackDeleted()` method to respond when the user deletes a track:

```
def onTrackDeleted(self):
    self.modified = True
    self.mapCanvas.refresh()
    self.actionDeleteTrack.setChecked(False)
    self.setPanMode()
```

With this map tool, we now have all of the necessary logic for adding, editing, and deleting tracks. We now have a complete mapping application for maintaining a database of forest trails, and you can use this program to enter as many tracks as you want.

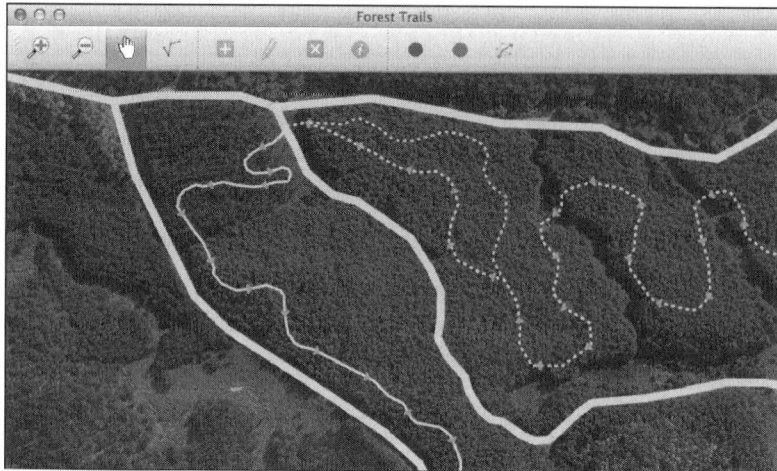

Of course, we're not finished yet. In particular, we can't yet specify the type of track; every track is a road at the moment. To get around this, our next task is to implement the **Get Info** action.

The Get Info map tool

When the user clicks on the **Get Info** item in the toolbar, we will activate a custom map tool that lets the user click on a track to display and edit the attributes for that track. Let's walk through this implementation one step at a time, starting with the `GetInfoTool` class itself. Add the following to your `mapTools.py` module:

```
class GetInfoTool(QgsMapTool, MapToolMixin):
    def __init__(self, canvas, layer, onGetInfo):
        QgsMapTool.__init__(self, canvas)
        self.onGetInfo = onGetInfo
        self.setLayer(layer)
        self.setCursor(Qt.WhatsThisCursor)

    def canvasReleaseEvent(self, event):
        if event.button() != Qt.LeftButton: return
        feature = self.findFeatureAt(event.pos())
        if feature != None:
            self.onGetInfo(feature)
```

This map tool calls the `onGetInfo()` method (which is passed as a parameter to the map tool's initializer) when the user clicks on a track. Let's now use this map tool within our program by adding the following code to the end of our `setupMapTools()` method in the `forestTrails.py` module:

```
self.getInfoTool = GetInfoTool(self.mapCanvas,
                               self.trackLayer,
                               self.onGetInfo)
self.getInfoTool.setAction(self.actionGetInfo)
```

We can then replace our placeholder `getInfo()` method with the following:

```
def getInfo(self):
    self.mapCanvas.setMapTool(self.getInfoTool)
```

This activates the map tool when the user clicks on the toolbar icon. The last step is to implement the `onGetInfo()` method, which is called when the user selects the map tool and clicks on a track.

When `onGetInfo()` is called, we want to display to the user the various attributes of the clicked-on track. These attributes will be displayed in a dialog window, where the user can make changes if he/she wishes. When the user submits his/her changes, we will have to update the feature with the new attribute values and indicate that the track has been changed.

The bulk of our work will be setting up the dialog window so that the attributes can be displayed and edited by the user. To do this, we'll create a new class named `TrackInfoDialog`, which will be a subclass of `QDialog`.

Add the following code to the `forestTrails.py` module, immediately before the `main()` function definition:

```
class TrackInfoDialog(QDialog):
    def __init__(self, parent=None):
        QDialog.__init__(self, parent)
        self.setWindowTitle("Track Info")
```

The `__init__()` method will set up the contents of the dialog window. So far, we've initialized the dialog object itself, and given the window a title. Let's now define a list of the available track types the user can choose from:

```
self.trackTypes = ["Road",
                   "Walking Trail",
                   "Bike Trail",
                   "Horse Trail"]
```

Similarly, we'll want a list of the available direction options:

```
self.directions = ["Both",
                   "Forward",
                   "Backward"]
```

We'll also want a list of the available track status options:

```
self.statuses = ["Open",
                 "Closed"]
```

With the preceding sets of options defined, we can now start to lay out the contents of our dialog window. We'll start by using a QFormLayout object that lets us lay out form labels and widgets side by side:

```
self.form = QFormLayout()
```

We next want to define the various input widgets we'll use to display and change the track attributes:

```
self.trackType = QComboBox(self)
self.trackType.addItems(self.trackTypes)

self.trackName = QLineEdit(self)

self.trackDirection = QComboBox(self)
self.trackDirection.addItems(self.directions)

self.trackStatus = QComboBox(self)
self.trackStatus.addItems(self.statuses)
```

Now that we have the widgets themselves, let's add them to the form:

```
self.form.addRow("Type",      self.trackType)
self.form.addRow("Name",      self.trackName)
self.form.addRow("Direction", self.trackDirection)
self.form.addRow("Status",    self.trackStatus)
```

Next, we want to define the buttons at the bottom of our dialog window:

```
self.buttons = QHBoxLayout()

self.okButton = QPushButton("OK", self)
self.connect(self.okButton, SIGNAL("clicked()"),
             self.accept)
```

```
self.cancelButton = QPushButton("Cancel", self)
self.connect(self.cancelButton, SIGNAL("clicked()"),
             self.reject)

self.buttons.addStretch(1)
self.buttons.addWidget(self.okButton)
self.buttons.addWidget(self.cancelButton)
```

Finally, we can place the form and our buttons within the dialog box, and lay everything out:

```
self.layout = QVBoxLayout(self)
self.layout.addLayout(self.form)
self.layout.addSpacing(10)

self.layout.addLayout(self.buttons)
self.setLayout(self.layout)
self.resize(self.sizeHint())
```

So much for the __init__() method. With the dialog box set up, we next want to define a method to copy the feature's attributes in the dialog window:

```
def loadAttributes(self, feature):
    type_attr      = feature.attribute("type")
    name_attr      = feature.attribute("name")
    direction_attr = feature.attribute("direction")
    status_attr    = feature.attribute("status")

    if   type_attr == TRACK_TYPE_ROAD:     index = 0
    elif type_attr == TRACK_TYPE_WALKING:  index = 1
    elif type_attr == TRACK_TYPE_BIKE:     index = 2
    elif type_attr == TRACK_TYPE_HORSE:    index = 3
    else:                                  index = 0
    self.trackType.setCurrentIndex(index)

    if name_attr != None:
        self.trackName.setText(name_attr)
    else:
        self.trackName.setText("")

    if   direction_attr == TRACK_DIRECTION_BOTH:     index = 0
    elif direction_attr == TRACK_DIRECTION_FORWARD:  index = 1
    elif direction_attr == TRACK_DIRECTION_BACKWARD: index = 2
    else:                                            index = 0
```

```
        self.trackDirection.setCurrentIndex(index)


        if    status_attr == TRACK_STATUS_OPEN:    index = 0
        elif status_attr == TRACK_STATUS_CLOSED: index = 1
        else:                                       index = 0
        self.trackStatus.setCurrentIndex(index)
```

The last method we need to define here is `saveAttributes()`, which stores the updated values from the dialog window back in the feature's attributes:

```
    def saveAttributes(self, feature):
        index = self.trackType.currentIndex()
        if    index == 0: type_attr = TRACK_TYPE_ROAD
        elif index == 1: type_attr = TRACK_TYPE_WALKING
        elif index == 2: type_attr = TRACK_TYPE_BIKE
        elif index == 3: type_attr = TRACK_TYPE_HORSE
        else:              type_attr = TRACK_TYPE_ROAD


        name_attr = self.trackName.text()


        index = self.trackDirection.currentIndex()
        if    index == 0: direction_attr = TRACK_DIRECTION_BOTH
        elif index == 1: direction_attr = TRACK_DIRECTION_FORWARD
        elif index == 2: direction_attr = TRACK_DIRECTION_BACKWARD
        else:              direction_attr = TRACK_DIRECTION_BOTH


        index = self.trackStatus.currentIndex()
        if    index == 0: status_attr = TRACK_STATUS_OPEN
        elif index == 1: status_attr = TRACK_STATUS_CLOSED
        else:              status_attr = TRACK_STATUS_OPEN


        feature.setAttribute("type",      type_attr)
        feature.setAttribute("name",      name_attr)
        feature.setAttribute("direction", direction_attr)
        feature.setAttribute("status",    status_attr)
```

With the `TrackInfoDialog` class defined, we can finally implement the `onGetInfo()` method (in our `ForestTrailsWindow` class) to display the clicked-on track's attributes in the dialog box, and save the changes if the user clicks on the **OK** button:

```
    def onGetInfo(self, feature):
        dialog = TrackInfoDialog(self)
        dialog.loadAttributes(feature)
        if dialog.exec_():
```

```
dialog.saveAttributes(feature)
self.trackLayer.updateFeature(feature)
self.modified = True
self.mapCanvas.refresh()
```

You should now be able to run the program, switch to the editing mode, click on the **Get Info** toolbar icon, and then click on a feature to display the attributes for that feature. The resulting dialog window should look like this:

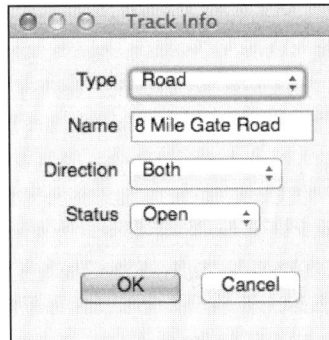

You should be able to change any of these attributes and click on the **OK** button to save the changes. As you change the track type, status and direction, you should see the change reflected in the way the track is displayed on the map.

The Set Start Point and Set End Point actions

The **Set Start Point** and **Set End Point** toolbar actions allow the user to set the start and end points in order to calculate the shortest path between these two points. To implement these actions, we're going to need a new map tool that lets the user click on a track vertex to select the starting or ending points.

> By positioning the start point and the end point on vertices, we guarantee that the points lie on a track's LineString. We could theoretically be more sophisticated and snap the starting and ending points to anywhere along a track segment, but that's more work, and we're trying to keep the implementation simple.

Go back to the `mapTools.py` module and add the following class definition to this file:

```
class SelectVertexTool(QgsMapTool, MapToolMixin):
    def __init__(self, canvas, trackLayer, onVertexSelected):
        QgsMapTool.__init__(self, canvas)
        self.onVertexSelected = onVertexSelected
        self.setLayer(trackLayer)
        self.setCursor(Qt.CrossCursor)

    def canvasReleaseEvent(self, event):
        feature = self.findFeatureAt(event.pos())
        if feature != None:
            vertex = self.findVertexAt(feature, event.pos())
            if vertex != None:
                self.onVertexSelected(feature, vertex)
```

This map tool uses the mixin's methods to identify which feature and vertex the user clicked on, and then calls the `onVertexSelected()` callback to allow the application to respond to the selection.

Let's use this map tool to implement the **Set Start Point** and **Set End Point** actions. Back in the `forestTrails.py` module, add the following to the end of the `setupMapTools()` method:

```
        self.selectStartPointTool = SelectVertexTool(
            self.mapCanvas, self.trackLayer,
            self.onStartPointSelected)

        self.selectEndPointTool = SelectVertexTool(
            self.mapCanvas, self.trackLayer,
            self.onEndPointSelected)
```

These two instances of `SelectVertexTool` use different callback methods to respond when the user clicks on a track vertex. Using these tools, we can now implement the `setStartPoint()` and `setEndPoint()` methods, which were just placeholders until now:

```
    def setStartPoint(self):
        if self.actionSetStartPoint.isChecked():
            self.mapCanvas.setMapTool(self.selectStartPointTool)
        else:
            self.setPanMode()
```

```
def setEndPoint(self):
    if self.actionSetEndPoint.isChecked():
        self.mapCanvas.setMapTool(self.selectEndPointTool)
    else:
        self.setPanMode()
```

As usual, we activate the map tool when the user clicks on the toolbar action, and switch back to the pan mode if the user clicks on the action a second time.

All that's left now are the two callback methods, `onStartPointSelected()` and `onEndPointSelected()`. Let's start with the implementation of `onStartPointSelected()`. This method will start by asking the feature's geometry to return the coordinates of the clicked-on vertex, which we store into `self.curStartPt`:

```
def onStartPointSelected(self, feature, vertex):
    self.curStartPt = feature.geometry().vertexAt(vertex)
```

Now that we know where the start point will be, we want to show this start point on the map. If you remember, we previously created a memory-based map layer called `startPointLayer`, to display this point. We'll need to first clear the contents of this memory layer, deleting any existing features, and then create a new feature at the given coordinate:

```
self.clearMemoryLayer(self.startPointLayer)

feature = QgsFeature()
feature.setGeometry(QgsGeometry.fromPoint(
                                    self.curStartPt))
self.startPointLayer.dataProvider().addFeatures([feature])
self.startPointLayer.updateExtents()
```

Finally, we'll redraw the map canvas to show the newly added point, and switch back to pan mode:

```
self.mapCanvas.refresh()
self.setPanMode()
self.adjustActions()
```

We'll need to implement the `clearMemoryLayer()` method, but before we do, let's also define the `onEndPointSelected()` callback method so that we can respond when the user clicks on the end point. The code for this is almost identical to the code for `onStartPointSelected()`:

```
def onEndPointSelected(self, feature, vertex):
    self.curEndPt = feature.geometry().vertexAt(vertex)
```

```
self.clearMemoryLayer(self.endPointLayer)

feature = QgsFeature()
feature.setGeometry(QgsGeometry.fromPoint(self.curEndPt))
self.endPointLayer.dataProvider().addFeatures([feature])
self.endPointLayer.updateExtents()
self.mapCanvas.refresh()
self.setPanMode()
self.adjustActions()
```

To finish off these two actions, we'll need to implement the `clearMemoryLayer()` method and initialize the `curStartPt` and `curEndPt` instance variables so that the program knows when these variables are set for the first time.

Here is the implementation for the `clearMemoryLayer()` method:

```
def clearMemoryLayer(self, layer):
    featureIDs = []
    provider = layer.dataProvider()
    for feature in provider.getFeatures(QgsFeatureRequest()):
        featureIDs.append(feature.id())
    provider.deleteFeatures(featureIDs)
```

We simply obtain a list of all the features in the given memory layer, and then ask the data provider to delete them. Since this data is transient and held in memory, deleting all the features is no big deal.

Finally, let's initialize those two instance variables. Add the following to the end of your `ForestTrailsWindow.__init__()` method:

```
self.curStartPt = None
self.curEndPt   = None
```

With all this implemented, the user can now click on a vertex to set the starting or ending point, as shown in the following screenshot:

The Find Shortest Path action

This is the last feature of the ForestTrails that we will have to implement. When the user clicks on this toolbar icon, we want to calculate the shortest available path between the given start and end points. Fortunately, the QGIS **network analysis library** will do the actual calculation for us. All we have to do is run the shortest path calculation on the track layer, build the LineString that corresponds to this shortest path, and display that LineString geometry in our memory-based map layer.

All of this logic will be implemented within the findShortestPath() method. We'll start our implementation with a bit of housekeeping: if the user unchecks the **Find Shortest Path** toolbar icon, we clear the shortest path memory layer, switch back to the panning mode, and redraw the map canvas to show the map without the previous path:

```
def findShortestPath(self):
    if not self.actionFindShortestPath.isChecked():
        self.clearMemoryLayer(self.shortestPathLayer)
        self.setPanMode()
        self.mapCanvas.refresh()
        return
```

The rest of the method will be executed when the user clicks on the **Find Shortest Path** toolbar action to check it. Add the following code to your method:

```
directionField = self.trackLayer.fieldNameIndex(
    "direction")
director = QgsLineVectorLayerDirector(
            self.trackLayer, directionField,
            TRACK_DIRECTION_FORWARD,
            TRACK_DIRECTION_BACKWARD,
            TRACK_DIRECTION_BOTH, 3)

properter = QgsDistanceArcProperter()
director.addProperter(properter)

crs = self.mapCanvas.mapRenderer().destinationCrs()
builder = QgsGraphBuilder(crs)

tiedPoints = director.makeGraph(builder, [self.curStartPt,
                                          self.curEndPt])
graph = builder.graph()

startPt = tiedPoints[0]
endPt   = tiedPoints[1]

startVertex = graph.findVertex(startPt)
tree = QgsGraphAnalyzer.shortestTree(graph,
                                     startVertex, 0)

startVertex = tree.findVertex(startPt)
endVertex   = tree.findVertex(endPt)

if endVertex == -1:
    QMessageBox.information(self.window,
                            "Not Found",
                            "No path found.")
    return
```

```
points = []
while startVertex != endVertex:
    incomingEdges = tree.vertex(endVertex).inArc()
    if len(incomingEdges) == 0:
        break
    edge = tree.arc(incomingEdges[0])
    points.insert(0, tree.vertex(edge.inVertex()).point())
    endVertex = edge.outVertex()

points.insert(0, startPt)
```

The preceding code was copied from the PyQGIS cookbook with some changes in variable names to make the meaning clearer. At the end, `points` will be a list of `QgsPoint` objects defining the LineString geometry that connects the starting point to the ending point. The most interesting part of this method is the following:

```
director = QgsLineVectorLayerDirector(
                self.trackLayer, directionField,
                TRACK_DIRECTION_FORWARD,
                TRACK_DIRECTION_BACKWARD,
                TRACK_DIRECTION_BOTH, 3)
```

This piece of code creates an object which converts a set of LineString features into an abstract **graph** of the layer's features. The various parameters specify which of the track's attributes will be used to define the various directions in which a track can be followed. Bidirectional tracks can be followed in either direction, while forward and reverse directional tracks can be followed in only one direction.

> The final parameter, with the value 3, tells the director to treat any track without a valid direction value as bidirectional.

Once we have the set of points that define the shortest path, it's easy to display those points as a LineString in the memory layer and make the resulting path visible on the map:

```
self.clearMemoryLayer(self.shortestPathLayer)

provider = self.shortestPathLayer.dataProvider()
feature = QgsFeature()
feature.setGeometry(QgsGeometry.fromPolyline(points))
provider.addFeatures([feature])
self.shortestPathLayer.updateExtents()
self.mapCanvas.refresh()
```

If you define the starting and ending points, and then click on the **Find Shortest Path** toolbar action, the resulting path will be displayed as a blue line on the map, as shown in the following screenshot:

If you look carefully at the preceding screenshot, you'll see that the path taken wasn't the shortest one; the starting point was at the bottom and the ending point was near the end of a one-way bike track, so the shortest available path involved taking the road back to the start of the one-way track, and then following it through to the endpoint. This is exactly the behavior that we would expect, and it is correct given the one-way nature of the tracks.

Adjusting the toolbar actions

Now that we've finished creating all the necessary map tools and instance variables, we can finally implement the rest of the `adjustActions()` method to adjust the toolbar and menu items to reflect the current state of the system. Firstly, we want to change the final line of this method so that the **Find Shortest Path** action is only enabled if the start and end points have both been set:

```
self.actionFindShortestPath.setEnabled(
    self.curStartPt != None andself.curEndPt != None)
```

In the final part of this method, we'll want to find the action that is associated with the current map tool and check that action, while unchecking all the others. To do this, add the following code to the end of your `adjustActions()` method:

```
curTool = self.mapCanvas.mapTool()

self.actionPan.setChecked(curTool == self.panTool)
self.actionEdit.setChecked(self.editing)
self.actionAddTrack.setChecked(
            curTool == self.addTrackTool)
self.actionEditTrack.setChecked(
            curTool == self.editTrackTool)
self.actionDeleteTrack.setChecked(
            curTool == self.deleteTrackTool)
self.actionGetInfo.setChecked(curTool == self.getInfoTool)
self.actionSetStartPoint.setChecked(
            curTool == self.selectStartPointTool)
self.actionSetEndPoint.setChecked(
            curTool == self.selectEndPointTool)
self.actionFindShortestPath.setChecked(False)
```

> Note that this code should go outside the `if...else` statement that you've already entered in this method.

This completes our implementation of the `adjustActions()` method, and in fact it also completes our implementation of the entire ForestTrails system. Congratulations! We now have a complete working mapping application, with all the features implemented and working.

Suggested improvements

Of course, no application is ever completely finished, and there are always things that could be improved upon. Here are a few ideas for things you could do to make the ForestTrails application even better:

- Adding labels to the trail layer, using the `QgsPalLabeling` engine to only show only the track names when the map is zoomed in sufficiently so that the names can be read.

- Changing the color used for the track based on the track type. For example, you might draw all bike trails in red, all walking trails in green, and all horse trails in yellow.

- Adding a **View** menu where the user can select the types of tracks to be displayed. For example, the user might choose to hide all the horse trails, or show only the walking trails.

- Extending the logic of the shortest path calculation to exclude any tracks that are currently closed.

- Adding another map layer to display various obstacles on the map. An obstacle would be something that is blocking a track, and could be represented by a Point geometry. Typical obstacles might be things like fallen trees, landslides, and ongoing track maintenance. Depending on the obstacle, the trail might be closed until the obstacle is cleared.

- Using **Print Composer** to generate a printable version of the map. This could be used to print maps based on the current state of the forest trails.

Summary

In this chapter, we finished implementing the ForestTrails mapping application. Our application now lets the user add, edit, and delete tracks; view and enter track attributes; set the start and end points; and display the shortest available path between those two points. As we implemented the application, we discovered an issue with tracks not connecting, and solved that problem by adding support for vertex snapping. We also learned how to write a custom `QDialog` to let the user view and edit attributes, and how to use the QGIS Network Analysis library to calculate the shortest available path between two points.

While the ForestTrails application is only one example of a specialized mapping application, it provides a good example of how to implement standalone mapping applications using PyQGIS. You should be able to use much of the code for your own mapping applications, as well as build on the techniques covered in previous chapters when you write your own mapping applications using Python and QGIS.

I hope you've enjoyed the journey, and learned much about using QGIS as a mapping toolkit within your Python programs. Map on!

Index

Symbols

[PACKT] open source

PUBLISHING   community experience distilled

Thank you for buying
Building Mapping Applications with QGIS

About Packt Publishing

Packt, pronounced 'packed', published its first book, *Mastering phpMyAdmin for Effective MySQL Management*, in April 2004, and subsequently continued to specialize in publishing highly focused books on specific technologies and solutions.

Our books and publications share the experiences of your fellow IT professionals in adapting and customizing today's systems, applications, and frameworks. Our solution-based books give you the knowledge and power to customize the software and technologies you're using to get the job done. Packt books are more specific and less general than the IT books you have seen in the past. Our unique business model allows us to bring you more focused information, giving you more of what you need to know, and less of what you don't.

Packt is a modern yet unique publishing company that focuses on producing quality, cutting-edge books for communities of developers, administrators, and newbies alike. For more information, please visit our website at www.packtpub.com.

About Packt Open Source

In 2010, Packt launched two new brands, Packt Open Source and Packt Enterprise, in order to continue its focus on specialization. This book is part of the Packt Open Source brand, home to books published on software built around open source licenses, and offering information to anybody from advanced developers to budding web designers. The Open Source brand also runs Packt's Open Source Royalty Scheme, by which Packt gives a royalty to each open source project about whose software a book is sold.

Writing for Packt

We welcome all inquiries from people who are interested in authoring. Book proposals should be sent to author@packtpub.com. If your book idea is still at an early stage and you would like to discuss it first before writing a formal book proposal, then please contact us; one of our commissioning editors will get in touch with you.

We're not just looking for published authors; if you have strong technical skills but no writing experience, our experienced editors can help you develop a writing career, or simply get some additional reward for your expertise.

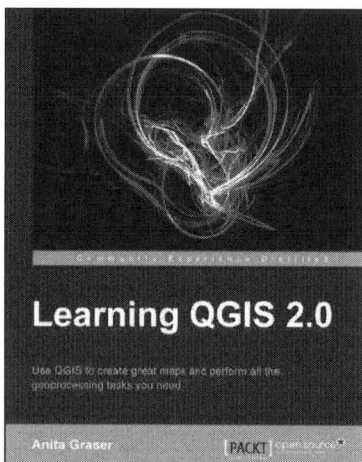

Learning QGIS 2.0

ISBN: 978-1-78216-748-8   Paperback: 110 pages

Use QGIS to create great maps and perform all the geoprocessing tasks you need

1. Load and visualize vector and raster data.

2. Create and edit spatial data and perform spatial analysis.

3. Construct great maps and print them.

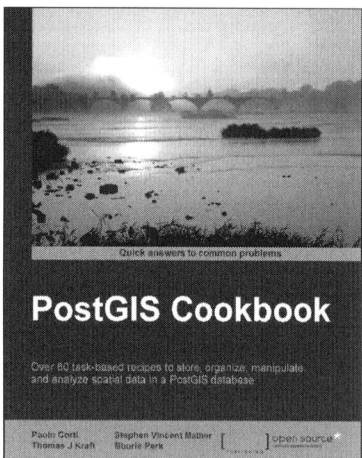

PostGIS Cookbook

ISBN: 978-1-84951-866-6   Paperback: 484 pages

Over 80 task-based recipes to store, organize, manipulate, and analyze spatial data in a PostGIS database

1. Integrate PostGIS with web frameworks and implement OGC standards such as WMS and WFS using MapServer and GeoServer.

2. Convert 2D and 3D vector data, raster data, and routing data into usable forms.

3. Visualize data from the PostGIS database using a desktop GIS program such as QGIS and OpenJUMP.

Please check **www.PacktPub.com** for information on our titles

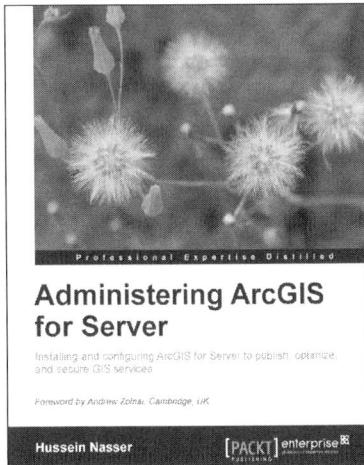

Administering ArcGIS for Server

ISBN: 978-1-78217-736-4   Paperback: 246 pages

Installing and configuring ArcGIS for Server to publish, optimize, and secure GIS services

1. Configure ArcGIS for Server to achieve maximum performance and response time.

2. Understand the product mechanics to build up good troubleshooting skills.

3. Filled with practical exercises, examples, and code snippets to help facilitate your learning.

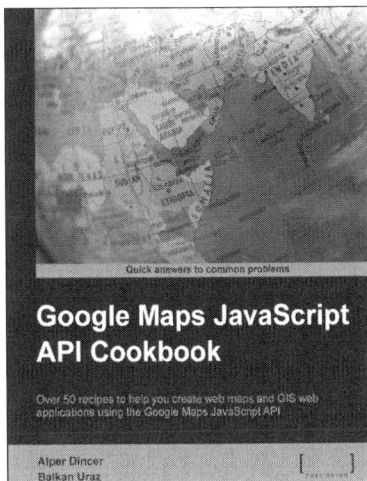

Google Maps JavaScript API Cookbook

ISBN: 978-1-84969-882-5   Paperback: 316 pages

Over 50 recipes to help you create web maps and GIS web applications using the Google Maps JavaScript API

1. Add to your website's functionality by utilizing Google Maps' power.

2. Full of code examples and screenshots for practical and efficient learning.

3. Empowers you to build your own mapping application from the ground up.

Please check **www.PacktPub.com** for information on our titles

12673879R00147

Printed in Great Britain
by Amazon.co.uk, Ltd.,
Marston Gate.